PRAISE FOR
STREET OF ETERNAL HAPPINESS

"A poignant microcosm . . . coursing under even the bleakest stories is a sense of optimism that tomorrow will be better."

—*The Economist*

"Enjoyable and illuminating . . . The great virtue of these books is that they offer Chinese people a voice, something that is often lacking in news coverage. Schmitz writes with great affection about the shopkeepers and other residents of his street: in telling their stories, he shows how the goals of the Chinese state have 'often stood in the way of individual dreams.'"

—*The Guardian*

"Hopes and struggles rise to the surface in this intimate portrait of modern China."

—*National Geographic*

"Educational and entertaining . . . rich with voices . . . The people [Schmitz] features . . . are fully rounded characters whose stories emerge in chat after chat, chapter after chapter, so we feel we are getting to know them as the writer does. [Readers] will feel so much wiser about China and the Chinese state than when they started."

—*The Telegraph*

"This beautifully conceived and written book conveys the joys, the tragedies, the comedy, and the vivid humanity of modern China. Years from now people will turn to this book to understand the China of this era."
—James Fallows, author of *China Airborne* and *Postcards from Tomorrow Square*

"A marvel of place-based reporting."

—Peter Hessler, author of *River Town* and *Country Driving*

"Rob Schmitz has given us a treasure: a patient portrait of an impatient country, a China that is utterly true to life in its beauty and heartache, tenderness and greed. Reading this is as close as most people will come to living there."

—Evan Osnos, National Book Award–winning author of *Age of Ambition*

Street of
ETERNAL HAPPINESS

BIG CITY DREAMS
ALONG A SHANGHAI ROAD

ROB SCHMITZ

B \ D \ W \ Y
BROADWAY BOOKS
NEW YORK

Published in the United States by Broadway Books, an imprint of the Crown
Publishing Group, a division of Penguin Random House LLC, New York.
crownpublishing.com

Broadway Books and its logo, B \ D \ W \ Y, are trademarks of
Penguin Random House LLC.

Originally published in hardcover in the United States by Crown,
an imprint of the Crown Publishing Group, a division of
Penguin Random House LLC, New York, in 2016.

Library of Congress Cataloging-in-Publication Data
Names: Schmitz, Rob.
Title: Street of Eternal Happiness: big city dreams along a Shanghai road /
    Rob Schmitz.
Description: First edition. | New York: Crown, 2016.
Identifiers: LCCN 2015041162 | ISBN 9780553418088 (hardback) |
    ISBN 9780553418095 (ebook)
Subjects: LCSH: Shanghai (China)—Biography. | Shanghai (China)—Social
    life and customs. | Shanghai (China)—Economic conditions. | Streets—
    China—Shanghai. | Neighborhoods—China—Shanghai. | City and
    town life—China—Shanghai. |Schmitz, Rob—Homes and haunts—
    China—Shanghai. | Americans—China—Shanghai—Biography. |
    BISAC: SOCIAL SCIENCE / Ethnic Studies / Asian American Studies. |
    HISTORY / Asia / China. | BIOGRAPHY & AUTOBIOGRAPHY /
    Cultural Heritage.
Classification: LCC DS796.S253 A26 2016 | DDC 951/.132—dc23
LC record available at http://lccn.loc.gov/2015041162

ISBN 978-0-553-41810-1
Ebook ISBN 978-0-553-41809-5

Printed in the United States of America

Book design by Elina D. Nudelman
Map and illustrations by Sophie Kittredge
Cover design by Elena Giavaldi
Cover photography by Sue Anne Tay

10 9 8 7 6 5 4 3 2 1

First Paperback Edition

For Lenora, Rainer, and Landon

CONTENTS

長乐路
Changle Lu

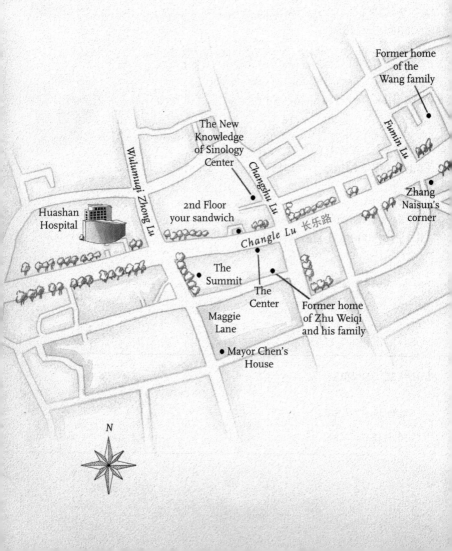

Former home
of the
Wang family

The New
Knowledge
of Sinology
Center

Changshu Lu

Fumin Lu

Zhang
Naisun's
corner

Huashan
Hospital

2nd Floor
your sandwich

Changle Lu 长乐路

The
Summit

The
Center

Maggie
Lane

Former home
of Zhu Weiqi
and his family

Mayor Chen's
House

N

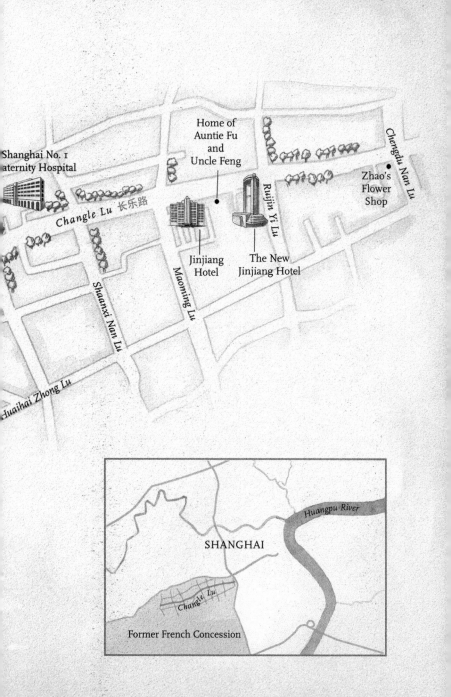

CK and the System

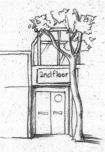

长乐路810号
Street of Eternal Happiness, No. 810

The Street of Eternal Happiness is two miles long. In the winter when its tangled trees are naked of foliage, you can see past their branches and catch a view of the city's signature skyline in the distance: the Jin Mao Tower, the Shanghai World Financial Center, and Shanghai Tower. The three giants stand within a block of one another, each of them taller than New York City's Empire State Building.

Below, people are too busy to take in the scenery. Today will be the first day of life for babies born at the Shanghai No. 1 Maternity Hospital along the street's midsection. For several souls at Huashan Hospital's emergency room at the street's western end, it will be their last. In between there is life, in all its facets: a bearded beggar sits on the sidewalk playing the bamboo flute, lovers pass him hand in hand, cars honk and lurch around two men spitting at each other and thrashing over whose car hit whose, a crowd of uniformed schoolchildren gathers and stares, an old woman with a cane yells at a vendor in disgust over the price of lychees, and the rest of the street pitches forward with a constant flow of people, cutting through bursts of savory-scented steam from pork bun stands and the sweet benzene exhaust of traffic. Life here is loud, dirty, and raw.

On a map, Eternal Happiness is a tiny squiggle to the southwest of People's Square, the center point of Shanghai. My home is at the western end of that squiggle. It looks out over a canopy of leaves that, most of the year, appears to hover two stories above the ground. Below, these plane trees are the only living things standing still. I spend mornings zigzagging around their trunks from sidewalk to road and then back again among pedestrians vying for space in their shade.

Few streets in China are lined with trees like these, and on the weekends the bustle of local workers is replaced by groups of tourists from other parts of China, pointing telephoto lenses down the street at rows of limbs, admiring their exotic beauty. The French had planted them in the mid-nineteenth century when Europeans and Americans carved up the city into foreign concessions. Nearly a century later, the French were gone, but the trees remained. The Japanese bombed Shanghai and took the city for a time, but they eventually retreated, too, leaving the French plantings unharmed. Then came the Communists under Mao with revolution, class warfare, and the untimely deaths of millions. The trees endured. The street is now a capitalist one, lined with restaurants and shops. When I stroll along its sidewalk, I sometimes catch glimpses of run-down European-style homes through the cracks of closed gates, and I think about the relentless churn of history this street has witnessed. Here, an empire rose, fell, and now rises again. Only the trees were constant.

I HAD LIVED ON THE STREET for nearly three years before I noticed Chen Kai's sandwich shop. It was less than a block away from my apartment, above a tiny boutique, but during the warm summer months, the leafy plane trees obstructed it entirely. A narrow spiral staircase led upstairs to the café's floor-to-ceiling windows. On the other side of the glass, a wall of leaves swayed in the wind, shielding the shop from the bustle of Shanghai below.

Inside, Chen—who goes by the nickname "CK"—often stood hunched over a counter, his black mop of hair obscuring his eyes, skinny fingers putting the finishing touches on a sandwich or a dessert before he flipped his mane back and mechanically swiped a cup of piping hot coffee from the espresso machine for a customer. Usually, though, the shop was empty. *That's okay,* CK told himself, *it's going to take time before business takes off. That's how dreams work.* During those times, he'd slouch atop a barstool, his boyish, acne-covered face turned away from the glass wall of trees. He'd quickly switch from one Chinese dialect to another over the phone, making deals for his side business: selling accordions.

The idea for the sandwich shop came to him after he visited one in Chicago, during his only trip to the United States. There would have been nothing extraordinary about the shop to American eyes, but CK was impressed and wanted to replicate the experience for Chinese diners. It was like an American returning from China inspired by a noodle stand. Such a seemingly reckless approach was typical of many small-business owners I met along the street. In a city as big and rich as Shanghai, you could sell anything if you put your mind to it.

CK dreamed that one day this artisan second-floor sandwich shop would become his main livelihood. He had invested years' worth of earnings from selling accordions into this place, pooling his savings with a friend's to create a space they hoped would attract young musicians and artists like them.

"One day I had an idea: maybe I can get all these people together and unite them," CK told me. "I want to find people who want to free themselves from the overall system. I want friends like me; entrepreneurs who have independent ideas in art, fashion design, lots of different industries."

Ambitions like CK's make the Street of Eternal Happiness a

fascinating stroll: tiny shops and cafés like his lined the narrow thoroughfare, the dreams of bright-eyed outsiders stacked up against each other, all looking to make it in the big city.

It wasn't easy. Neither CK nor his friend Max had any experience working at—much less *owning*—a restaurant. The two had met in 2011 at an antique-camera shop in the former French Concession where CK had taken a part-time job to learn more about photography. Like CK, Max had an entrepreneurial background; through long conversations during their shifts at the camera shop, each had come to appreciate the other's savvy approach to making and selling product. Eventually, CK convinced Max to team up with him to open a sandwich shop.

They named it *Your Sandwich*. It was two blocks from a busy subway station, in the shadow of a forty-five-story skyscraper that spit out hundreds of office workers each day at noon, all searching for a quick lunch. But nobody could see *Your Sandwich*. It was obscured by the plane trees. No one ever looked up through the canopy as they rushed along the Street of Eternal Happiness.

So they changed the name to *2nd Floor*—a hint to passersby that they should elevate their gaze as they passed. Below the new name, in diminutive typeface, were the words: Your Sandwich. They also hired a new chef, constructed a bar with mixed drinks and imported beer, and obsessively fiddled with the menu. One day I dropped by CK's apartment and noticed a pile of electronic tablets stacked in the corner. "Touchscreen menus!" CK told me with a smile. Certainly, he figured, their drab, noninteractive menus *had* to be the reason *2nd Floor* wasn't attracting the iGeneration.

Although he had built a profitable accordion business quickly, CK was a naïve restaurateur. Lunch crowds—typically office workers struggling to pay rent—tended to opt for meals that were cheap and local, and they preferred eating cooked food aided by the distance of chopsticks. In the coming months, CK would adjust to these realities. He introduced affordable lunch specials, and tweaked the sandwiches on offer. Through it all, CK didn't worry about his deli. Selling accordions was still a reliable source of revenue, and he felt fortunate to manage both businesses from his own place, like a resourceful squirrel stashing nuts for the winter inside his cozy tree house.

THE SANDWICH SHOP was a sanctuary within a sanctuary. The neighborhood was established as a refuge for outsiders. After losing the first Opium War in 1842, the Qing dynasty court handed over parts of Shanghai and other Chinese port cities to Western colonial powers. The French occupied this section of the city and transformed what was once an expanse of rice paddies into an exclusive neighborhood, establishing the French Concession in 1849. Since then, one marginalized group after another had sought shelter there. In 1860, the French offered residence to tens of thousands of local Chinese looking to escape the Taiping Rebellion, a violent peasant uprising against the dynasty. Later on, theaters, cinemas, and dance halls—frowned upon by the ever-changing Chinese leadership of the city—were allowed to flourish under French protection. Churches, temples, and mosques soon followed.

When the Communist Party took over in 1949, it vilified the foreign concessions, considering them to be humiliating symbols of outside aggression. Missing from Party propaganda, though, was that in 1921, the twenty-eight-year-old Mao Zedong secretly met with other young radical thinkers at a girls' boarding school deep within the French Concession, convening the first congress of the Chinese Communist Party there. Mao and his comrades chose the site precisely for the type of refuge it provided others. It was less likely that authorities controlling the Chinese-run part of the city would find them, arrest them, and put them on trial, a fate that would have prevented the Communists from gaining ground, forever altering the course of China's history.

The French had built their neighborhood with a layout typical of a Parisian arrondissement: narrow, winding boulevards lined with trees that locals still call *Faguo Wutong*, "French Phoenix Trees," though they are neither French nor phoenix trees. Like the muddled history of Shanghai, they were much more cosmopolitan: London plane trees, a hybrid of the Oriental plane—native to

Central Asia—and the American sycamore. The first London plane tree was discovered in Spain.

Baron Georges-Eugène Haussmann made the London plane famous. The urban planner loved the leafy look of the tree, and he had them planted throughout Paris in the nineteenth century when he transformed the city from a chaotic mess of tiny streets into neighborhoods connected by wide, tree-lined avenues. Soon after, London planes appeared across the globe. They still dominate the streets of world-class cities like Rome, Sydney, and New York City. Its leaf, similar to a maple, is the official symbol of New York City's Parks Department.

Two out of every three trees in Shanghai is a London plane. City planners call it the "Supertree" because of its shallow root systems and its high tolerance to smog, extreme temperatures, and pests. They're planted between eighteen and twenty-four feet apart and pruned with a technique known as pollarding, which stunts their growth and forces the branches to grow toward the trees on the opposite side of the street, where they intertwine to form dark green tunnels between two and three stories high. The resulting arched canopy offers pedestrians shade from the sweltering summer sun and cover from the fierce storms that frequently come rumbling off the East China Sea.

By 2010, when I moved to the neighborhood, the Parisian layout and its plane trees remained, but the Chinese had reclaimed the street names. Rue Chevalier and Route Garnier had become Jianguo Lu and Dongping Lu—Build the Nation and Eastern Peace Roads. Other streets once commemorating notable dead Frenchmen had transformed into Rich People Road, Famous People Road, and Lucky Gold Road. On walks through my new neighborhood, I practiced my Chinese by reading their auspicious-sounding names. There was 安福路 (Peaceful Happiness Road), 永福路 (Eternally Fortunate Road), and 宛平路 (Winding Peace Road). I lived on what was perhaps the most auspiciously named one of all: 长乐路—literally "Long Happiness Road," which I took to calling the more eloquent-sounding "Street of Eternal Happiness."

When locals read the names of these streets, eloquence and auspiciousness aren't the first things that come to mind. The street south of my apartment, Anfu (Peaceful Happiness), is a small city in Jiangxi province famous for processing pig parts for ham. Maoming, Famous People Road, is a thriving Cantonese port city. And Changle, my own Street of Eternal Happiness, is the name of a coastal town in Fujian province from which Ming dynasty explorer Zheng He had set sail to explore much of Asia. When the Chinese renamed these French streets, those running south to north had been named after Chinese provinces or provincial capitals, while streets running east to west were named after prominent Chinese cities of the time, which themselves had been auspiciously named so many dynasties ago.

Whenever I pedal my bike along the Street of Eternal Happiness, I need all the luck I can get. The narrow street is one of the neighborhood's few two-way thoroughfares. Taxis often use it to escape the traffic of the nearby expressway, but they must contend with droves of electric motor scooters that seem to pour into every open space. Scooters often barrel down the wrong side of the road in packs against oncoming traffic, dispersing just in time to make way for the cars cutting through the hordes, horns blaring, headlights flashing. Survival is the rule of the road, and the right-of-way cedes to the biggest, most aggressive vehicles. City buses top the food chain. Their sheer size commands respect from the scooter and car drivers who pull over to make way for the behemoths, a survival instinct akin to diving out of the way of a rampaging elephant. All this activity leaves bicyclists to fend for themselves near the curbs or on the sidewalks, where riders often take out their frustrations by plowing through pedestrian traffic.

I choose to ride with the electric scooters. I can usually pedal fast enough to keep up with them, and their riding habits—traveling as an integrated unit like a peloton in the Tour de France—help protect me. Each morning's ride requires a constant awareness of my surroundings. Despite the appearance of vehicular pandemonium, many drivers possess a conditioned athlete's mental focus, behaving according to the unspoken rules of the road. They move in concert with one another as they speed and swerve down the Street of Eternal Happiness, a system disguised as chaos.

ON A COLD DAY in the winter of 2012 I ascended *2nd Floor Your Sandwich*'s spiral stairway to warm up with a cup of coffee in a corner booth. The branches of the plane trees outside were like nude, brittle chopsticks, pointing in all directions, making scraping sounds across the second-floor windows whenever a freezing wind came swirling down the street.

On a shelf in the middle of the sunny dining room sat CK's accordion, a massive black instrument with "Polverini" engraved across the front in elegant cursive. The shop was empty that day, so CK heaved it off the shelf, slumped into a sunlit booth, bowed his head, and pressed the air release button, slowly opening the bellows. The instrument exhaled, a sigh so deep it seemed to be coming from CK himself. The day before, his head chef had quit in a fury, taking half the waitstaff with him. If any customers arrived today, CK and Max were on their own.

He paused for a moment, and then launched into a furious, fast-paced ballad, his fingers racing across the keyboard. He closed his eyes as the melody took shape, expanding and contracting the instrument with a fluid motion, his fingers moving so quickly they seemed to have minds of their own. It was a patriotic song from his childhood, and as his head bobbed back and forth, memories suddenly came to him, driving the song forward, faster and faster.

CK WAS ELEVEN YEARS OLD when it dawned on him: killing himself wasn't going to be easy. For two straight months, he had explored his options each day after school. Swallowing sleeping pills should be the most comfortable way to do it, he thought, but the pharmacist wouldn't sell them to him. "You're too young," she said. Walking off the roof of his family's apartment building was a possibility.

Nah, he concluded: too painful. "I realized I didn't have the courage to jump," he said.

There was another problem. He rarely had a moment alone. The boy was an only child with overbearing parents and a *nai nai*—his paternal grandma—who left his side only when he used the toilet. Each day he ate a porridge breakfast seated inches from them. At the school down the dirt road from his family's rural home, teachers took over. After that, it was back to *nai nai* and his parents for homework, music lessons, and a vegetables-and-rice dinner. He couldn't even steal a minute alone at bedtime: *nai nai* slept on a thin bamboo-matted bed beside him.

One afternoon while his father was writing at his desk, CK took a final, determined inventory of his family's cold, bare apartment. Outside, the air was thick with the exhaust of neighboring chemical and mining-equipment factories. He walked through the apartment, quietly foraging for household objects with the most promising life-ending potential. His quest ended in the only room where he had a reasonable excuse to be alone: the bathroom. He settled on a straightedge razor he discovered in his father's shaving kit. One night before turning in, he slipped the folded razor into his pajamas pocket.

It was a chilly autumn evening. Moonlight filled the room. The night was quiet, save for *nai nai*'s steady breathing and the occasional train in the distance. It announced itself with a soft, sustained horn blast, followed by the soothing rumble of freight rolling along track before dissipating into the silence. As he waited for his grandmother to fade into deep sleep, CK thought about his family.

FROM AN EARLY AGE, the boy had listened to his father talk about "the system." He was never sure what the words actually meant, but he could usually predict when his father was about to utter them. His father had a way of pausing before he said the words, pronouncing the phrase slowly and deliberately, making them stand apart from the rest of a sentence so the boy would take note.

"You see, Kai Kai, you just can't fight . . . *the system.*" The phrase was imprinted onto the boy's memory in italics.

After a difficult day at work, his father would return home and sit his son down, a ready audience for his rants. *The system* didn't allow him to choose his career. *The system* didn't reward intelligence. *The system* discouraged individual talent. You could never get ahead in *the system*. "*Zhongguode guoqing buhao!*"—"China's state of affairs is terrible!" his father would rage.

"My father thought he was an intellectual," CK said. "He wasn't happy with his job and the fact that he didn't choose what he wanted to be. He knew he was smarter than others. He wanted to succeed based on his talents, but he couldn't. *The system* wouldn't allow it. He didn't think my mother was very smart, and that frustrated him, too. He didn't like his colleagues at work, and he hated China."

When CK tried to ask questions, his father shushed him, continuing his tirade. Eventually, CK felt it made little sense to talk in a home where no one listened. So he stopped talking altogether.

CK didn't have any brothers or sisters. He was born in 1981, two years after the implementation of China's planned-birth policy. His shared living quarters with his mother, father, and *nai nai* were on the top floor of a run-down four-story brick building assigned to them by the city railway bureau, his grandmother's work unit. The stairwells were littered with garbage. CK's father employed *the system*'s propaganda of the day—Leader Deng Xiaoping's Four Modernizations campaign and President Jiang Zemin's Three Represents slogan—to describe the place. "He called it a 'three no-managements' area: nobody cleaned it, nobody administered it, and nobody cared about it."

The same could be said for the city where CK grew up. Historically, Hengyang, as far from Shanghai as New York is from Chicago, was a place to avoid. Located in the central province of Hunan, it made brief appearances in Chinese records beginning fourteen hundred years ago, when Tang dynasty emperor Gaozong punished a rebellious assistant by banishing him to administer the city. Later, emperors used an appointment there again and again as retribution for other dodgy high-ranking court officials, all sent to govern a far-flung municipality on the edge of the empire, from where they were seldom heard again.

Modern times hadn't been much better for the people of Hengyang. On a freight rail map of China, the north–south and east–west lines crisscross there, creating an X in the heart of the country. It's one of the region's most important centers of heavy industry. Chemical factories abound, as do coal, lead, and zinc mines. The air was polluted and rancid, but there were jobs: CK's grandmother worked at the railway bureau, his mother at a phosphate fertilizer factory, and his father at the Hengyang City Number Two Construction Company.

CK's parents were born in the early 1950s alongside the birth of Communist China. Their generation grew up with the Party's schizophrenic campaigns, revolutions, and counterrevolutions that left tens of millions dead, persecuted, and imprisoned. There was rarely a calm moment in those years. Survival depended on a keen ability to adapt to an ever-changing political environment, understanding that, like someone caught in a riptide, you must resist the urge to swim against a much stronger force. There was always the possibility of patiently maneuvering your way to safety, but you first had to cede control to *the system*.

As teenagers, CK's parents were sent to the countryside to farm for several years, a fate typical for city kids under the policies of Chinese leader Mao Zedong. Mao dreamed of a China where urbanites worked alongside farmers in a proletariat utopia; but when he died in 1976, his dreams went with him. Most "sent-down youth" promptly dropped their hoes and returned home to their families. Upon their arrival, the Party stepped in again, assigning them jobs at local state-owned enterprises. By the time they turned thirty, CK's parents hadn't yet made a single career decision for themselves.

"WOULD YOU LIKE to draw or play the violin?" CK's parents asked him one day in 1985. The three sat at the dinner table, the adults searching the boy's face for an answer. His father had always aspired to be a writer or a musician. He was convinced that had he mastered an artistic skill as a boy, he might have been able to wrest some control from *the system* that had robbed him of any choice in how he made a living. Pushing his son into the arts would serve as a safety net in case China's economy took another treacherous turn someday, he reasoned.

CK's parents had whittled the boy's options down to skills other family members had shown talent for. The boy's grandmother was a gifted illustrator. His father had once happened upon an *erhu*—a two-stringed traditional Chinese instrument vaguely similar to the violin—in the garbage, and had taught himself how to play. The two choices were clear.

"Draw or play the violin," his father demanded, staring at his son. The boy thought for a moment.

"Draw," he replied.

His parents turned away from him, whispering to each other, before turning back to him. "You will play the violin," announced his father.

CK had just turned four.

CK'S LESSONS started when his family shelled out six months' salary for a new violin. They ended a couple of years later when the government launched a series of reforms that privatized parts of China's economy. This put employees at the most inefficient state-owned enterprises, such as Hengyang City Number Two Construction Company, on the chopping block. CK's father lost his job, and with that went money for the violin teacher. The family scrambled for an alternative, and someone remembered that an uncle owned an accordion. A new instrument was chosen. CK's uncle taught the boy the basics for half a year until one night when an electrical fire burned down the government-owned shop where the man worked. CK's uncle was the manager, so the government held him responsible and sent him to prison.

"It wasn't his fault," CK's father said about the incident; "it was *the system's* fault."

CK's dad, who had no idea how to play the accordion but plenty of time to learn, took over as instructor. It didn't take long for CK's knowledge to surpass his father's, and practice became a subtle power reversal as son began to instruct father. Lessons turned tense at unpredictable moments, with CK's father screaming and slapping his son for any perceived misstep.

CK's father was insecure, temperamental, and so scrawny he looked feminine. His mother was calm and confident, with the strong hands of a peasant. The Chinese say such characteristics often spring from childhood. CK's father grew up in the city, while his mother was raised on the shores of Dongting Lake in the Hunan countryside. She seemed to have absorbed the resolute stillness of its serene waters. "She was somehow more masculine," CK said. "She demanded self-esteem and independence."

CK's father hit his mother, too. CK sometimes heard screaming from their bedroom at night. He usually noticed a spattering of purple bruises on his mother's face and arms at breakfast the next morning. As he got older, the boy would try to step in between his parents at the height of these arguments. "I would try to protect her, but he was too fast," he said.

CK spoke of his father not with bitterness, but with the resignation that the Chinese often feel toward people they despise yet also love out of duty. It wasn't his father's fault, he says, nor was it *the system*'s. It was his father's spleen.

The Chinese believe the spleen is the receptacle for a person's temperament and willpower. This belief is immortalized in the Chinese character for *spleen:* 脾, or *pi*. Add in the Chinese character for *energy*, 气, *qi*, and together *piqi*—literally "spleen energy"—comes to mean "temperament" in Mandarin. Many Chinese believe that any damage to the spleen threatens your *piqi*, making you unable to control your emotions. When CK's father was a boy, he was punched so hard in a fistfight that his spleen ruptured. CK said once his dad had injured his spleen, his *piqi* had been lost forever.

In the spring of 1989, CK's father ratcheted up his politically inspired rants. CK was eight, too young to understand the news of student protests and hunger strikes from Beijing. There were whispers of democracy and the possible end of one-party rule in

China. Hundreds of miles away in Tian'anmen Square, protesters had erected a white statue, the *Goddess of Democracy*, that towered over a sea of students. She held aloft a torch with both hands and her gaze was fixed on the oversized portrait of Mao hanging at the entrance to the Forbidden City, and, beyond that, to China's current patriarchs ruling the country from inside their guarded compound, like a mother protecting her children from the tyranny of their father. But the students had swiftly assembled the goddess from metal, foam, and papier-mâché in just four days, and they were pitting it against a style of governance that had lasted millennia. It was hardly a surprise when China's patriarchs prevailed, employing their brute strength to kill thousands, silencing the discussion about the system—a system that would endure.

In the aftermath of the Tian'anmen crackdown, CK was again forced to play audience to his father's political tirades. "I was a kid and I didn't understand much of it," he told me, "I just felt depressed. I wanted to be alone. I didn't want to be stuck at home, left to face my father."

Soon after, CK's mother sought an audience of her own. She sat him down and delivered some news. "Ma's going to be staying somewhere else from now on," she told him. "How about every Wednesday or Thursday I come back here to see you?"

At the time, divorce was uncommon in China. Marital strife was typically worked out behind closed doors, moderated by older generations to ensure the family unit—the backbone of Chinese culture—remained unbroken. CK's mind raced. His classmates would soon find out. His teachers would know. He would have to live alone with his father, with only his grandmother as buffer. CK's father stepped into the room. Would his father blame his mother's departure on *the system,* too? the boy wondered. Family, he concluded, was the only *system* that mattered.

"I want to go live with Mom," CK announced.

His father didn't pause. "It's been decided," he said. "You'll live with me."

THE FIRST SONG CK learned on the accordion was *"Caoyuan Gechang Mao Zhuxi,"* or "The Grasslands Sing for Chairman Mao." CK obediently mastered it, playing the refrain over and over like a machine under the stern watch of his father, who was always ready to strike the boy at any hint of attitude. Between lessons, his father would complain. "Your mother is no good," his father told him, "how could she leave us?"

At school, it seemed everyone had learned about his parents' separation. His classmates asked questions, wondering what it was like to have parents who lived apart. His teachers used the news to embarrass him in front of other students when he wasn't paying attention in class. CK began to feel anxious. He yearned to isolate himself from his classmates and his family: to become *chouli*—detached. "The only quiet time to myself that I had was my walk between home and school. I was basically walking from one source of pressure to the other."

CK LAY AWAKE that autumn evening of his eleventh year, staring at the ceiling, far from *chouli* as *nai nai*'s breathing grew deeper. He felt the weight of the folded straightedge razor pressing lightly on his thigh through his pajamas. When he was certain *nai nai* was asleep, he sat up in bed and withdrew the razor from his pocket. He unfolded it. He took a breath. Holding the handle firmly in his right hand, he pressed the blade to the inside of his left wrist.

He penetrated skin, cutting into flesh. He watched as blood rose to the surface. He began making swift cutting motions, pressing left to right again and again. He was bleeding, but it wasn't the geyser he'd expected. He switched hands and tried the other wrist. The family matriarch continued to doze peacefully beside him. His blood seeped into his pajamas, but the wounds kept clotting.. He couldn't find a vein. And his wrists began to hurt. "I continued to cut, but it was useless. I couldn't see well, and my wrists were so thick," CK told me.

CK slowly folded up the razor and returned it to the pocket of his bloodstained pajamas. *This is just too difficult,* he thought to himself before falling asleep.

THE BELLOWS OF THE ACCORDION expanded and compressed like the lungs of a runner in mid-sprint. The fingers of CK's right hand frantically raced up and down the keyboard, staccato bursts of treble notes trickling over a shifting landscape of bass controlled with a swift mechanical reflex of his left fingers, the two sides chasing each other. CK's eyes were still closed in concentration. A freezing wind blew down the Street of Eternal Happiness, sending the branches outside clattering against the windows of the shop. All appeared to be in harmony, but then CK hit a wrong note. Then two. He opened his eyes, looked at me, and laughed, giving up.

"Wow. What was that?" I asked him.

" 'Taking Tiger Mountain by Strategy,' " he said, still laughing.

The song was a revolutionary epic that opened one of eight Beijing operas allowed during Mao's Cultural Revolution. It borrowed heavily from *Water Margin*, a fourteenth-century Chinese novel known as one of the four classics of Chinese literature. Party leaders turned the novel's tales into musical propaganda—a portrayal of a proletariat hero to rouse the masses in support of *the system*.

CK shook his head, embarrassed he had forgotten how to play a song he had spent his childhood practicing.

"I used to play traditional Chinese songs, but I later discovered I didn't like to play them," CK told me, wiping sweat off his forehead to reveal two bright, oval brown eyes that seemed larger than they were because of his face, which had become thinner in recent weeks. "I preferred something different. It took me a while to realize I can play my own songs."

With that, CK began playing one: a slow, sad melody that conjured up a cold, lonely street in Paris. Or Shanghai.

CK'S FIRST JOB INTERVIEW after college was at Pearl River Piano, China's largest accordion manufacturer. All the practice as a child had finally paid off. After the encounter with his father's razor blade, he'd come to accept the idea that he would spend the remainder of his teenage years living under his father's roof. So he decided to focus on what would come after. He worked hard in school, practiced the accordion, and earned a spot a few hundred miles from home at a college in the southern metropolis of Guangzhou, where he studied music. His Pearl River interviewer was impressed that he played the instrument, and within minutes CK found himself in the office of the president, who handed him an accordion and removed his own from a case next to his desk. The two played a duet together, and when CK was asked to play a solo, he thought about it carefully.

"I picked a very complicated piece: Liszt's 'La Campanella.' I got the job."

CK was assigned a position in the company's accordion sales and marketing department. For the first time in his life, CK's father was proud of him. Pearl River was one of a handful of state-owned musical instrument makers that had survived the country's ambitious market reforms. Sales were picking up, thanks to China's rising consumer class. CK would receive a competitive salary, health benefits, and a generous state pension. But the work was mind numbing. "Each day you'd work two or three hours and then you'd run out of things to do, so you'd just sit around chatting, reading the newspaper," CK said. "Others used the time to cultivate relationships with each other, but I didn't see the point of that."

Instead, CK spent his free time looking for a more interesting job. After a quick search, he found one: Polverini, an Italian accordion maker, had opened a tiny factory a dozen miles west of Shanghai. The company sought an assistant to liaise between its Italian factory manager and its Chinese workers.

Polverini's accordions were world-class—Pearl River accordions seemed like plastic toys in comparison. The job would be technically challenging: CK would have to learn every step in the manufacturing process so that he could help teach low-skilled assembly line workers how to do it.

CK read the job posting over and over.

"It sounded interesting," he told me. "I could finally learn something."

When CK called home to say he found a new job outside the state system, his father was livid. "You can't just walk away from the iron rice bowl!" his dad screamed over the phone. He would earn less at Polverini, and he'd also lose the state benefits package he'd gotten at Pearl River.

"Suddenly, my dad felt unsafe," CK said. "He was extremely angry with me. He kept repeating the same thing: 'When you work for the state, your future is unlimited!'"

In the early 2000s, though, that was no longer true. CK's father still hadn't found a job since he was laid off from Hengyang City Number Two Construction Company. At forty-seven, CK's mother was pressured into early retirement after Hengyang Chemical Factory's orders were decimated by new competition from China's nascent private sector. In 2001, China had entered the World Trade Organization, and cushy jobs at state-owned enterprises were becoming rare. Capitalism was the new norm. CK began to feel that his parents, exhausted from a lifetime of dependency on the state, were now adrift in these new surroundings, and each had begun looking to him for financial stability.

CK explained his decision patiently. He wasn't learning anything by watching others socialize at Pearl River. At Polverini he'd at last acquire the skills to develop himself and his individual talents. This is something you should be able to relate to, he told his father gently.

The system had turned out exactly as CK's father had explained it to him as a boy: it was there to restrain and control you, rather than to enable you to learn and grow. But as his father got older, he began to realize the importance of money, and the stability that *the system* provided. "When I started working at Pearl River, he suddenly embraced *the system*. I didn't know how to talk to him about escaping it."

CK took the job with Polverini and left for Shanghai. His new roommate—a middle-aged Italian engineer—also happened to be his new boss. The two shared a passion for tinkering. As boys, each had spent afternoons taking things apart and piecing them back together; now they would get paid to do it. At Polverini's cramped factory on the outskirts of Shanghai, their mission was to modify the brand's classic accordion to bring its price down. Chinese accordion players tended to either drop thousands of dollars on an expensive Italian instrument, or penny-pinch to buy the cheapest Chinese brand they could find. There was no accordion between the two price points, and therein lay CK's mission: Creating an affordable Polverini, tailored for China's rising middle class.

CK spent months on the assembly line, learning about every part of the instrument. In Italy, his boss designed Ferraris. An accordion was an even more complicated machine, he told CK.

"An accordion is very small, and you have more than three thousand tiny parts inside of it, so a millimeter misstep is a huge mistake," CK explained. "You must have a good understanding of chemicals, wood, steel, how they interact inside the machine, and the sounds they create."

Within a year at Polverini, CK had mastered every step. In the years to come, CK's boss encouraged him to learn more, and he became a jack-of-all-trades. "I was a manager, a translator, a supply chain point person, a customer service agent, I made the prototypes, I was in charge of sound QC, and by the end, I could build an accordion from scratch."

Within four years, CK went from making $400 a month to $4,000, jumping from the average salary in China to that in the United States. For the first time, Shanghai—with its fancy cars, scenic tree-lined boulevards, and international appeal—began to feel like home.

"CAN YOU PLAY something else?" I asked.

It was eleven o'clock and CK had been playing for over half an hour. *2nd Floor Your Sandwich* had been empty all morning. The lunch hour was approaching, and soon hundreds of hungry office workers would be spewed onto the sidewalks of the Street of Eternal Happiness. CK checked the clock, paused, and then nodded, his hands expanding the instrument, letting it breathe.

"I wrote this for a girl I once loved. It's called '2-27.' That's the date we met."

It began with a sustained note in a minor key, and then another, and another, haunting tones patiently repeating like the deep breaths of someone fast asleep. Then, a playful melody arose, unpolished at parts, like a boy strolling down the street without a care in the world, whistling to himself.

CK closed his eyes again, and I stole a glance at his wrists. The wounds of his childhood had long since healed. His music filled his shop. And for the moment, *the system* disappeared.

2

Better City, Better Life

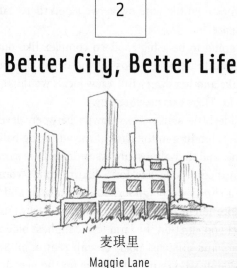

麦琪里

Maggie Lane

While the north side of my apartment had a view of the Street of Eternal Happiness, the southern floor-to-ceiling windows overlooked a walled-in vacant lot of weeds and stray cats. It was punctuated here and there with the burned-out corpses of traditional gray-brick homes. Occasionally, I saw people emerge from the hollow structures, looking skyward and moving slowly as if the daylight was an interruption.

Homeless squatters, I assumed.

I often stood at my window and wondered about the carnage. It seemed strange that a space the size of three football fields in the middle of one of Shanghai's—and China's—swankiest neighborhoods was left to rot. I asked the owner of the apartment upstairs about it. He nodded, pensive, taking a draw from his cigarette and exhaling fumes onto his window as we stood there, taking in the expanse of space.

"It was going to be a big modern complex like ours, and the developer began to demolish most of the neighborhood," he said, pausing to take another drag. "But a few locals wouldn't budge. *Mei banfa*," he said. *There was no other way.*

This made little sense. Showdowns between developers and local residents standing in the path of the wrecking ball were common in China, and they almost always unfolded the same way: City officials identified a good site for a luxury condo complex, there was usually a run-down neighborhood in the way, and they would negotiate relocation deals with the residents. They would demolish the neighborhood, auction the land to the highest bidder, and then fill city coffers and officials' pockets with renminbi. Should there be angry residents who refused to budge for the new development, there was usually a way to deal with them. There was always a *banfa* for Chinese developers.

When I had asked the landlord upstairs about the neighborhood our own complex had replaced, he brushed away the question. "Just a bunch of old, run-down hovels," he said with a swipe of his hand.

Later, when a historian showed me an old browned map of the neighborhood from the 1940s, I noticed a maze of alleyways snaking south from the Street of Eternal Happiness down through dense rows of tiny residential plots where my high-rise apartment building now stood. I peered closer and counted well over a hundred structures inside one square block. I thought about the hundreds of families who had lived where my family now slept. Where did they go? Did they leave peacefully?

MY WIFE AND I had left our home in 2010 to move to Shanghai with our eighteen-month-old son, Rainer, whom we nicknamed "Rainey." We were welcomed by a smiling blue cartoon character with rubbery arms and legs—a cross between Gumby and a Smurf—waving hello. His name was Haibao, the official mascot of the 2010 world's fair, and he was on nearly every billboard on our ride from the airport. Tens of millions of visitors from the farthest reaches of China were descending upon Shanghai to celebrate the city's arrival on the world stage, and Haibao followed them everywhere. He waved hello from the island of the luggage carousel, the airport's greeting hall, taxicab seatbacks, and inside subway stations. He was the twenty-first-century version of the Mao portrait that had adorned public spaces throughout Communist China decades ago: ever-present, always watching. Mao looked dignified, confident, and a little scary. Haibao's deer-in-the-headlights gaze made him appear slightly lost and vacant.

Rainey shouted and waved back whenever he caught a glimpse of him, screaming "Blue!" each time.

"That's Haibao," I told him.

"Hai-bao," Rainey said slowly. He repeated it, smiling. "Hai-bao . . . Haibao . . ."

It was his first word in Chinese.

One of the Haibao billboards caught my attention, too. Haibao posed politely with his arms behind his back, in front of the glowing Shanghai skyline. Above loomed bright yellow characters: 城市让生活更美好.

"The city . . . makes life more beautiful," I said out loud, translating the phrase to no one in particular, struggling to salvage the remnants of a language I hadn't spoken in years.

The slogan was the official theme of the world's fair. Its English equivalent was simpler: "Better City, Better Life." Shanghai was being showcased as the model Chinese city, and China's government was moving forward with an ambitious urbanization campaign, working hard to convince hundreds of millions of rural Chinese that a city life was a better one.

It was a stark departure from the Chinese propaganda I had grown accustomed to years ago. I first came to China near the end of the twentieth century. I was in my early twenties, working as a Peace Corps Volunteer in the countryside. My salary was $120 a month, twice as much as the 800 million Chinese—roughly two-thirds of the population—who lived on less than $2 a day.

Hand-painted signs on the edge of my town reminded residents in bright red characters that little girls were people, too—a warning against the quiet tradition of infanticide among farming families who preferred boys.

Fifteen years later, as I arrived with my family to work as a foreign correspondent in China's wealthiest city, the change was remarkable. The country was about to oust Japan to become the second-largest economy on the planet. Hundreds of millions of Chinese had worked themselves out of poverty. The view from our apartment was a jagged skyline clogged with hundreds of gleaming high-rises. Still, the prominent displays of government-issued directives remained. Sure, Haibao's rollicking billboard presence was more adorable than the propaganda of the '90s, yet it was there for the same reason: to remind people of what was right and what was wrong in today's China. Killing your baby daughter is bad. Cities are good.

Shanghai, with its mix of sleek, modern skyscrapers and green, leafy neighborhoods of nineteenth-century European homes, was a city at its peak. The government had spent the equivalent of $45 billion remaking it, building seven subway lines in five years, the world's longest subway network. Journeys to and from this city now took place on bullet trains traveling at 200 miles per hour. If this century belonged to the Chinese, Shanghai led the way.

Yet change had come quickly, and old habits remained. Social etiquette wasn't part of China's growth strategy; people commonly spat on sidewalks along the Street of Eternal Happiness, threw refuse onto it, and elbowed one another to get to the front of any line. Elderly Shanghainese men in the neighborhood commonly wore pajamas in public. Children were accustomed to squatting and urinating in open view of passersby. Pet owners left dog feces to ferment on sidewalks. This was all standard conduct in urban China, where millions of migrants just off the farm mingled with sophisticated urbanites, each faction wary of the other.

What would visiting foreigners think? Beijing had been trying to eradicate these habits since the run-up to the 2008 Olympics, with varying degrees of success. Alongside "Better City, Better

Life," the characters 文明 littered Shanghai's advertising space. Pronounced "Wen-Ming," the words translated to "Civilized," and signs instructed citizens to help make a "civilized city." The Shanghai government stepped up its efforts in the months leading to the fair. Copies of an etiquette book were mailed to residents. *How to Be a Lovely Shanghainese* was compiled by the city's Commission for Cultural and Ethical Progress in 2006. The guidebook's 242 pages contained pointers on everything from how to cut your hair ("Your hairstyle should not be flashy; just natural and simple") to how to eat Western food ("Don't pick up the bowl or plate with your hands and tilt it toward your mouth to eat").

For native Shanghainese along the Street of Eternal Happiness— those whose ancestors were from the region—the need for such a book was an uncomfortable topic. They had always considered themselves among the most sophisticated Chinese. They'd been ruled by Europe's most civilized powers and had enjoyed the culture and comforts introduced to them by Western residents. Its unique history had made Shanghai one of the great world cities. What use would the "Paris of the East" have for an etiquette guide?

The truth was, nearly half the people who now lived in Shanghai—up to 10 million of its 24 million residents—were workers who had recently moved from poorer parts of China. They were known pejoratively as *waidi ren*—literally, "outside people"—and *How to Be a Lovely Shanghainese* seemed to be written with them in mind.

One chapter began with the stark admission "Shanghainese are generally considered to be cold, detached, and unemotional, unlike people from other places who are rather warm and exuberant," before setting the record straight:

> Urban residents, especially those from the city, are generally cold to strangers because of the current population flow, vast differences between people, and a low trust level. Even in the U.S., people from New York or Chicago are less warm-hearted to those from small towns . . . Most of Shanghai is now occupied by *waidi ren*.

The city government authors were on the defense, inside a twenty-first-century China where everyone else was on the move. The section "Competition and Modesty" implored Shanghainese to accept more menial work and keep an open mind, as migrants were pushing Shanghai residents out of parts of the labor force:

> Shanghainese aren't willing to sell vegetables at the wet market or run barbershops. They aren't willing to be construction workers. There are even fewer Shanghainese starting businesses outside Shanghai or abroad. To fight over small things and to remain ambivalent over the big things remains a negative spirit of the Shanghainese.

One of the main conclusions from how to "Correctly Understand the Shanghainese Character" was that their dominant flaw seemed to be blaming others for those defects. But *How to Be a Lovely Shanghainese* didn't discuss that.

OUR NEW HOME stood eight stories above the Street of Eternal Happiness, nestled inside a complex named the Summit. The development contained seven white-tiled high-rises, one of them standing forty stories. Had it been plopped down in my home state of Minnesota, the Summit would have been the seventh-tallest building. But in Shanghai, it was just another collection of towers woven into a tapestry of hundreds of skyscrapers of all shapes and colors. The Summit towers surrounded a rectangular courtyard with a curved pond, a grassy pitch, and two playgrounds.

Underneath was a multilevel garage jammed with the spoils of China's rising economy: millions of dollars' worth of neon-colored luxury vehicles. A year later I would stroll through this same garage with Rainey, horrified by his expanding Chinese vocabulary, parroting the propaganda of consumerism.

"*Baoma! Benchi! Baoshijie! Falali!*" he'd yell: BMW, Benz, Porsche, Ferrari.

The south side of our apartment faced a road named Peaceful

Happiness; the north side, Eternal Happiness. Wherever we looked, there was happiness.

Except when we happened to glance past the stucco wall lining Peaceful Happiness Road and into the burned-out neighborhood beyond. That autumn, I took walks with Rainey around the perimeter of the abandoned lot. From the ground level, it appeared nothing was amiss. The ten-foot-high wall surrounded it on all sides, world's fair posters greeting us every five steps or so. "Haibao! Haibao!" Rainey screamed.

The only entrance was a creaky metal gate that was usually locked. One afternoon, I knocked on the door. A skinny security guard poked his head out.

"What do you want?" he barked, taking in the blond foreigner standing before him.

"I'd like to come in and take a look around," I said.

"I don't suppose you know any of the residents?" he asked, chuckling at the thought of a foreigner dropping by for tea.

"No."

"Sorry. Foreigners can't come in here. It's not allowed. *Mei banfa.*"

With that, he slammed the door, waking Rainey from his stroller nap. Chinese people might have better luck, I thought.

The next time I visited, I brought some, and I didn't knock.

After the security guard left for lunch I pushed through the unmanned metal gate with a Chinese colleague and a homeless man named Old Kang. Old Kang's full name was Kang Chenggang. He'd lived in this neighborhood for twenty years before his home was demolished, leaving him to wander from one friend's place to another seeking shelter. I'd found Old Kang on an online forum devoted to the neighborhood's history. He was a big man with a potbelly and a face that rarely smiled. His eyes were shaped like downcast crescent moons, topped with droopy eyelids that encircled a stone-cold stare, the look of someone who sought revenge.

We walked underneath a gray-brick archway, one of a handful of structures still standing. Once inside the lot, the first thing I noticed was my apartment building towering above us, dozens of living room windows reflecting the sun's rays onto the field of rubble we tiptoed through. Next door was the glass and steel skyscraper full of office workers that stood across the street from CK's sandwich shop. We were trespassing, and it felt like everyone was watching.

We trudged through chest-high weeds and walked for several minutes before finally stopping at a three-story structure on the edge of the lot. Its roof had caved in and all of its windows were now jagged shards of glass. "Welcome to my home," said Old Kang softly.

A bright yellow string of plastic police tape was wrapped around the building like a ribbon around a gift box. Old Kang lifted it and motioned us through a gray-brick doorway underneath a concrete stele of carved flowers. The absent door appeared to have been ripped off its three rusted misshapen hinges. We stepped inside what used to be Kang's dining room. Sunlight shone through a hole in the roof three stories above us, casting a spotlight onto a floor littered with splintered lumber, broken glass, and rotting furniture.

The sounds of the city poured in from the other side of the wall: a bus braking for a stoplight, the ringing bell of a junk peddler's cart, a baby crying in the distance. We followed Old Kang up the creaky stairs to his third-floor apartment; he'd once shared the home with two other families. Lime-green wallpaper lined a living room that was missing a ceiling and a floor, leaving only a few crossbeams to tiptoe across. I peered down to the floor of the apartment below, trying not to lose my balance. It was as if a meteorite had crashed through the roof, plummeting through the house, ripping through ceilings and floors in a single instant. I looked out the kitchen window. Across a field of weeds were the blackened, empty shells of three homes that had burned down. The neighborhood looked like it had been firebombed.

MORE THAN THREE THOUSAND people had once lived here, packed into rows of three-story homes made of gray and red bricks called *shikumen*, "stone framed gate." Each one abutted the next, creating narrow alleyways in between called *longtang*, whose entrances were capped with massive brick arches. Step inside the gateway of each *shikumen* home, and you'd enter a cramped courtyard with a patch of grass. Beyond that, a single door opened into a hallway and a staircase that led to the various rooms of the house.

The *shikumen* was one part traditional Chinese courtyard home and one part Western townhome. Like everything that was to become synonymous with Shanghai, it fused the most popular styles of East and West. Around the turn of the twentieth century, 60 percent of Shanghai's housing stock—more than 9,000 homes—were built in the *shikumen* style, tucked away in quiet neighborhoods along narrow alleyways off the city's main thoroughfares.

According to municipal records, Maggie Lane, pronounced "My-Chee-Lee" in Chinese, was one of the most orderly, well-kept *shikumen* neighborhoods in Shanghai. In 1958, officials singled it out with an "excellent community" award, and included it in a national propaganda video. Back then, each house had a terrace teeming with flowers and, on the ground level, two big black wooden doors marking the entrance underneath the stone gate. Hanging on the doors were elaborate bronze rings used as knockers, later removed and melted down for steel during Mao's Great Leap Forward campaign.

The lane was named after Maggie Road, a French Concession thoroughfare that Shanghai's Communist leaders later renamed Wulumuqi Road after Urumqi, the capital of the newly incorporated region of Xinjiang. Construction on Maggie Lane's 178 buildings was finished in 1937, but it turned out to be a terrible year for Shanghai real estate. That August, the Japanese began striking the city from the air, the sea, and the ground, marking the beginning of the second Sino-Japanese War. The three-month assault was known as the Battle of Shanghai. By December, the Japanese had killed a quarter of a million people in the city, destroying entire neighborhoods.

Maggie Lane was brutally wiped off the map, but the perpetrators weren't Japanese. They were local officials. And they did so sixty-four years after the Battle of Shanghai. In 2001, the city was developing faster than it ever had. Construction cranes crowded the horizon, and news of violent showdowns between local residents and demolition dominated headlines. That year, Beijing had been selected to host the Summer Olympics of 2008, and now Shanghai was locked against Yeosu, South Korea, in a neck-and-neck bid to host the 2010 world's fair. Members of the Bureau International des Expositions, the Paris-based organization that would choose the winning city, were concerned with Shanghai's human rights record. How would the proposed theme of "Better City, Better Life" fit with the frequent news of enraged Shanghai residents being thrown out of their homes to make way for the city's development?

Responding to that criticism, municipal officials tried a kinder, gentler development path that year called "Urban Renewal." Should an old neighborhood be designated an appropriate project, the developer was required to set aside homes for former residents on the same lot. In return, the developer was exempt from paying land use fees, a savings of millions of dollars.

Maggie Lane was designated as one of Shanghai's first Urban Renewal projects. By the new decree, residents were supposed to be given the right to live on the land following demolition and rebuilding. In February of 2002, Xuhui District officials auctioned the land to a developer named Chengkai Group. In the summer of that year, Chengkai slipped paper notices under the doorways of Maggie Lane residents: they were to be permanently relocated to an outer district of Shanghai—banished to the boonies.

Residents protested. They had a right to return, they said. The Urban Renewal project promised this. But they'd been hoodwinked. Chengkai had saved millions of dollars by developing Maggie Lane as an Urban Renewal project, but district officials had quietly changed its designation to reserved land. It was December 2002. A group of city politicians—including Shanghai's own mayor—was accepting bribes and making shady land deals that would eventually send them all to prison. Party officials had tricked thousands of Maggie Lane residents out of their homes. And Shanghai had won its bid to host the 2010 world's fair. The winning theme was "Better City, Better Life."

The Xuhui government's maneuver reminded me of an etiquette rule I had read in *How to Be a Lovely Shanghainese*. In a section named "Talking and Conversing," government authors educated Shanghai residents about the finer points of gaining trust:

> You should truthfully reflect the truth. Some people like to boast of themselves and make unrealistic promises. That usually ruins things later.

IN MANY RESPECTS, turn-of-the-twenty-first-century Shanghai reminded me of turn-of-the-twentieth-century New York City. The rapid economic growth and the rise of a wealthy class in New York during America's Gilded Age was now repeating itself on the other side of the planet. So, too, were shady land grabs. Seizures like that of Maggie Lane were reminiscent of the New York neighborhoods destroyed in the wake of urban planner Robert Moses, who also helped plan two world's fairs for the city, in 1939 and 1964.

Yet it was the sudden mix of people that struck me as one of the most obvious similarities. The dialects of Chinese spoken by migrants along the Street of Eternal Happiness from provinces like Sichuan, Hunan, and Fujian were just as unintelligible from one another as Italian, French, and German among the European immigrants who flocked to nineteenth-century New York. Both melting pots of new arrivals had been driven to the big city by poverty and a risk-taking ambition that propelled them to drop everything, leave home, and try and make it anew. The immigrants who had arrived on Ellis Island—like their Chinese *waidi ren* counterparts a century later—came straight from the farm, where their ancestors had lived for as long as they could remember.

Many lacked education and refined manners, too. In film footage from the early 1900s taken by a trolley car passenger, New Yorkers scramble around one another to cross the street. They step in front of cars, duck between horse-drawn carriages, and fail to acknowledge those they're cutting off. In another scene, pedestrians jab each other with elbows in a rush to get going. The film was shot at Broadway and Union Square, but swap the trolleys and carriages for honking cars and speeding scooters, and it could have been any intersection along the Street of Eternal Happiness.

I didn't have to dig through too much of my home country's history to find a similar period of economic upheaval that demanded a civilization campaign for the masses, either. Hundreds of etiquette books were published in America at the turn of the twentieth century that bore a striking resemblance to *How to Be a Lovely Shanghainese*:

"It may seem a very simple thing to eat your meals, yet there is no occasion upon which the gentleman, and the low-bred, vulgar man are more strongly contrasted, than when at the table," began the chapter on Table Etiquette in *The Gentlemen's Book of Etiquette*, published in 1879 in Boston by Cecil B. Hartley. "I have seen men who eat soup, or chewed their food, in so noisy a manner as to be heard from one end of the table to the other; fill their mouths so full of food, as to threaten suffocation or choking; use their own knife for the butter, and salt; put their fingers in the sugar bowl, and commit other faults quite as monstrous, yet seem perfectly unconscious that they were doing anything to attract attention."

The Chinese authors of *How to Be a Lovely Shanghainese* appear equally aghast at such boorish behavior, managing to sound like a nagging parent in a section titled "Civilized Eating": "Sit up straight, don't put your elbows on the table, and avoid sticking your feet out at will or kicking others. Don't take too much food at once; if you don't have enough you can take more later. Close your mouth when you chew your food and don't make any licking or smacking sounds. If the food is too hot, wait until it's cooled off. It's not polite to blow your nose or belch during a meal."

"Never put a knife into your mouth, not even with cheese, which should be eaten with a fork," lectures Hartley. "Never use a spoon for anything but liquids. Never touch anything edible with your fingers. Forks were, undoubtedly, a later invention than fingers, but, as we are not cannibals, I am inclined to think they were a good one."

"Pay attention to your chopsticks," *How to Be a Lovely Shanghai-nese* continues. "Don't use them to bang on cups, and don't throw them up in the air. You shouldn't throw chopsticks at someone be-fore a meal . . . You shouldn't fumble with your chopsticks while picking up food or 'fight' with other people's chopsticks."

"Do not be persuaded to touch another drop of wine after your own prudence warns you that you have taken enough," cautions Hartley to nineteenth-century Americans.

It is acceptable, though, explains *How to Be a Lovely Shang-hainese*, to secretly spill alcohol on the floor if excessive toasting is making you drunk. "Don't drain the glass in one swallow," it cau-tions. "Don't get carried away at the sight of alcohol and avoid losing control and speaking nonsense, making a scene out of yourself."

A government-issued publication, *How to Be a Lovely Shang-hainese* lacked the charm of Hartley's *Gentlemen's Book of Etiquette*. Its chapters were sprinkled with laundry lists of behavior modifi-cation, steeped in the Chinese obsession with numerology: "Five kinds of consciousness," "four kinds of spirit," "five dares," and "four forevers." There were also the Seven Don'ts: "Don't spit; don't litter; don't damage public property; don't damage greenery; don't jaywalk; don't smoke in public areas; don't utter vulgar words."

Still, Shanghai's government failed to realize its ambitious goals by the time the world's fair came around. Public property remained largely undamaged, but other than that lone abided re-striction, I commonly saw locals *do* these don'ts within minutes of walking down the Street of Eternal Happiness.

"YOU'RE NOT ALLOWED in here! Hey you! Get out of here!"

It was one o'clock. Lunch was over, and Maggie Lane's security guard had reported back to work, right on schedule.

"Old Kang! Is that you? Who's with you?" the guard demanded, yelling up toward the hollowed third floor.

I peered outside the third-story window of Old Kang's aban-doned house to see the skinny guard standing obediently behind the police line. His blue jacket hung loose on his bony shoulders, his hat tilted to the side; the entire uniform was too big for him. He looked like a boy ready to go trick-or-treating.

"They're my friends!" hollered Old Kang from inside.

"He's a foreigner!" yelled the security guard, pointing at my face in the broken window.

"That doesn't make him any less of a friend!" quipped Old Kang.

We gingerly descended the stairs and came outside to face the guard, who seemed nervous at having to deal with a foreign intruder in what was usually as quiet a beat as a guard could get.

"What are you doing here?" he asked.

"I'm a foreign journalist. I'm interviewing him," I said, indicating Old Kang.

This was the last thing a security guard wanted to hear from an intruder. His anxiety level ticked up a notch, and he shifted from one foot to another.

The guard searched for words. "Well, you can't interview him here," he declared.

"Of course he can! This is my home. I've invited him here to interview me!" said Old Kang.

I carried a copy of the Chinese government's "Regulations on Foreign Journalists" for moments like this. I took the yellowed paper out of my bag, unfolded it, and handed it to the guard. "It says here I can interview anyone in China as long as they give me permission," I said, pointing to Item 17 of the regulations.

"I give him permission," announced Old Kang, smiling at the clarity of this particular Chinese law.

The guard ignored him, scanning the document. "It also says here you have to show police your press card," he said, pointing.

I pulled out my press card and gave it to him. He inspected both sides, holding it at an angle in the sunlight as if he were checking for a watermark on a hundred-yuan bill. He returned it to me.

"You're trespassing," he announced decisively.

"No, he's not," said Old Kang. "Is this not my home?"

The guard thought for a second, lifting his white-gloved fingers to scratch the back of his head. "Yes, it's your home," he finally admitted.

"And did I not give him permission to interview me?"

"Yes."

"Then this is all perfectly legal," concluded Old Kang, turning back to me. "Don't mind him."

The guard kept quiet and followed us as we walked around the partially demolished house, lifting his oversized policeman's hat above his ears to hear Old Kang tell the story of what happened the night they destroyed his home.

It was a clear October evening in 2004. Most of the lane's residents had negotiated relocation packages with Chengkai Group and had moved to tiny apartments on the edge of Shanghai. But dozens of people remained in Maggie Lane, refusing to budge on the principle that the Xuhui government had auctioned the land illegally. But after two years, district officials grew impatient. They put Chengkai Group's demolition crew in charge of getting rid of the holdouts.

"At least twenty thugs surrounded my house," recalled Old Kang. "They cut my water and gas, and then they pulled my front door off the hinges. I refused to leave. Then they threw rocks through my windows and poured buckets of raw sewage into the house. It was disgusting and the smell was horrible, but I mopped it all up. I still didn't leave."

Ever patient, the crew waited for a change in the weather. One night it began to rain, and Old Kang was relaxing in his living room when he heard the noise of a loud engine outside. An excavator slowly pulled up to his house and lifted its arm high above Old Kang's roof.

"*Peng! Peng! Peng!*" Old Kang shouted, remembering the smashing noise he heard from above. The roof collapsed, sending lumber and plaster everywhere and nearly crushing him. Debris, along with a torrent of rain, began to soak his furniture. "Everything got wet," said Kang, "so I left."

Old Kang has been homeless ever since, bouncing around friends' apartments, living on social welfare checks, and petitioning the government to compensate him for his demolished home. "You can't leave me roaming around outside on the streets like this," he told me. The skinny security guard leaned in as Old Kang grew more impassioned. "You've got to give me a shelter to live or rent a place for me. Why not repair the house so that I can move back?" he asked.

The security guard let out a loud guffaw, bending over to laugh at the absurdity of such an idea before shouting *"Bu keneng!"*— *No way!*

Old Kang ignored the guard. "The least they can do is to pay my rent. I don't need a nice house; just a place to live is enough. It doesn't matter where," he said. "A ten-square-meter room would be sufficient, where rent is around two thousand yuan a month."

Old Kang spoke as if I had a say in the matter. Maggie Lane residents had sued the district government, but a local judge had dismissed the suit. They had filed petitions with the government, but those were ignored. The Party controlled the judiciary and the press, so people who had been dealt injustices by the government typically sought out the only people who refused to be influenced by the Party: foreign journalists. Unlike local media, which were strictly censored in their coverage, I was allowed to report whatever I wanted under the protection of a foreign journalist visa. When I first met Old Kang, I wondered how much he told me "truthfully reflected the truth." Was he embellishing some of the details to attract the government's attention? Officials had the chance to refute his story when I contacted them, but they didn't—they refused interview requests. Later, I found police reports that corroborated his story. Plus, the physical evidence was right here, directly above us: a massive hole in his roof in an empty neighborhood of demolished homes.

"I've been without a home for more than eight years," Old Kang said as we hiked over a pile of rubble, walking away. "Do things like this ever happen in your country?"

I thought about the eminent domain cases I had covered back in the United States. "Yes," I said, "but contractors aren't allowed to harass people in the process. That's against the law. And people usually don't end up homeless."

"That's the big difference between your country and mine," said Old Kang, nodding. "We have laws here, but none of them are enforced. Nobody has rights here. It doesn't matter how developed China is—the system is what's important. If they don't change the system, economic development is useless. The government only seems to care about progress in science and technology or the economy, not in its overall system."

Old Kang had raised the proverbial question for China's future, a pivotal issue that scholars have debated for years. Establishing fair legal rights would require an independent judiciary and open the door to lawsuits filed by the people against their government, threatening the Party's power. For years, many China-watchers assumed an independent legal system would gradually evolve alongside the flourishing of capitalism and the economic development of the country, but it hadn't happened yet.

We arrived at the burned-out shell of a *shikumen* home in the center of the lot. We were standing in a vacuum at the center of the world's fastest-moving city, a void that had been left for dead.

A group of old women emerged from the partially destroyed homes of Maggie Lane to say hello.

"He's a foreign journalist!" announced Old Kang, proudly.

The security guard shot me a nervous glance. "Don't talk to them," he told the women.

"Why not?" asked one of them, sarcastically. "We'd just tell him how happy we are to live here! So happy! And what a dignified life! Just look at this lovely place!"

The women's cackling laughter embarrassed the guard and he looked away. Old Kang motioned to a man standing behind them to come forward. "That's Old Chen. He and his wife live in that house over there. He's leading the fight!"

I shook Chen's hand. His full name was Chen Zhongdao, but I later came to nickname him Mayor Chen.

The Mayor of Maggie Lane was a thin man in his sixties. His

hair was neatly trimmed and he had calm, kind eyes, a large nose, and a gentle smile that revealed two large buckteeth. His house stood near the entrance to the lot. Mayor Chen had obtained police records, court documents, and all sorts of evidence of wrongdoing related to the lane. As a result, demolition crews had largely left his house alone. It was well kept, surrounded by a grove of trees. A weeping willow stood in front of the stone gate entrance. Mayor Chen and I traded phone numbers, and I asked him how he and the others were still allowed to live here.

"Oh, they try to kick us out from time to time," he said in a thick Shanghainese dialect, "but we keep fighting."

But their tenacity wasn't the reason they were allowed to remain here, Mayor Chen explained. It was the double murder.

In the early-morning hours of January 9, 2005, three men from the demolition crew arrived carrying canisters of gasoline. The previous year, the group had threatened and intimidated most of the lane's residents out of their homes; in the weeks leading up to that evening, they set more than a dozen fires to scare those who remained, but residents had learned to have buckets of water at the ready to put them out.

On that January night, the three men sprayed gasoline throughout the ground level of an elderly couple's home. Zhu Shuikang and his wife Li Xingzhi were in their seventies and had lived in Maggie Lane for more than sixty years. Zhu was a retired veteran who had fought with the People's Liberation Army in the Korean War. According to court documents, at one o'clock in the morning, the men ignited the gasoline. Within minutes, flames consumed the house. Zhu's and Li's charred bodies were found in what was left of their bed the following morning.

Months later at trial, Zhu and Li's daughter-in-law told the judge through tears that her father-in-law had survived a war, yet he and his wife, aged and defenseless, were murdered on the orders of corrupt local officials. The judge found the three men, all employees of Chengkai Group, guilty. Wang Changkun and Yang Sunqin received reprieved death sentences and Lu Peide was sentenced to life in prison.

This sentence was handed down the same year Shanghai officials published and distributed *How to Be a Lovely Shanghainese* to residents as part of the city's "civilization" campaign. The term is defined on page 75:

> It refers to the state and extent of social progress when human society has rid itself of ignorance, brutality, and backwardness. It is the hallmark of a country, a nation's advancement and enlightenment. It includes material civilization, political civilization and spiritual civilization. It shows a new type of interpersonal relationship that reflects an equal, united society marked by mutual help and amicableness.

THE MAGGIE LANE MURDERS came at a vulnerable time for Shanghai. The city was preparing for the world's spotlight, and it couldn't afford bad press about a burned-out, partially demolished neighborhood—the site of a grisly murder at the hands of a developer—in the very center of the city. Xuhui District officials purchased the land back from the developer at a loss and promptly fenced it in with cream-colored stucco that stood ten feet tall. China's leaders had always been good at building walls, and this one prevented passersby from witnessing the carnage.

Mayor Chen, his wife, and four other families continued living inside their partially demolished houses, refusing to budge until the district met their demands: new homes in the same neighborhood. The district government had restored water, gas, and electricity to the lot, and now the only complaint Chen had was about his leaky roof. (An excavator damaged it years ago, but it wasn't anything a properly placed pail couldn't handle.) Much as it was decades ago, Maggie Lane was a quiet place to live, and residents could come and go as they pleased through a locked gate guarded twenty-four hours a day by a rotating shift of police officers. The lane's remaining residents had even built their own community garden in a sun-drenched expanse in front of what was left of Zhu and Li's home that included onions, chili peppers, and zucchini. I often watched them work from my window above. It was a collective farm in the middle of China's biggest city.

On a sunny day later that autumn, I took a walk around the perimeter of the wall with Rainey. It was October 2010, and the world's fair was wrapping up. Rainey trailed me with a rope in his hand along Peaceful Happiness Road, pulling his favorite toy behind him, a white wooden duck with clicking wheels.

As we kicked through the fallen yellow leaves of the plane trees, the clicking abruptly stopped. I turned to see him pointing to the wall, smiling.

"Haibao! Haibao!" he screamed.

The wall was covered with the same posters we had seen when we first arrived here: the blue, smiling, rubbery figure vacantly staring into the distance as he floated atop Shanghai's skyline. Underneath him, in giant red letters, there it was: "Better City, Better Life." The phrase appeared on posters every ten feet as we strolled alongside the wall: Better City, Better Life . . . Better City, Better Life . . . Better City, Better Life . . .

It was a repeated chorus backed by the steady rhythm of Rainey's clicking duck as he ran ahead, chasing one Haibao after another, ecstatic at each appearance, unaware of the blackened corpse of a neighborhood that lay on the other side.

Hot and Noisy

长乐路109号

Street of Eternal Happiness, No. 109

I met Zhao Shiling while looking for a place to buy flowers for my wife. Zhao's flower shop is at the eastern end of the Street of Eternal Happiness, right before it turns into Golden Hill Road and continues east to the Bund, a raised walkway along the Huangpu River fronted by a row of colonial-style buildings that were built by the European powers in the nineteenth century. Zhao's corner shop is well located—a block from the city's congested North–South Elevated expressway—and I sometimes biked past it on my way home from work.

Competing stores along the street also offer roses, lilies, and tulips, but I prefer Zhao's because her corner is so lively. Shops along this part of the street are tiny. They take up, at most, fifteen-foot-wide sections of the block, and go back only ten feet, like a row of walk-in closets. Shop owners and their wares are forced to spill out onto the sidewalk. I often found Zhao sitting in a lawn chair under her shop's awning, fanning herself while watching a toddler whose parents ran a store a few doors down. In between Zhao and that shop was a clothing boutique run by a woman from Anhui and a motorcycle repairman from Jiangsu who was usually hunched over a dismembered scooter, its parts scattered all over the sidewalk. The three would trade neighborhood gossip in loud bursts of rural dialect while each of them did what they could to prevent the toddler from falling over sharp scooter parts or wandering down the sidewalk beyond their stores, gently nudging the child between them like a pinball as shoppers scurried by.

The Chinese have a name for the warm bustle of a street corner like this: *renao,* literally "hot and noisy." And for urban Chinese, life is an eternal quest for more hot and noisy.

I had grown up surrounded by the opposite of *renao.* Few places were colder and quieter than rural Minnesota. But after living in China for years, even I had come to seek places that were hot and noisy. There was something else that drew me to the intersection at Zhao's, though. She had a countryside sensibility that reminded me of the Sichuan students I had taught. She laughed easily and spoke loudly and confidently. She poked fun at others but mostly she made fun of herself, something the status-conscious Shanghainese rarely did. The only wrinkles on her face laid a gentle path from the edge of her eyes toward her forehead—a face shaped by smiling.

Zhao had two grown sons, a fact everyone learned within a minute of meeting her. Both were named Sun. Big Sun was tall, like his mother. He was thin and handsome, and he had tranquil, almond-shaped eyes and a long, slender nose. Little Sun stood shorter than his brother, his eyes were narrower, and he was built like a bull. Her regular customers knew everything about these young men— how proud Zhao was of Big Sun's intelligence, how guilty she felt about his path in life. Her customers knew she worried about Little Sun's business smarts and whether he would make it in the big city. At least Little Sun had produced a grandson for her, Zhao would chuckle; Little Sun was good for something. Everything inside this shop—the roses, the lilies, the special-order bouquets—was here to provide better lives for her two Suns.

Zhao didn't slouch. Standing on the hot and noisy corner outside her shop, her sturdy frame towered over the lithe, petite local women who passed by, tiny purses clutched to their fragile bodies. However, Zhao had lived in cosmopolitan Shanghai long enough to have gained a fashion sense. On the rare occasion when she dressed up and let her hair down, she was a pretty, middle-aged lady who carried the confidence of one who had conquered the hardships of the country. We often spent afternoons whiling away the time on stools in her shop's doorway, eating sliced fruit, deep in conversation, immersed in the hot and noisy rhythms of the big city.

YEARS AGO, inside a concrete block apartment at the edge of a coal mine, Zhao daydreamed about Shanghai. Growing up seven hundred miles away, she knew only two things about the city: its legendary wealth and its evocative name. The Chinese characters for Shanghai, 上海, mean "on the sea." The city center is actually dozens of miles away from the coast. It's built along a bend of the Huangpu River, one of the many narrow tributaries of the Yangtze that, from an airplane, look like capillaries branching off a bulging, muddy mother artery.

Zhao hadn't flown over Shanghai before. She had never boarded a plane. She used her imagination instead. She visualized waves pounding Shanghai's beaches. Beyond the white sand, she imagined rows of glass and steel rising from the city like the towering stalks of corn at the height of summer near her hometown. One day in 1995, her curiosity overpowered her. She packed a plastic tarp bag with her belongings, said goodbye to her husband and two young sons, and boarded an overnight train.

"Shanghai wasn't what I had imagined," says Zhao, giggling.

Shanghai was crowded with soaring office buildings and noisy traffic. Everywhere you looked, there was construction. Cranes filled the horizon, and there was a ring of smelly factories around the city, polluting its skies.

Zhao had been Shanghaied.

She had saved money for an outfit to wear her first day there: red dress, red socks, and a red hat with a big plastic flower stapled to its front. "I figured that's how they dressed in the city," Zhao once told me with a laugh.

Zhao had envisioned dipping her toes in the ocean when she arrived. "I walked past a bridge and asked a few factory workers, 'Is that the sea?'"

The workers took one look at her and then at the narrow river full of garbage and had a good laugh.

When it came time for her to take the subway, she thought it was a long tractor. "I had never seen a subway before and tractors were all I knew," she said.

Zhao didn't have family in Shanghai, only a handful of friends who had made the journey from her village in Shandong province. They were too busy to send her a detailed description of the city. They all worked at the same factory—Beishang Electronics—a company that assembled televisions for Sony in an industrial Shanghai suburb. Like many migrants back then, Zhao arrived with a vague promise of assembly line work secured through the oldest known system in China: *guanxi*—relationships. In the belt of factories surrounding Shanghai, hometown *guanxi* was the door to a coveted job making foreign products, earning a salary several times more than what you could make back home. Each assembly line at Beishang Electronics was staffed with workers from the same hometown speaking dialects unintelligible to the next line over.

Zhao was twenty-nine years old—nearly a decade her coworkers' senior, and the eldest arrival from her hometown. Back home, her departure was the talk of the Zaozhuang Coal Mining Bureau, her husband's work unit. What kind of man would allow his wife to up and leave him and his children for the big city? Zhao's husband had the habit of squinting when he listened to others, his mouth slightly agape—a face that looked perpetually confused. He was a short man of few words who had married a tall woman of many. He didn't have an answer for his jocular comrades in the mine, nor could he muster an objection when his wife sat him down one day and, with a booming voice cultivated by yelling across fields of sorghum as a girl, lectured him on the facts: China was changing, people were now allowed to make money, and she was going to go and make some before others made it first. After all, how would their children survive in this fast-changing China merely on the fifty dollars a month he was making at the mine? Zhao remembers her husband answering with his enigmatic squint, silently puzzled at her restlessness.

Their village was *luohou*, backwards, she said. It was a term I often heard while teaching in Sichuan in the '90s. While biking in the countryside, I would stop to talk to villagers and I would comment on how pretty the terraced rice paddies were. Inevitably I would receive a *"luohou"* in response. *Backwards.* "In your country, does anyone live like this?" a villager once asked me, defending his word choice.

I looked around: a child sat cross-legged on a dirt courtyard, barefoot, doing his homework, his clothes stained with the manure he had just spread in the fields. Chickens and piglets wandered in and out of the house, while a shit-stained duck quacked incessantly. "Not much, anymore," I said slowly, fumbling nervously with my bike helmet.

"Exactly," the man said, spitting on the ground. "We're *luohou*."

It wasn't their fault. When I first arrived in China in the mid-'90s, the country was emerging from four decades of *luohou* economic policies. It didn't take much to resurrect it. "To get rich is glorious," announced Chinese leader Deng Xiaoping in the early 1990s. To this day, historians quibble over whether Deng actually coined the phrase, but it didn't matter: The masses attributed it to their diminutive and feisty leader, nobody in the Party appeared to refute it, and the phrase stuck. In 1992, Deng boarded a train for a monthlong journey through Southern China. At each stop, the leader encouraged workers to pull themselves up by their bootstraps, promising that the government would get out of their way. After decades of being forced to follow one harebrained campaign after another, the Chinese could finally make some money. *"Gaige Kaifang"* was the term Deng repeated: "Reform and Opening."

Reform our economy, Deng pronounced, and open the country up to the outside world. China's Communist Party called this "Socialism with Chinese Characteristics." Others called it capitalism.

Zhao had her own response to *Gaige Kaifang*: After losing out on an education during the Cultural Revolution, being forced into a marriage arranged by her parents, and then raising her children in a village with trees stained jet black from the surrounding coal pit, she seized this new autonomy as an opportunity—and moved to Shanghai.

Like Deng, she planned to get there by train. Before she left in the spring of 1995, the women in Zhao's village suddenly stopped talking to her. "They looked at me in disgust," she said. "Why on earth would a woman move so far from home? All of them stayed at home knitting, and most of them were unemployed. They thought I was leaving to take part in some immoral business," she said coyly.

When the Chinese New Year holiday arrived the following year, Zhao and her coworkers returned to their village wearing blue jumpsuits with the Beishang Electronics patch emblazoned on the breast pockets, dispelling any myths about working girls in the big city. "We were proud, and we looked it," she said. "We showed them we weren't working in some dirty massage parlor. We were working hard, eating bitter," she said, repeating the familiar phrase *chi ku* in Chinese, an expression that came to define the country's first wave of industrious migrant workers.

"RED ROSE, WHITE ROSE, tulip, *Lilium* 'Casa Blanca' . . ." Zhao took inventory of her shop while I looked on, asking about prices. "Lilies sure are expensive this year—I sell them for 150 yuan a bunch, and still the quality is poor! *Aiya!*" (That was about 25 U.S. dollars.)

It was early 2012, the final year of Chinese president Hu Jintao's leadership, and the nation's economy—a juggernaut that had grown more than 8 percent a year for the past two decades—was beginning to cool. One thing I had learned as an economics reporter in China was to take what economists say about the country with a grain of salt. It's difficult to know what's happening when its own leaders admit—like a smiling future premier Li Keqiang did to U.S. ambassador Clark Randt over dinner in 2007—that the country's GDP growth figures are "man-made."

Economists have other ways, of course, to gauge China's economic health: trade figures, industrial electricity output, local government debt. I have my methods, too: small-business owners like Zhao. "Look at these orders yesterday," Zhao said, showing me a price list from her wholesaler. "Fifty red roses cost 500 yuan, and nineteen blue roses are 570 yuan. Just a couple of years ago, it cost 3 yuan per rose. Now it's three times that! I used to give baby's breath to customers for free—I can't do that anymore."

The year before last, Zhao earned ¥100,000 of profit—around $15,000—but not this year. Prices were going up and she was losing customers. "I have a feeling we're in for tough times," Zhao told me.

The red characters on the awning above the door to Zhao's shop read *Jin Le Hua Dian*: "Bright Happiness Flower Shop." The first character is borrowed from the name of the Jinjiang Hotel, one of Shanghai's oldest establishments, situated two blocks from her corner. The second character means "happiness," taken from the Street of Eternal Happiness.

Each morning at eight o'clock, Zhao hoists the rickety metal gate to her Jin Le Flower Shop and drags a waist-high table in front of a window filled with the bright fuchsias and yellows of her wares inside. Atop the table sits a basket with pink tissue paper; underneath, a few buckets. Shortly after opening, a delivery van arrives with an order of fresh flowers from a wholesale market near the Hongqiao airport, where they're flown overnight from Kunming, the flower capital of China in the southwestern province of Yunnan. Zhao and the delivery boy exchange a *"Zao"*—"morning"— and they unpack the van together onto the sidewalk in front of the motorcycle repair shop, which won't open for another hour. Zhao begins cutting flowers on her table, discarding the stems in the buckets below, and wrapping the top sellers—roses, lilies, and tulips—in tissue to fill orders for bouquets phoned in the day before. She'll then place the rest of the flowers in plastic white vases neatly arranged on three levels of shelves lining the window and inside wall.

When the shelves are full, it's hard to walk inside the shop without brushing up against rows of Technicolor petals smelling of spring. On the floor there's room for just two stools, a green plastic container of boiled water for tea, and a tiny table Zhao will unfold for lunch each day. At the back of the store, a counter is littered with the trappings of floral retail: a calculator, a phone, a television remote, and a large mirror, to which the week's order forms are taped. Bright Happiness Flower Shop measures ten feet by ten feet—every inch has a purpose.

While the prices from Zhao's wholesaler were steadily on the rise, Internet vendors had begun to battle for her customers. The invisible competition prevented her from charging more, and she swallowed the difference. Two workers helped with deliveries, but before long, she wouldn't be able to afford them.

"What about your sons?" I asked. Big Sun and Little Sun were now in their mid-twenties, and they'd left the coal mine to live with her in Shanghai. She cackled, as if her offspring were hopeless vagrants.

"*Aiya*. Neither of them wants to work for me. Big Sun asked me the other day, 'What if it rains? I don't want to deliver flowers in the rain!' They don't know what it's like to eat bitter."

Both men had found jobs servicing the city's wealthiest residents. Little Sun cooked at a Greek restaurant, and Big Sun worked the counter at one of the dozens of golf courses emerging from the suburban swamps on Shanghai's outskirts. "I make more than my sons," she told me, "but they say they're happier."

" 'We have a lot of coworkers and we have fun together,' they reminded me again yesterday," Zhao said in a mocking voice. "They're just like all young people today, who don't want to actually work. They want jobs with freedom, rest, good pay, and a happy work environment. They ask for too much and they'll never be satisfied. We asked for nothing."

AFTER TWO YEARS of eating bitter on the assembly line at Beishang Electronics, Zhao's supervisor had news for her: "You're too old to work on the line," he announced coldly. "You're fired."

Zhao was thirty-one years old.

It was 1997, the year Deng Xiaoping died. He had left the legacy of Reform and Opening, and it was working splendidly. Factories along China's coast were quickly becoming the largest manufacturing force the planet has known: the workshop of the world. Over the next ten years, 250 million people—a number close to the entire population of the United States at the time—would pick up and leave rural China to be part of the largest human migration in recorded history. "It was almost scary to walk into a factory during that era," recalled an acquaintance who worked in the boomtown of Dongguan then. "You would have hundreds of people lined up in circles around the gate, pushing to get forward to read the signs about what kind of worker they were hiring. You've seen the movies where people are trying to leave the city before the invading army comes? It was like that, but they weren't trying to leave. They were trying to get in."

And that's why Zhao was out. Chinese factory bosses preferred to hire young women. Their fingers were more agile, Zhao's boss told her, plus management had decided to fire everyone over the age of twenty-five. "You should feel good you made it this long," he told her. Zhao cried, pleading with him, but factory bosses didn't trust older workers. They were more likely to complain about working conditions, and their seniority meant they had sway over their younger coworkers.

Another line worker introduced Zhao to an older man who ran his own flower business. Zhao tended the shop and made deliveries, and in return the man taught her how to arrange flowers and how to write calligraphy. "His son studied in Australia and married a Japanese girl," Zhao said. "His wife is a deputy schoolmaster. His *suzhi* is very high."

Suzhi was a term I often heard Chinese say with reverence. Its meaning had evolved through thousands of years of Chinese history, and it was a difficult word to translate. Essentially, it referred to the "inner quality" or the "essence" of a person. Confucian tradition held that a person's *suzhi* was determined by qualities such as birth, education, and knowledge of classic texts. Today, it has evolved to mean "educated and civil." The phrase was now *en vogue* again, thanks to its use in China's state-run media and other state propaganda, and Chinese citizens whose *suzhi* was high, the message went, would better represent the People's Republic.

"When I first arrived in Shanghai, I was a stupid peasant," Zhao told me. "I didn't know anything about saving money. If I made a thousand yuan, I'd waste it on clothes. When I met my *laoshi*—teacher—it changed my life."

Laoshi's most important directive, Zhao said, was to never rely on a man.

"He told me, 'You have to become independent, master skills, and manage your money,'" she said.

It was a fitting lesson, considering how her marriage had turned out.

ZHAO HAD GROWN UP sickly and therefore useless to the family farm in rural Shandong province. As a teenager, she had frequent bloody noses and her gums bled. The first time she visited a hospital she said she was so tired she couldn't walk.

Her father called her lazy. It turned out she had leukemia.

As families often do in the countryside, hers promptly sold their pigs, chickens, sheep, and a single ox to pay for a medical regimen that combined East and West. Between weekly blood transfusions and bone marrow transplants, Zhao slurped down live mudfish. She spent her days in a hospital ward with seven other leukemia patients. Within months, all seven had died.

She was surely next. Her parents sold a few more animals to make one last purchase: a coffin. Zhao's mother attended a Christian church in the village, and she arranged to baptize her daughter before she died. Others were called on to pray for Zhao's health. They even killed a lamb, believing it would help save her.

When she recovered, they considered it miraculous. "Was it God who saved me?" Zhao wondered. Regardless, she began attending church, thankful for her good fortune.

But while she had found Jesus, she had lost her chance at finding a good husband. Zhao could no longer bear children, villagers whispered. The family had no assets except for an unused coffin, others said. Zhao wasn't bad-looking, but her illness kept the village men away.

Her aunt found a man whose family knew nothing about Zhao's medical history. The man was short, ugly, and "from the mountains"—meaning desperately poor—but he was her lone suitor. The family was thrilled.

Zhao was not. Nineteen at the time, she took one look at the confused-looking peasant, and immediately described her bout with leukemia in great detail. His family didn't believe the story. "People from the mountains in China are born suspicious, and his mother thought I was trying to trick him out of a dowry," she said.

A month after the couple married, Zhao was pregnant. Two years later, they had their second son and were fined a month's wages for violating China's one-child policy. Money was tight, and her husband would argue with her about finances after a long day at the coal mine. He would often hit her, and Zhao began to think about leaving. She couldn't pursue divorce, because her husband threatened to kill her father in return. One day, Zhao asked him: "Can you be nicer to me? I promise to stay here with the children."

The short, fat mountain man didn't answer.

So the married mother of two left for Shanghai alone, becoming a pariah to her husband, her family, and to everyone else in the village except her mother.

"People from my hometown value emotions and relationships above money," she told me, shaking her head. "They'd die, they'll cry, they'll sacrifice their parents, their homes, their money, all for a man."

Zhao motioned to the shelves of colorful flowers. Her life was full of ugliness, but her shop wasn't.

"Life is endurable here, but the whole situation is still very bitter. I cry when I think about how things have turned out," she told me. "But it's not about me anymore. I'm living for my sons now."

SOON AFTER Zhao established her corner flower shop on the Street of Eternal Happiness, her husband sent their firstborn to Shanghai. Big Sun, Mountain Man had determined, would be a resident of China's richest city. Zhao was thrilled.

"If he could make it to college, everyone in my hometown would be so proud of him and we would have a chance to change our family's fate," she said.

Big Sun was in the sixth grade at the time. The boy had inherited his mother's tall, broad body and high cheekbones. He was popular among his classmates at the Zaozhuang coal mining bureau school; he was a fast runner and had earned good grades.

Big Sun's prowess in the coal town followed him to Shanghai; he earned top marks in his new school. A year after attending a neighborhood primary, officials from a local junior high recruited him for his athletic ability. Later, he graduated from Shanghai's Bi Le Middle School as the champion of the thousand-meter dash and the first-prize winner in essay writing. He was at the top of his class. If he kept at his studies, he would test into an elite university. In the meantime, Zhao's flower shop had taken off and she was fielding orders from all over Shanghai. Dreams of making it in the big city were coming true for both mother and son.

Eight-year-old Little Sun, however, was suffering back home. His father was busy with multiple shifts at the mine, and he was often alone. The boy grew withdrawn, often locking himself in his room to read books. He hung up on Zhao when she called, and refused to speak to her during her visits. When she invited village kids to play with him, he hit and kicked them. They didn't come back. Little Sun was a *liushou ertong*, a "left-behind child."

Soon after a quarter of a billion Chinese had migrated to the coast, doctors began to recognize psychological problems among the children like Little Sun who didn't make the journey. They had inferiority complexes. They had low self-esteem. They were afraid to interact with others. They were often unwilling to take their parents' calls, and they were emotionally detached. According to one government study, half of them suffered from depression and anxiety disorders.

State media estimated there were 61 million left-behind boys and girls: one out of every five children in China.

Zhao was too busy to read research about left-behind children. She sought advice from Little Sun's teacher, who guessed that her son was autistic. She promptly removed him from school and sent Little Sun to a special institution dozens of miles away in the county seat.

Back in Shanghai, Big Sun would soon encounter problems, too. He'd graduated from middle school and was enrolled in one of the city's most prestigious high schools, just a block down from his mother's flower shop on the Street of Eternal Happiness.

But before classes were set to start, Zhao received a call from the school, inquiring about her son's residency status.

Zhao had dreaded a call like this. Chinese household registration laws—which, among other things, govern where a child may attend high school—are strict, and neither she nor Big Sun was registered to live in Shanghai. However, the city was in the process of reforming these laws, and some of her friends from other parts of China had successfully become Shanghai residents. Zhao ran her own business in the city and Big Sun was excelling at one of its top schools. She hoped these things would help him gain entrance to a Shanghai high school.

Zhao told the truth: "I told them our household registration permits were from Zaozhuang."

There was a long pause on the other end of the line. Finally, the woman spoke. "He'll have to return there if he ever wants to attend college."

Chinese law required students to sit for the national college entrance exam in the place tied to their household registration permit, forcing them to attend high school there, too.

Zhao thought about all the work she had done so that her children could have better lives, the hopes she had for Big Sun, and the promise he had shown. All of it—the endless studying, his high class rank, his prize-winning writing—suddenly seemed like a big waste.

Big Sun was going to have to return to the coal mine.

MUCH OF CHINA may be on the move, but the country's household registration system—known as *hukou*—ties Chinese families to their hometowns. If you ever want to hear a Chinese farmer curse, rant, and complain, utter *"Hukou."* After nearly a decade living here, I had yet to meet any rural Chinese who were happy with the system.

The grumbling went back millennia. Rulers since the Shang dynasty 3,500 years ago had understood the importance of keeping a meticulous registry of all households in China. It ensured steady tax revenue and a continual stream of young men to serve in the military. It was also useful for keeping close tabs on any potential sources of social and political unrest. Chairman Mao later discovered an additional use for the *hukou* system: building China's command economy.

After taking power in 1949, China's Communist Party began its push to industrialize, looking to Stalin for help. The USSR's *propiska*—or internal passport—system had helped the Soviet leader build a socialist economy by keeping workers in industry and agriculture separated, restricting their movements inside the country.

And so, beginning in 1958, Chinese who lived in Shanghai were granted urban *hukou*. Most everyone who lived along the Street of Eternal Happiness—like their urban counterparts in cities all over China—were assigned to work in factories. In villages like Zhao's—which comprised a vast majority of the population at the time—they were assigned rural *hukou* and forced to join collective farms. Checkpoints at train stations and along roadways prevented either group from traveling outside the city or village where they were registered. China's new government could control who worked where, and account for each citizen's economic output for the state in minute detail.

There were problems with the system. During the Great Famine, a rural *hukou* was, for many, equivalent to a death sentence. At the time, more than half a billion rural *hukou* holders worked for collective farms where the government took its share of the harvest before farmers were allowed to eat. Much of the forfeited food went straight to China's urban residents.

This scheme backfired when rural government officials—under pressure from the central government to raise agricultural output—wildly exaggerated their crop numbers. When state tax collectors came around, many rural communities like Zhao's were forced to give up all their food to meet what was promised. From 1958 to 1962, it is estimated that 36 million rural Chinese starved to death while their urban *hukou*-holding compatriots—factory workers along the Street of Eternal Happiness included—dined on the food they had grown, oblivious to the body count in China's countryside.

Yet from an economic perspective, the *hukou* system sped up the country's industrialization. One *hukou* expert called it "China's secret recipe for its unprecedented economic success." But a report written on the fiftieth anniversary of the modern *hukou* system laid out the brutal cost to Chinese society:

> By immobilizing the peasantry, forcing them to tend the land at mostly subsistence levels of compensation, and excluding them from access to social welfare and ability to move to cities, this approach created two very different societies. And given the immutable, hereditary nature of the *hukou* classifications, the peasantry de facto became an underclass.

After the Reform and Opening era of the 1980s, China's government removed the *hukou* checkpoints and gradually allowed its citizens more freedom of movement, restoring a right that had originally been guaranteed in the country's constitution, but ignored by law enforcement.

Despite the change, the impact on Chinese society remained. By 2000, the *hukou* system had created two Chinas: one like

Shanghai, filled with gleaming skyscrapers and modern public transportation that drew migrant workers from undeveloped areas and tourists from abroad; and the other China, which looked like Zhao's hometown: an impoverished, *luohou* countryside, where hundreds of millions still eked out livings as farmers on less than $2.00 a day. That other China was a place that visitors didn't care to go, and that most Chinese were eager to leave.

Once they did, though, they learned a rural *hukou* was worthless in a city like Shanghai. Rural Chinese like Zhao had to journey back to their *hukou*'s origin if they wanted a marriage license, a passport, or health insurance.

The biggest complaint I heard from non-native Shanghainese along the street was the system's impact on their children. Tens of millions of children were born to couples that had moved to the cities to find work. Like Big Sun, these kids grew up in the city, went to primary school in the city, made friends in the city, and considered the city their hometown. Yet their *hukou* belonged to the countryside. So when it came time for high school, they were forced to move back to the town of their parents' birth. If they weren't left-behind children by then, odds are when they were sent to the countryside to live with their grandparents in a town they had visited only a handful of times, they would become textbook examples by the time high school was through. Social scientists wrote condemning stories about this aspect of the *hukou* system, often comparing it to the apartheid system in South Africa before Mandela came to power.

Doing away with *hukou* wouldn't be easy for the government. It had helped leaders gain control over the economic output of its 1.3 billion citizens, aiding in China's rise to become the world's second-largest economy by 2011. This restriction on the flow of migrant workers' families had also helped prevent the emergence of shantytown suburbs commonplace in the cities of other developing countries, like India or Brazil. It wasn't uncommon even for migrant workers to acknowledge the dangers of dismantling the system. A factory worker from Anhui once told me, "Without the *hukou* system, there'd be a flood of outsiders into Shanghai, and many of them wouldn't be able to find a job. Pretty soon there'd be poor people everywhere, their kids all over the streets. Can you imagine how much crime we'd have?"

These were all valid points I had heard from government officials whenever they defended the system—arguments Western media usually ignored. When you considered that China was a developing country with more than a billion people and a rapidly widening wealth gap, it was astonishing how safe its biggest cities were. The harmless streets of Shanghai were one of the biggest draws of moving back to China with my family. Here was a city of 25 million people where we could take a neighborhood stroll at night without worrying about being harassed or mugged. Doing the same thing in our former home along the outskirts of downtown Los Angeles could sometimes draw out our survival instincts.

In addition to preventing the shantytown effect, China had forced more than 250 million people to retain connections with their rural hometowns, and this, too, had a long-term positive impact. As China's economy sped along with double-digit growth, workers who flocked to the cities as young men and women were now making enough money to return home to their children, buy a house, and apply the skills they'd acquired in the cities to help build the economies of their rural hometowns.

In 2013, I returned to the town in Sichuan where I'd lived fifteen years earlier, and I marveled at the changes there. My former Chinese colleagues used to live in Stalinist cement-block hovels with chickens roaming around their courtyards, but now they inhabited luxury condominium complexes and owned cars for weekend family road trips. The region's economy was also flourishing thanks in no small part to the money and skills sent home through a network of migrant workers: trickle-down economics with Chinese characteristics.

In the minds of China's economic planners, the *hukou* system may have treated hundreds of millions of people like illegal immigrants in their own country, but, like the one-child policy, it was a necessary evil if the country was to raise the standard of living for its 1.3 billion residents.

IN 2002, Zhao's oldest had gone as far as he could in Shanghai with a Zaozhuang *hukou*. Big Sun moved back to the Zaozhuang mining bureau to start the tenth grade. His father was working double-time at the coal mine, so they rarely saw each other. China had just entered the WTO, and the Olympic committee had selected Beijing to host the upcoming 2008 summer games. A record amount of coal would be needed to fuel China's growing economy—an average of one coal-fired power plant would be built each week to maintain the country's growth. With his father at the mine and his brother away at a special education school, Big Sun tried to fend off loneliness by focusing on his studies, something he excelled at in Shanghai. He'd outshone his Shanghai classmates, and he figured high school in a *luohou* place like Zaozhuang would be a cinch.

"I'll be one of the top students in my class," Big Sun guessed.

But on his first day of school, he panicked. His new classmates were years ahead of him. He showed his instructor a physics textbook from Shanghai.

"My teacher paged through the book, started to laugh, pointed to the worst student in class, and said, 'You could be first in class if you moved to Shanghai!' The rest of the students laughed out loud."

Big Sun suddenly wished he could transport himself back to his mother's shop on the Street of Eternal Happiness. As his first day of school crawled by, he realized rural students used textbooks tailored to prepare them for a college entrance exam that was far more challenging than the one given in China's biggest cities. The exam was designed to be harder because there were simply more students to filter out. Shandong province has nearly 100 million people, his teacher explained. "He'd said, 'Among a sea of people, the test needs to sift through the sand to find the elite.'"

Big Sun came to understand he was an insignificant grain of sand. His new classmates worked harder than he did, and the school day in Zaozhuang was twice as long as the one in Shanghai, with students arriving at 7 a.m. and sticking around for evening study sessions until 9 p.m.

"All that extra time was devoted to memorizing textbooks—students wouldn't even rest during break time," Big Sun told me. Shanghai students could sometimes consult books during exams, but hometown kids had to rely only on their memories, he said.

Memorizing textbooks was the natural outcome of an education system that culminated with a single college entrance exam known as the *gaokao*. In a culture that emphasized connections to get ahead, the *gaokao* was the great equalizer: anyone, no matter his or her background, could, if they studied hard enough, do well on the test and take control of their family's destiny. Because of its ability to transform the fate of an entire bloodline, though, the *gaokao* has meant that Chinese students spend much of their time studying for and taking tests.

With his new classmates a few years ahead in their memorization, Big Sun was drowning. He began failing exams. He lost interest in school. He started playing videogames at Internet bars instead of attending evening study sessions. Good students didn't talk to him anymore, and he slept through class. His high school teacher thought the sixteen-year-old should re-enroll as a seventh grader and repeat middle school.

"I'd have been close to thirty years old by the time I could graduate from college. It would've had a huge impact on the rest of my life," Big Sun said.

The alternative was more attractive: he dropped out.

Big Sun would return to Shanghai not as a decorated student, but as a migrant worker, just like his mother had twenty years earlier.

FEBRUARY MARKS THE BEGINNING of the busy season for flower vendors in China with the one-two punch of the Lunar New Year—China's most celebrated holiday—and Valentine's Day. Roses are in high demand.

It was 2012. Zhao had barely recovered from the Year of the Dragon celebration, ushered in with an all-night blitzkrieg of fireworks. Her shop floor was a mess of ribbon, tissue, and banners, surrounded by shelves of red, pink, and white roses to be sold for the forthcoming holiday.

She looked tired. She was up most of the night taking care of her new grandchild, who had been born two months ago when it was still the Year of the Rabbit. The chubby boy was the son of Little Sun, now living with Zhao. When Big Sun dropped out and returned to Shanghai, Little Sun saw his chance to finally escape the County school for autistic children and tagged along on Big Brother's trip to the big city.

Both moved in with their mother. Little Sun was twenty-four. Folks in his hometown had heard about where he attended school, and at first, few families offered up their daughters in marriage. It reminded Zhao of her bout with leukemia years ago and the stigma it earned her. But now she had a trump card: the money she had made in the big city, which was also well-shared gossip back in the coal town.

Everyone knew about the two apartments she'd purchased near the high-speed rail station in the county seat. The same local women who had refused to speak to Zhao when she first left for her factory job fifteen years ago were now vying for her attention. It was decided that marrying a son of Zhao was a ticket out of the countryside, and Zhao selected Zhang Min, the confident young daughter of farmers, to be Little Sun's bride.

"Valentine's Day is exhausting," Zhao said as she wrapped a bouquet of roses, "but it always makes me happy to know the flowers I've arranged will be given by young people as a token of love."

Zhao bound the stems tightly together—an order of fifty-seven roses that would be picked up the next day—and a smile emerged as she thought about this. It was just above freezing outside, and her door was opened a crack to let the chilly, humid air inside to prolong the lives of her slowly dying merchandise. It was late afternoon, and the smog had turned the setting sun into a reddish-orange ball suspended just above the bare branches of the plane trees lining the Street of Eternal Happiness. The faint, intermittent car horns of rush hour began to honk, the soundtrack to the end of the workday in Shanghai.

Big Sun was away, working at a golf course. After spending several years playing videogames and subsisting on an allowance from Zhao, he had pulled himself together and found a job. "He thinks golf will be big in China, so he's learning how to play—he wants to be a golf coach someday," Zhao told me. "The other day he said, 'Mom, I can hit a ball from here to the Yan'an expressway!'"

Shanghai's busiest thoroughfare was visible from Zhao's shop 200 yards to the north.

Zhao looked relieved. The past few years had been tough for Big Sun. His classmates from his Shanghai middle school had graduated from the country's best universities. That should've been him, Zhao told me, and it killed her to think about that.

"Sometimes I feel like I've ruined my son," Zhao said, putting the roses aside for a moment. "I always told him to be a good worker, to work hard for the country. But look what's happened to him."

Just the other day, Zhao said, a couple from Fujian arrived in the big city and had their eyes on renting a storefront across the street. They wanted to bring their child here.

"I told them, 'Go back to Fujian! We were fooled.'"

Zhao had given the same advice to all her friends from the countryside. "I tell them if they come, they'll ruin their kids' lives."

This seemed melodramatic to me, and I said so. She had done well in Shanghai and people back home envied her success. Her sons may not have attended perfect schools, but they were working hard, just like she did when she came to the big city.

"Is Big Sun's life really ruined?" I asked her.

Zhao let the question hang in the cold fragrant air of the shop.

"We are all Chinese," Zhao said, motioning to the people walking along the sidewalk. "We are under the same leadership, and we are part of the same country. Why aren't we allowed to have the same rights?"

She had come with a dream and worked hard to achieve it, only to watch the fruits of this labor spoil because she didn't have the correct household registration. Still, Zhao enjoyed other rights her ancestors hadn't. She had freely left her hometown. She had worked hard and earned more money than anyone in her family. Her boys may not have received a Shanghai education, but they would enjoy the material benefits of their mother's decisions for years to come.

Zhao sat on the stool beside me and released a big sigh, exhaled with a cloud of vapor that slowly dissipated inside the freezing shop.

"After my husband retires and I find a wife for Big Sun, I need to rest. I've been here in this tiny room for fifteen years. I've never traveled or even gone out to eat. Sometimes I wonder if there will ever be a day when I start to live for myself."

It's a question often pondered by Chinese mothers, and the answer is almost always: no. Tradition requires them to take care of their husbands, their parents, their children, and their grandchildren. Living for yourself is considered selfish.

But Zhao had done away with tradition. She had left her husband behind. She had started her own business and made her own money. She had seized control of her life. Now she felt responsible for her children and she worried about them incessantly—and she'd feel the same anxiety for their children, too.

"After my eldest son gets married, I'll have to take care of his child, right?" she asked. "Chinese people just can't let things go. We always live for others, for the next generation. It's endless. Aren't we stupid?"

There were several unanswered questions at the Jin Le Flower Shop this afternoon. That one went unanswered, too.

Zhao's telephone rang. "*Wei?* Hello? Big Sun!" Her face immediately reverted to her usual beaming smile. Her son was calling to tell her about his day.

I stepped outside to give her some privacy. The sun had set over Shanghai, the lights of office buildings shining brightly above me through the bare branches of the plane trees. The repairman next door tinkered with a scooter underneath a streetlamp, and his wife was inside the shop serving noodles to their little boy.

Above the din of traffic along the street, I heard Zhao laughing, listening to her son recount his day. She was happy again.

4

Re-Education

长乐路169号
Street of Eternal Happiness, No. 169

Morning on the Street of Eternal Happiness begins earlier than it does in much of the rest of China. The first signs of life are minivans stocked with fresh fish that pull into the neighborhood wet market near the street's midpoint at four in the morning. Then come the stacked boxes of fruits and vegetables, strapped to scooters with a tangle of bungee cords, their drivers racing down the dark, empty street. At five o'clock, vendors set up their wares, tossing yesterday's rotten produce onto the sidewalks. Minutes later, garbage trucks full of street cleaners dressed in pale blue jumpsuits arrive and pick up the mess. Then comes the street-cleaning machine, an enormous water tank on wheels that glides slowly over the pavement like a Zamboni, speakers on top of it blasting an eerie electronic version of "It's a Small World."

On this brisk November morning in 2013, the sun peeks over

Shanghai's horizon at nine minutes after six o'clock. Three thousand miles west in Kashgar, a former Silk Road trading town in the Chinese region of Xinjiang, the sky is still pitch black, sprinkled with stars. If China adhered to more than one time zone, it would now be three in the morning in Kashgar. But it's not. It's 6 a.m. there too, and the sun won't come up for another three and a half hours. The city is as far away from Shanghai as Los Angeles is from New York, but clocks on the city squares, train stations, and high school classrooms in the two cities display the same time.

No matter where you are in China, it's Beijing Time.

It's going to be a sunny autumn day in Shanghai. The high temperature will hover around 50 degrees Fahrenheit. It's currently 40 degrees with an occasional breeze pushing smog eastward into the city from the manufacturing empire of the Yangtze Delta. The plane trees' foliage is a spattering of green trending yellow, and when a strong wind blows down the street, banana-colored leaves break free from their branches, gently falling onto the honking cars and scooters of the morning traffic below. I check the air quality index on my phone, and it reads an orange-colored UNHEALTHY.

I've spent the morning visiting with Zhao Shiling at her flower shop. On my way home along the Street of Eternal Happiness, I spot steam rising from an open window just above the sidewalk, obscuring the faces of the people who pass me with their hands stuffed in their pockets, rushing to work.

I'm hungry, so I stop, lock my bike, and join the line in front of the window.

"Try it. If it doesn't taste good, don't pay," a gruff voice booms from inside the shop. I see a weathered, wrinkled hand emerging from behind the frame to shove a *congyoubing*—a scallion pancake, a popular Shanghai snack—into the slender hands of a young woman in a fashionable pink coat. The line is beginning to grow behind her.

"*Shifu*," she says, using the honorific *master* to refer to the old cook, "I don't want a scallion pancake. Do you have *youdunzi*?"

Youdunzi—literally "oily block"—are fried turnip cakes, another

Shanghai treat. The man wipes sweat from his forehead, the oil on his hand making his silver bangs stand straight up.

"Yes, of course!" shouts the old man. "You'll have to wait, though, while I make a batch. Why don't you take a scallion pancake instead?"

"Your pancakes cost a *kuai* more than anywhere else."

"That's because mine taste better than anyone else's! I won't charge you one *fen* if you don't like them." The young woman pushes her lips into a pout. She eventually orders three more.

Snacks are big in Shanghai. From *xiaolongbao*—"little basket buns"—to *xie ke huang*—crab shell pie—it's hard to walk a block without catching a whiff of the homemade goodies vendors cook from pushcart stovetops or from their own street-level apartments. Inside the old cook's kitchen is a mess of partially cut garden onions, carrots, and lotus root on a tree stump cutting board, a red plastic bucket filled with batter, an electric griddle jam-packed with scallion pancakes, and a wok full of oil over a high gas flame. He plops dollops of turnip cake batter into the wok—it's a mess of shredded turnip, mushrooms, and celery packed inside raw dough—and a scalding sizzle drowns out the sound of scooters buzzing through the neighborhood outside the old man's window.

His kitchen is inside a stucco building that is more than a hundred years old. An intricate, colorful tile pattern on the floor suggests this structure used to be a wealthy residence. But, like many houses and mansions in the former French Concession, its occupants had vacated at some point during decades of war and Communist campaigns, and repopulated with commoners who divided the structures up into tiny, crowded apartments.

The old cook lives in a dark room tucked into the back of the ground floor. He shares the kitchen with tenants in four other apartments upstairs. When each of them descends the stairs and walks by on their way to work, they nod a cheerful *"Zao,"* "Good morning," to the old man. The fact that he's taken over the entire communal space to run his business doesn't appear to be a problem. He's the senior resident and he owns the deed to his room, so he notches above the younger renters in the apartment block hierarchy. Although they might complain among themselves, they pay the old man the appropriate amount of respect.

"Hey you! Buy a scallion pancake, will you?" shouts Shifu to passersby.

The line outside the window has dissipated, and he's trying to unload the rest of his pancakes. A middle-aged man in glasses slows down to read the poorly written blue Chinese characters on a dry erase board hanging from Shifu's window, but he doesn't order anything.

The old cook's name is Feng Jianguo, "Veng Jiguo" in his native Shanghai dialect. I simply call him Uncle Feng. Uncle Feng rarely flashes a full smile. He smirks when he's trying to sell snacks, or when he hears something he doesn't believe, but his face is usually locked into a skeptical Bruce Willis look—wondering when the other guy will strike first. Uncle Feng's stocky torso makes him look ready for anything, and his broad chest is nearly always covered with a white apron.

On a busy day, he makes 180 scallion pancakes. He sells them for three yuan—fifty cents—each, one yuan more than most other snack stalls in the neighborhood. "They have a special flavor everyone loves," he says.

He used to work in the kitchen at the Old Jinjiang Hotel farther down the Street of Eternal Happiness. Minutes later, four of his former coworkers stop by. They're dressed in aprons, too. All but one smokes during their break. As a foreigner inside Uncle Feng's tiny kitchen, I arouse their curiosity, and they take me for a potential customer.

"Nobody makes *congyoubing* like Old Veng!" one of them yells in a thick Shanghai accent, laughing. Feng doesn't say a word as he flips a batch of them onto the griddle. He just smirks.

This block of the Street of Eternal Happiness is bookended by two hotels of the same name: Jinjiang. To the west is the Old Jinjiang, Uncle Feng's old workplace. The fifteen-story brick hotel was established in 1934 by Dong Zhujun, a former prostitute who became one of Shanghai's first successful businesswomen. It was one of the tallest buildings in Shanghai at the time. When the Communist Party came to power in 1949, Dong wisely partnered with them, offering up her hotel to house state leaders like Ho Chi Minh, Kim Il Sung, and in 1972, U.S. president Richard Nixon during the signing of the Shanghai Communiqué, which opened Communist China to a surge in foreign investment.

It was a bad deal for the Jinjiang. Like many state hotels of the era, it lost its status to a new wave of luxurious hotels opened during Shanghai's economic revival. The New Jinjiang, forty stories of glass and steel with a revolving restaurant on top, was the city's tallest building when it was constructed on the opposite end of the block in 1988.

The stretch between the old and new hotels is a timeline that connects an icon of 1930s Shanghai prosperity to a symbol of the city's power today. To compare the two, all you have to do is walk a single block along the Street of Eternal Happiness, from the Jinjiang Hotel on Maoming Road to the Jinjiang Hotel on Ruijin Road.

That's all it takes. One block.

Uncle Feng's kitchen is in the middle. Metaphorically it makes sense. The major events of his life transpired in the three decades of chaos and poverty under Mao between the boom years of the Jinjiangs. "Before he was our leader, Mao made a big contribution to China," Uncle Feng once explained to me. "But afterward, he seemed to want everyone to memorize his heroism. Had he opened his mind to capitalism, China would be much more advanced today. Back in the time of the Old Jinjiang, Hong Kong and Taiwan were much poorer than Shanghai. Later on, they learned from the foreign countries. Shanghai was left behind."

So was Uncle Feng.

HE WAS BORN IN 1951, two years into Mao's tenure. His parents and four siblings lived in a small alley home just a few blocks south of the Street of Eternal Happiness. Mao's influence was at its peak during Uncle Feng's childhood, and he became so immersed in the propaganda and campaigns of the era that by the time he was in middle school, he yearned to leave China's richest city for the countryside. He wanted to toil alongside the proletariat masses he had read so much about in school.

On May 25, 1965, Feng noticed posters along the halls of his school inviting students to join a mass rally that night at the Shanghai Cultural Plaza. There, the posters said, they would learn about a place called Xinjiang.

Xinjiang, "new frontier" in Chinese, is smack dab in the middle of the Eurasian landmass, the place on earth farthest from any ocean. It spans an area the size of California, Nevada, Utah, Arizona, and New Mexico combined. The region had been occupied by a group of Central Asian ethnicities dominated by the Uighur people until the Qing dynasty annexed the territory in the nineteenth century after decades of war. The ancient Silk Road ran through its middle. During the 1940s, Xinjiang slipped away from Chinese control, but after the Communists came to power in 1949, the new leaders were determined to dominate Xinjiang for good. China's military built garrisons throughout Xinjiang; all it needed was hundreds of thousands of settlers to occupy the desolate region.

Uncle Feng was just fourteen years old when he saw the posters. He'd never heard of Xinjiang, but he skipped dinner to attend the rally with classmates. They joined tens of thousands of young people in the stands. On the lit stage below were dozens of People's Liberation Army soldiers who had served in Xinjiang.

"The organizers choreographed the rally very carefully," Uncle said. "The soldiers told us Xinjiang was just amazing—it was a very nice place to work and the food there was plentiful. You could eat all the melons and grapes you wanted."

Uncle Feng remembered this part of the speech resonated with the crowd. It had been just a few years since tens of millions starved to death in the famine that followed Mao's Great Leap Forward campaign. Shanghai had escaped the famine largely unscathed, but food was still in short supply.

The following day, news of the youth rally dominated the headlines of city newspapers. "50,000 Shanghai Youth Display

Dedication to the Full Construction of Xinjiang" read the top line of the *Liberation Daily* on May 26, 1965. The two-page spread included reports about young men and women from China's cities, dubbing them "pale-faced pedants who had zero knowledge about farming." The report claimed the former urban know-nothings were transforming Xinjiang's arid soil into rice paddies. "Each young person on the farm manages 25 acres of paddies, 20–25 acres of cotton, or 50 acres of wheat. They are 'little tigers' who have endured pain and hardship to create wealth for China."

One story highlighted an eighteen-year-old Shanghai native who became a deputy platoon head within a year of arriving in Xinjiang: "When I learned I had come to Xinjiang to raise pigs, I was unhappy," the young man said. "But after being re-educated, I realized that being a 'pig class head' is meaningful work. Serving pork will improve the meals for all the workers!"

The young Feng had never been to such a large rally. He was so excited that he couldn't sleep that night. The next day, he announced to his parents he was dropping out of middle school to help develop Xinjiang. His mother and father were unemotional.

"By then, Mom and Dad had four other children to feed, so they didn't care," Uncle Feng told me. The day after that, he boarded a train that would take weeks to reach China's new frontier. He was farther from home than anyone in his family had ever gone.

An estimated 17 million young people were uprooted from China's cities in the 1950s and '60s. The purpose was twofold: The country's brightest could be "re-educated" by the peasantry, and also help develop the nation's poorest and most remote areas in the process. This mass migration of China's youth became known by four of the simplest characters in Chinese: 上山下乡. "Shangshan Xiaxiang," or "Up to the mountains and down to the villages."

Uncle Feng was among 100,000 young men and women from Shanghai assigned to work in Xinjiang in a group known as *bingtuan*, the Xinjiang Production and Construction Corps. The Corps harnessed dozens of rivers that bordered two of China's largest deserts and built 96 reservoirs and 117 dams. After controlling the region's waterways, the Corps young members dug irrigation ditches and turned 140,000 hectares of scrubland into farmland, an area the size of the state of New York.

On December 7, 1963, the *Liberation Daily* published an article about developing a farm at the foot of the Tianshan Mountains. The area would later become Uncle Feng's sent-down home. "Alongside old soldiers: Shanghai youth active in Tianshan," read the article, which included a poem by the leader of the No. 19 Victory Farm:

Saying goodbye to Shanghai's Huangpu River,
Advancing to Xinjiang with loud songs,
Wade through the dust of tens of thousands of roads,
Young men must have high ambitions.
The country holds limitless goodness,
The youth must be more courageous,
By the desert we thresh the wheat fields,
And the sea of sand rolls by in waves.

"What a shithole," Uncle Feng told me later, shaking his head at the memory of his new desert home. "It was a wasteland—an uninhabited wasteland. Most of us immediately regretted going there, but it was impossible to return to Shanghai. The place was so barren and remote that you couldn't leave even if you wanted to—there was no food, no roads. You'd starve to death trying."

Uncle Feng and his new coworkers began to question everything they had heard in that rally back in Shanghai, now three thousand miles of treacherous roads and rail away. "We had been told how great this place was, so we never asked what we'd be doing. When we got there, we realized they had tricked us and that our job was to try and turn this dry wasteland into farmland."

Feng was assigned to a division outside the town of Aksu, less than a hundred miles from the mountainous border of Kyrgyzstan, at the time a part of the Soviet Union. "There were no homes in Aksu. Nothing, really. The people there were so poor they lived inside mud houses covered with grass. When we first arrived, we didn't even have a place to sleep, so we dug holes, covered them with dry scrub, and collapsed. That's how we slept for two years."

There were 150 young people—mostly men—in Feng's work unit, and they came from all over China: Hebei, Shanxi, Sichuan. Some were soldiers who had fought against local Uighur and Kazakh resistance forces to take control of the area. Nobody seemed to have much food. "They gave us three buns a day. That was our breakfast, lunch, and dinner. That was it."

It was a race against starvation. Feng and his coworkers frantically learned how to drive tractors imported from the Soviet Union. They flattened and tilled the white salinized soil, eventually managing to grow vegetables alongside the Tarim River. A few years later, they grew enough produce to barter for small game with local Kazakh and Uighur hunters who would come down from the mountains. The whole affair gave new meaning to "Up to the Mountains and Down to the Villages."

"NI-HAO!" Uncle Feng's wife bursts through the door carrying bags of giant purple grapes, and then stops when she notices a foreigner in her husband's kitchen.

"Oh! Hello! Would you like some tea? You haven't offered our guest tea, have you?" she asks Feng, scolding him. He ignores her, suddenly becoming quiet as he pours more batter into the wok.

I decline the tea. "Here! Have some grapes! They're delicious. They're from Xinjiang. I've washed them all."

The conversation with Uncle Feng screeches to a halt. It's as if his wife has pointed a remote control at him and put him on mute. I address Auntie Fu with an honorific as she spews questions.

"Are you American?" Auntie asks.

"Yes."

"Are you married?"

"Yes."

"Your wife must be Chinese, that's why you speak Chinese, right?"

"No, she's from America. I learned to speak in Sichuan."

"Sichuan! I'm from Sichuan! Have you been to Songpan? It's close to Jiuzhaigou. *Wah!* It's a shame you didn't marry a Sichuanese girl! So your wife is American, then?"

"Yes. Actually, she's Chinese American."

"*Wah!* Mixed blood! What a blessing! Your children will be very smart. It's genetic."

This woman is a frantic, whirling force of nature. While her husband sits like a rock watching his scallion pancakes sizzle, dollops of dough turning crisp on the griddle, she is like the wind—in constant motion, always talking.

Auntie Fu is short and fat. She wears a pair of glasses that always slip down to the bottom of her nose, the top edge of the frame lining up neatly with her eyes. Instead of pushing them up, she repeatedly tilts her head either up or down to get a clear look at her surroundings. Auntie is two years older than her husband. The two met in Xinjiang. She arrived as a laborer at the farm in Aksu five years after he had arrived. By then, Uncle Feng and his team had developed a range of crops and they had built proper wooden homes to house everybody. Auntie Fu, an educated youth fresh from Sichuan, ate more than three buns a day upon arrival thanks, in part, to years of Feng's labor.

"Are you a Christian?" Auntie Fu asks me excitedly.

I tell her I grew up Catholic. Thank God, she tells me, and promptly invites me to church to meet her preacher.

"Preacher Shen used to be a bandit. He's illiterate, but someone recited the Bible to him in prison and he's memorized the whole book! He's amazing."

This seems odd to me. A bandit who reformed in prison and was now running a church? It sounds like Shen might still be a bandit.

I turn to Feng, unmuting him: "Have you been to this church?"

"I don't believe in those sorts of things. Somebody needs to run the family," he says.

"When you get older and have more time, you need to come and listen," she yells at her husband. "God created the world and everything on Earth. He created human beings, too. We belong to Him."

Uncle rolls his eyes. He turns toward the open window, this time muting himself. Auntie turns back to me. "You must come! There are many young people like you there! Preacher Shen is so good."

Unmute. "Just leave, then!" yells Uncle. "Stop talking so much! If you're going to go, go!"

"The church is owned by a rich man from Wenzhou!" Auntie tells me, ignoring her husband.

Auntie's talk of illiterate bandit preachers and businessmen from Wenzhou—a prosperous city in the South infamous for exporting scam artists—leaves me wondering if it's a sanctioned church. China's government keeps a tight lid on religion, and only sanctioned mainstream faiths whose local leaders vow allegiance to the Party are allowed.

"Is it a legal church?" I ask.

"I don't think so," Auntie answers, with a wave of her hand.

Uncle Feng has something else to say. "If she keeps going to church, pretty soon she won't be able to afford to eat."

I glance at Auntie Fu and she shakes her head, waving her hand again. "God tells us 'What I've given you will be enough.'"

"Ha! Then don't bother returning home!" yells Feng.

I DIDN'T KNOW MUCH about illegal churches in China until one moved in next door to me. A year after we arrived in Shanghai, a blonde American woman in her twenties had rented the apartment next to ours. Like the rest of our neighbors, she kept to herself and was rarely home. But on Friday nights, I began to notice an unusually long queue for the elevator. What was on every other day of the week a quiet ascent to my floor became a ride crowded with young, smiling foreigners and Chinese, all gabbing with one another in English. When the elevator arrived at my floor, they would stream past me to my neighbor's apartment, where there were usually at least a dozen more twenty-somethings inside, singing about Jesus.

It became a Friday night ritual for Lenora and me: dinner with a view of Shanghai's lights accompanied by live gospel music, filtering in from the apartment across the hall.

The church next door was called a *jiating jiaohui* in Chinese—a house church. By 2010, house churches were becoming popular in Shanghai, especially among the city's young office workers whose careers, education, and upbringing often left them feeling spiritually empty and morally adrift. At a house church, they could seek faith among a small group of peers, forgoing large state-sanctioned churches where sermons had to be preapproved by a Party official.

China's leaders had always been suspicious of foreign religions, especially those that had spread as quickly as Christianity had throughout the rest of the world. Theirs was a paranoia that sprung from the bullying and colonization by foreign powers in the nineteenth and twentieth centuries. It helped explain the name the Party bestowed on the country's only state-sanctioned Protestant church: the Three-Self Patriotic Movement. Originated by nineteeth-century foreign missionaries to China, the name was designed to give an impression of "localizing" Christianity and reassuring the Chinese that they—and not foreign powers—were in control of the spread of faith inside their borders.

Early Communist leaders retained the title and gave it a twist, emphasizing the word *patriotic*. Believers should be loyal first to China's Communist Party, the leadership reasoned. Of the four other religions allowed under Communist rule, only one other was forced to include *patriotic* in its name: Catholicism.

Christianity is now China's fastest-growing religion, a trend that Party officials are keeping their eyes on. In an internal government report leaked in 2014, the religion was singled out for tight regulation. In a central government directive, provincial officials were ordered to remove crosses and "religious activity sites" near national and provincial highways. The secret policy came to light after the forced demolition of a Protestant church in Wenzhou, which was topped with a 180-foot spire and a cross that were visible citywide. It was not an illegal church; in fact, it belonged to the Communist Party's own Three-Self Patriotic Movement. But tearing it down was an indication of uncertainty in Party ranks about how to treat the religion.

Auntie Fu's church was neither a sanctioned church nor a house church. It was an underground church—*dixia jiaohui*—a well-organized illegal church with money and logistics behind it, and too many congregants to fit inside a house.

When Auntie and I arrived there, the sun had gone down and she couldn't immediately locate the right building in the dark. We finally caught sight of a few other people who walked with purpose, and we followed them toward a six-story building under construction. Outside, a group of workers were mixing cement. They stopped to stare at me—the lone foreigner—as the man in the lead used his cellphone to light our way through a mess of piping, stacked drywall, and dangling electrical wires. We climbed a stairway to the second floor, where, through a set of double doors, a bright worship hall awaited us.

"ZIMEI HAO! Dixiong hao!" Auntie greeted the others when we arrived. *Sister, brother, hello!* She grabbed my arm and led me past the main hall to a long, narrow dining room filled with more than a dozen cafeteria-style tables. Windows were concealed behind wooden shutters that were padlocked shut.

The name of the church was "Central Church," and its objectives were painted in brown Chinese characters on the walls. One must be centered around, the banners proclaimed, Christ, the Bible, Love, Oneness, Discipleship, Preaching, Community, and, finally, Career.

I paused at the last one. It seemed oddly secular to include career as an objective. It was obviously aimed at young Chinese professionals. Here, through church, they could help one another find work, make new connections, and guide one another up the ladder to financial success. Church was providing an alternative *guanxi* network to family and friends.

A glaring absence, I noticed, was a slogan centered on "family." Chinese society had brought up its older generation to believe the Marxist view of religion as an opiate of the masses, and I sensed that Mom and Dad's generation was unwelcome here.

"Is he with you?" a young, bespectacled church leader named Zhang asked Auntie Fu. She nodded.

Confusion flashed across Zhang's eyes, and I spoke to him in Chinese, which put him at ease. I expected to get looks as the only foreigner inside a secret church tucked inside a half-finished building. But other than Zhang's initial surprise, no one paid any mind to the squat woman in peasant clothes trailed by a blue-eyed foreigner in the dinner line, filling their stainless steel bowls with mushrooms and rice. People from all walks of life—poor, rich, young, old—were too busy eating and chatting happily. We were among family. All were civil with one another: No pushing, shoving, spitting, or cutting.

Zhang told me the church had three other branches in Shanghai, and had quietly established churches in twenty-seven other Chinese cities. He also broke the news: Preacher Shen—the illiterate bandit—wasn't coming.

Fu's face dropped. "*Aiya!* I told the foreigner all about him!"

"Don't worry," said Zhang. "Preacher Jiang will lead the service. He's a former crime boss."

"Did he memorize the Bible in prison, too?" asked Auntie, hopefully.

"Not quite—Preacher Jiang can read and write. But he also found Jesus while he was in prison—just like Preacher Shen!"

Auntie Fu sighed in relief. Even if we weren't going to witness a sermon by an illiterate reformed criminal with a photographic memory, this was clearly in the same genre.

Dozens of people began streaming into rows of orange chairs in the main hall. Fu and I sat in the front. On a raised stage, a young man with hair hanging into his eyes assembled a drum kit beneath a wooden cross that was nailed to the wall. Flat-screen televisions showed a mountainous landscape, with the photo changing in tune to an upbeat rock song that blared over speakers suspended from the ceiling. As lyrics began to scroll across the foot of the mountains, five women dressed in black miniskirts stepped up to the stage and began to sing. They were young and lithe, and they swayed to the beat:

JESUS, COME INTO MY HEART . . . SHOW ME YOUR LOVE!

The congregation stood in unison and began singing along. Some began clapping; others lifted their hands up in the air. They belted out lyrics in Mandarin with the soul of a Southern gospel choir, their heads bobbing in unison, several clenching their fists and closing their eyes as they sang. Auntie Fu pulled me out of my chair and began to sing, too.

I mouthed the few lyrics I understood from the television screen, but I soon became distracted by the five singers on stage, who had begun to contort their bodies into hip-hop dance moves. Two men with long black hair suddenly appeared, stepping around the dancing girls. One picked up a guitar and the other a bass. They began tuning them, turning up their amps over the rock music, a jarring cacophony of fantastically off-key noise. It had little effect on the congregation, which only adjusted by singing even louder.

OPEN THE SKIES . . . AND THE FIRE OF REJUVENATION WILL BURN . . . RAINING DOWN ON US . . . PLEASE REVITALIZE US!

The lyrics rang in my ears. I began to sweat; the room was large, but there was no ventilation. I glanced over at the padlocked windows.

When hundreds of Chinese come together to sing, it's usually for a staged, televised performance of a choir singing nationalistic songs. Overly energetic singers would show off their patriotic fervor in state-sponsored hooey that was amusing to watch. It was hard to be cynical, though, when I looked around: a man with his head down, eyes shut tight, arms up in the air, bellowing; a young woman staring at the ceiling, her eyes swollen with tears; a mother across the aisle singing to her baby, who smiled back at her.

No one was putting on a show—this felt completely personal. They were all lost in the music, undergoing a spiritual release by singing.

Auntie elbowed me.

"Come on!" she yelled, taking my hands in hers and pushing them together with the beat. "It's good for your health to clap!" So I did.

After the young Chinese Christian rock band had finally tuned their instruments, Auntie turned to me.

"How did you find *Yesu*?" she shouted to her new Catholic friend. *Yesu* is Mandarin for Jesus.

"Um, I'm not sure I remember. I grew up going to church," I screamed, directing my mouth toward her ear over the sounds of an electric guitar.

"I found *Yesu* a long time ago! I was pregnant," Auntie yelled. "In my eighth month!" She paused to sing along with a stanza floating across the screen:

LORD, YOU ARE MY GUIDE, THE SHEPHERD OF MY LIFE,
THROUGH THE HILLS AND VALLEYS YOU'LL ALWAYS BE BY MY SIDE.

Auntie Fu had gotten pregnant at the Xinjiang camp, and as her belly grew, Uncle Feng decided he wanted her to give birth in Shanghai. They started out for the long journey, but the road was bumpy, and she went into labor in Turpan, in the middle of the desert.

"A son! Premature!" Auntie yelled. "My body was in so much pain and the baby was suffering, too. But he made us go back to Shanghai without my month of rest. I've suffered my whole life because of him!" She took another break to sing.

CALLING ME BY NAME,
YOU'VE CHOSEN ME WITH LOVE.
BLESSING ME ABUNDANTLY,
YOUR PROMISE WILL NEVER CHANGE.

A year later they were back in Xinjiang, her body still recovering from the birth. Chinese medicine didn't ease her pain, and that's when a doctor told her that *Yesu* could cure her.

"She told me all about *Yesu*! She held masses in her home. The leaders of my work unit found out and told me to stop attending, they said religion was nonsense, but I didn't listen to them. Thank God for her!" she yelled.

Auntie Fu closed her eyes, threw her hands up in the air, and let the music of *Yesu* wash over her.

AUNTIE FU had grown up hungry.

She was born in 1949, the year Mao took control of China. Home was a small farming village in the mountains of western Sichuan province, near the border of Tibet. When she was in the third grade, Mao's Great Leap Forward swept through the country, and the village was split into ten farming collectives. Families were required to eat at communal kitchens. Land was snatched from local families and redistributed to teams of more than five hundred people each. For those accustomed to tilling individual plots of the challenging mountainside terrain, working collectively didn't come naturally.

Worse still, the village was required to hand over nearly all its output to government officials. Within a year, the town ran out of food.

Auntie Fu scrambled for anything to put in her stomach. There was no school, and she'd spend days foraging for wild vegetables in the mountains. When the trees bloomed in the spring, she ate their flowers. In the river valley below, boats docked next to the granaries. She learned to lie in wait for careless tractors that would sometimes cut through bags of wheat while transporting them to the warehouses. Fu and her brothers and sisters would follow the trail with brooms, sweeping up stray kernels of wheat for dinner.

When she was nine, her father was labeled a counterrevolutionary. They'd attended a town meeting where every farmer was expected to give a speech praising the collective. Instead, her father, a stubborn, no-nonsense farmer, spoke his mind.

"He told the leaders more food was needed. The people weren't able to feed themselves properly. They were too weak to work for the collective," Auntie Fu said.

Villagers respected Auntie Fu's father, but they were too afraid to publicly agree with him. Doing so would amount to treason. "He stuck his neck out for the farmers, and they accused him of hating communism."

Her father's name appeared on a list nailed to the communal canteen. His name was among those of other "class enemies, counterrevolutionaries, and rightists." He was forced to sit among them during village meetings. When work shifts were announced each morning over the crackly village megaphones, he was relegated to the worst of them, with multiple back-to-back shifts and evenings worked alongside former landlords and other "enemies of the people."

In the end, it was too much work and too little food. He collapsed in the field. He died at thirty-seven.

"I blame his death on Chairman Mao," Auntie told me. "Mao instigated people to fight against each other. He launched one campaign after another, and anyone who had the know-how to come up with a better way to govern was killed."

Years later, Auntie Fu heard about work on a farm in Xinjiang. She'd never heard of the place, but she reasoned that anywhere was better than her hometown. She joined her brothers on the long journey north. "The air in Xinjiang was better," she said. "And there was food. Lots of food. The fruits and vegetables tasted so good and they were cheap. The climate was dry and cool in the mountains. Once I save enough money, I'm going to go back there to retire. Xinjiang is like heaven."

It was even better, she added, than Shanghai is today.

ON OUR WAY to church that evening, Auntie had described her Xinjiang retirement plan. A friend from church had invited her to an investment seminar. She paid one hundred yuan to attend.

"It was worth it," she reasoned. "It was a company that'll sell you shares before they go public; a joint venture between a British and a Chinese company. My friend spent tens of thousands of yuan, so I bought some shares, too."

In all, she bought shares worth ¥30,000, or around $5,000. "It's already worth double that! I can check it all online. The company will be listed on the London stock exchange in January! When it does, I'll make half a million," she said, before putting her hand on my shoulder. "You should invest, too!"

I thought about this for a moment. How did Fu have $5,000? That was a lot of scallion pancakes. How could she check her shares "online"? She was too poor to afford a computer, and she didn't have a smartphone. And why was she asking me to invest? In my reporting on China's economy, I'd heard of investment schemes like this. They often targeted the elderly. I weighed my response carefully.

"Are you worried this could be a scam?" I asked.

Fu laughed. "Definitely not! They told me there was *zero* risk. Come to our investment meeting next week." She bowed her head to peer at me over the top of her glasses, looking me in the eye. "You should never give up opportunities to make money."

She then climbed up the stairs to Central Church.

PREACHER JIANG SMILED with his entire face. It was the sort of grin that pressed his cheeks so far upward that his eyes closed, leaving a pair of eyebrows shaped in an inverted *V*. "Today we will explore what it means to be grateful," Preacher Jiang announced in a booming voice.

We'd been singing for an hour, and the congregation of Central Church finally lowered themselves into plastic orange chairs for the evening's sermon. They leaned forward, straining their necks to catch a full glimpse of the former crime boss.

Preacher Jiang certainly looked the part. A black vinyl jacket reflected the lights overhead as it clung to his thick, muscular torso. He tucked his left sleeve underneath a Rolex watch, and he waved this display of prosperity as often as he could. His hair was closely cropped around a football-sized head that swiveled back and forth to address the congregation. He was in his fifties.

"Your gratefulness is proof that you've experienced God's life," he began, dramatically raising his arms. His Rolex glinted. "Let us pray: Dear Father, we praise You. We thank You for establishing this Central Church . . ."

The congregants raised their hands, shouting "Amen" after each pause, allowing Preacher Jiang to find his stride.

"Gratitude is important! Gratitude allows us to sacrifice for God!" he shouted.

Preacher Jiang told us he had much to be grateful for. He said he was a sinner born to a sinner—the criminal son of a local Communist Party official.

People laughed, nodding along. Many in the audience considered city officials worse than criminals, because the Party often shielded their crimes. Preacher Jiang said his father had used *guanxi* to spring him from prison, but when his crimes became too serious, even the Party couldn't protect him. He was sentenced to ten years in prison for robbery and assault.

"And that's when Daddy severed his relationship with me!" he shouted. "And where did he end up? In a mental ward!"

"*Aiya!*" shouted Fu, shaking her head at the thought of this.

Preacher Jiang tilted his head back, lifting the microphone to his mouth. "My only God was *ren-min-bi*!" he shouted, slowing down to linger over the pronunciation of China's currency.

The audience roared with laughter. Preacher Jiang laughed with them, his eyebrows arching upward to form an M. His sermon unraveled like a Chinese blockbuster action film: it had a big-shot criminal, a corrupt but powerful father figure, prison time, and a mental ward. The audience was rapt.

"What do the two characters of *grateful* share in common?" Preacher Jiang asked the congregation, tracing the Chinese characters on his hand: 感恩.

Both characters included the radical for the word *heart*—心— and everyone shouted the word in unison. "Heart!! Heart!! Heart!!"

"Now—raise your hand if you can control your heart!"

Four hands shot up.

"Really? There are people here who can do that?" Preacher Jiang asked, making eye contact with the four brave souls. They lowered their hands sheepishly.

"Yes, that's right." Preacher Jiang grinned. "Everyone has a heart, but nobody can control it," he said slowly. "Repeat after me! 'I have everything, yet I can't control anything!'"

"I have everything, yet I can't control anything!"

In a society where parents controlled the decision-making process for their children through adulthood, where students were taught never to question their teachers, and where leaders often ruled with an iron fist, this message of powerlessness was, well, powerful.

"Our parents can't even control their own lives!" Preacher Jiang shouted. "My father was a member of the Communist Party! What a joke! Even he had no power over me!"

The congregants laughed. Preacher Jiang took a deep breath, and plunged in.

"But then God took control of my tongue! Amen!"

"Amen!"

"And He gave me wisdom and eloquence! Amen!"

"Amen!"

"And then I realized the Bible surpasses all kinds of knowledge! Amen!"

"Amen!"

The pronouncements came out like a rapid-fire cheer, and he pumped his fist with each one. Each Amen fed his energy, and he met the audience's responses by turning up the volume.

"It was written by the Holy Spirit! Amen!"

"Amen!"

"You are all shaped by God, revealed by God, blessed by God! Amen!"

"Amen!"

"And we must be grateful for God! Amen!"

"Amen!"

Preacher Jiang stood motionless with his fist up in the air, his head bobbing with each breath. He abruptly broke his stance to take a sip of water. I looked around the hall. People were pushed up against the edge of their seats. Fu elbowed me in the ribs. "Isn't he great?" she asked, gripping her knees, her eyes fixed on him.

Preacher Jiang had likely delivered this sermon dozens—perhaps hundreds—of times before. He'd been able to refine his oratory and the timing of his jokes. His dark, rebellious past captivated people. The Chinese spoke often of *hei shehui*—"black society," known popularly as the Triads—and these criminals were popular because they offered an alternative source of power to the Communist Party. But few had ever met a real-life boss. Jiang's jokes about Communists were a hit, too, as they gave permission to make fun of corrupt officials and a government that looked down on their beliefs. His delivery had a distinct rhythm with a call-and-response cadence, which made it irresistible. Rote repetition followed by plainspoken lecturing was a feature of Chinese classrooms all over the country. For Auntie Fu and others old enough to remember, this style also conjured up political rallies in the 1960s where thousands of Red Guards would scream slogans like "Long live Chairman Mao!" Repeating phrases like this induced a kind of hypnosis. If anyone—mortal or immortal—had control over the congregation at Central Church this evening, it was Preacher Jiang.

"The establishment of a church is a gift from God! Amen!"

"*Amen!*"

"The establishment of a church means lost souls are being saved! Amen!"

"*Amen!*"

"Then the establishment of a church needs capital!" Preacher Jiang shouted, inflecting the last word with a descending tone of finality.

He paused to let this sink in. He wiped his brow with a handkerchief.

Aha, there it was, I thought. I looked over at Auntie Fu. She was fixated on Jiang.

"Where does this money come from?" he asked, looking around the room for an answer.

For the first time that night, the hall fell silent.

"It comes from God!" he barked. "Don't think that it's *your* money. You might think the money you earn is yours, but it isn't. It's a blessing from God! God created you, so everything you have belongs to Him."

I looked around, scanning the faces of the congregants. Were they still in step with Preacher Jiang's logic? Most of the people here were among the first generation of Chinese allowed to make their own money. Telling them what they had earned wasn't theirs seemed to me a risky test of their faith. It had worked for Mao, but he had an army behind him. If anyone tonight questioned Preacher Jiang's reasoning, it didn't show—everyone's gaze remained locked on him. I quietly withdrew my phone from my pocket to check the time. It had taken Preacher Jiang exactly one hour to get to this point. It was an hour filled with subtle hints carefully dropped after he had landed a good joke or had made a point that resonated with people. These moments were followed by readings from the Bible supporting his points. He had masked the message with terms like "gratitude," "receiving additional grace," and "the meaning of being grateful to God." After an hour he had an audience happy to repeat or laugh at anything he said. Mission accomplished. Time to switch gears and allow the polish to begin to chip from the euphemisms. In the end, like most things in China, this sermon boiled down to *ren-min-bi*.

"Why should we sacrifice?" Preacher Jiang asked. "Maybe you've been talking about the one-tenth rule, maybe not. It's a sensitive topic. But it's the best rule. It's a sacred rule, and it opens the door to heaven."

I turned to Auntie Fu. Before she could whisper back, Preacher Jiang cut in.

"Today's churches often deviate from God's rules, but not ours. Which rule?"

"The one-tenth rule!" echoed the congregation.

Since the 1990s I'd lived and worked in rural and urban parts of the country. In all that time, I'd never witnessed a group of Chinese agreeing to part so willingly with their money.

"Whether you're a boss or a worker, if you've got ten yuan, you can only take nine yuan from your pocket. That one yuan must be given to our God. Amen!"

"Amen!"

Growing up Catholic, I was familiar with the custom of tithing, but it was a subtle, unspoken pact to the church and community. I'd never heard giving described in such precise terms, nor had I ever heard an entire sermon devoted to it. In my childhood church, baskets were quietly passed around to collect donations at the end of mass, but no priest would dare specify an amount. You simply gave what you could. Clearly, Preacher Jiang felt Chinese Christians needed a defined directive, and for good measure, he sealed it with a threat.

"Repeat after me: tou qie!"

"Tou qie!" responded the congregation in unison. The word meant "to steal."

"The original meaning of the word tou qie is to withhold—to steal—your one-tenth offering. Did you know this?" Preacher Jiang asked, with a wave of his arm.

"The Bible says that if you tou qie, where will the curse fall upon?" He paused dramatically.

"On you! The curse will fall on you! Repeat after me: 'On you!'"

"On you!"

"What kind of curse?"

The audience murmured, unsure of how to answer. Preacher Jiang had led his flock into uncharted territory. Auntie Fu looked to me for help, but I had nothing to offer.

"You will suffer from disease!" he spat. "I once met a sister in the city of Luoyang who loves God very much. She was very sick. I took her to many curing sessions and doctors, but she did not get better. I began to wonder whether she had given her one-tenth. Her colleagues confirmed my hunch." Jiang paused, scanning the faces assembled before him.

"I went back and told her, 'God cursed you with disease!'"
Jiang screamed.

The congregation erupted in whispers again. He continued. "I told her what I told you tonight! 'If you turn to God, God will turn to you!' She started giving one-tenth. The last time I met her, she was cured! Amen!"

"Amen! Amen! Amen!"

Auntie Fu nodded her head in approval for the sick sister from Luoyang. I slouched in my chair. Preacher Jiang was a crime boss, a former prisoner, the prodigal son of a Party official, and now a healer who miraculously cured the sick. This church had expanded to twenty-seven cities. How many Preacher Jiangs were out there, delivering the exact same pitch?

Jiang again wiped his forehead. The Rolex gleamed as he moved, and the vinyl of his jacket was luminescent on stage. He sensed fertile ground.

"Repeat after me: People who are saved and given a new life must give one-tenth of their income."

The audience chanted the phrase back to him.

"How can you prove you are Christian if you don't give? How can you prove you love God?"

The men and women repeated his words.

"If you don't give God one-tenth of your income, you are *stealing* from God!" he screeched, waving both arms over the congregation. The accusation hung in the cavernous hall.

No one said a word.

A FEW DAYS LATER, I stopped by Uncle's shop and ordered a scallion pancake. It was four thirty in the afternoon, and the thick smog of winter obscured the glowing red ball setting over the plane trees. I asked Auntie Fu about Preacher Jiang's sermon.

"I was really moved," she said.

I pulled a stool into the shop and sat down. She continued. "Wenzhou churches always find the top preachers from across the country. Preacher Jiang gave all of us a spiritual shock!"

Uncle Feng was fiddling with his griddle. He snickered loud enough for Fu to hear.

"*Aiya!*" Auntie snapped. "You don't understand! What do you know, old man?"

"I don't understand? And you do?" he asked her, still laughing.

"Preacher Jiang talked a lot about giving one-tenth of your income," I said slowly.

Uncle stopped what he was doing and listened.

"Did you feel compelled to give money?" I asked her.

"No! Who can afford that?" Auntie Fu replied loud enough for Uncle to hear. She shot a nervous glance at her husband. "Some older *senile* people might be persuaded to do that, but not me. It's based on everyone's capabilities. Actually there is no such rule, but I guess it's written in the Bible somewhere. Usually people don't give very much."

A neighbor arrived at the window, distracting Uncle Feng. They began to chat. Auntie bent over and whispered to me: "I was very moved by the sermon. I gave fifty yuan!"

Uncle reached for a spatula and removed a pancake. He gingerly placed it into a thin plastic bag and handed it to me. I waited for him to turn back to his neighbor, and then quietly placed three silver yuan coins into his plastic container bank. Auntie saw this and put the money back into my pocket. I waited until she left the room, and then returned the coins to the container. It was a game of money tag I often played with friends along the street.

It was getting dark. Uncle switched on a solitary lightbulb dangling from a black wire, projecting a perfect square of light onto the sidewalk in front of his shop. Auntie returned with an Advent calendar and a teacup with a cross.

"Free gifts from the church," she announced, brandishing the items.

Uncle laughed. "Nothing's free," he said.

"You don't have faith now," Auntie told him, "but after you get old and idle, I'll drag you to church."

"I won't go even when I get old."

"You'll suffer later if you don't go," warned Auntie.

"Once people die, they're gone. You could grind them up into meat, and they wouldn't even know," Uncle muttered slowly, his face lit by the bulb.

Auntie turned to me. "I'll get another Advent calendar for you, too."

"I've escaped death once," Uncle interrupted, ignoring his wife.

"What happened?" I asked.

"I fell through the ice once in a frozen river in Xinjiang," he responded, staring out into the darkness. "I pulled myself out, walked a few steps, and fell down again. I crawled to the banks of the river and up onto a road. My clothes were all frozen, turned to ice. I couldn't feel anything. It was one of the coldest days of the year.

"Nobody helped me," he said. "Nobody. It took me a long time to walk back to the village. When a friend saw me, he thought I was a ghost. I made it home and changed my clothes by the fire and drank sorghum liquor. That was December 19, 1989. I'll always remember that date."

Auntie listened, clutching her Advent calendar, silent.

"I don't believe in the things she believes in," Uncle said. "You've got to have a sober mind. That's the only way you can survive. That's why I don't believe in God."

Uncle looked out and saw no customers. He began to clean up his workspace, wiping down the counter and griddle in a mechanical fashion.

Outside, the Street of Eternal Happiness was growing quiet. I looked at Uncle Feng. He had survived in Xinjiang on next to nothing, turning desert into farmland. It taught him to never trust any authority.

Auntie stood up. To Uncle Feng, she must have seemed frustratingly gullible. "The only reason you didn't die that day was because of God," she proclaimed. "He gave you the strength to pull yourself out of that river. Think about it! Nobody could have survived falling into that frozen river!"

"Nonsense," said Uncle, turning to look at his wife for the first time that evening. "After I fell into that frozen river in Xinjiang, I didn't believe in anything except myself."

Box of Letters

长乐路682弄70号

Street of Eternal Happiness, Lane 682, No. 70

There were just three hours left in the Year of the Dragon when I saw the letters. It was Chinese New Year's Eve, 2013, and my friends Lei Lei and Rich had invited me to their apartment to usher in the Year of the Snake. The previous two New Years, Lenora and I had downed dumplings with her Chinese relatives and lit fireworks on the street at midnight alongside millions of others in the city. They erupted around us with a deafening pop, and ash fell from the sky in what felt like a sustained missile strike. This year Lenora had found a reason to escape. Our second son was a year old, and she took both boys to the U.S. for a couple of weeks.

Lei Lei handed me a stack of yellowed letters. "Take a look at the return address," she said.

I glanced at one of the frayed envelopes in my hand: *Lane 682, number 70, Street of Eternal Happiness.*

They had heard my radio series about the street and thought I'd be interested. As we drank scotch, fireworks began to explode outside. We rifled through the letters.

There were more than a hundred of them, neatly tucked into a shoebox. Rich and Lei Lei had a side business refurbishing old lane homes in the former French Concession, and they'd come across the collection in an old antiques shop two blocks south of the Street of Eternal Happiness.

The earliest ones were written in the 1950s, between a wife and her husband, who was serving time in a labor camp near Tibet as a political prisoner. Others were addressed to the same prisoner, but written by different hands. The last letters were from the 1990s. All were stamped with the same return address on the Street of Eternal Happiness.

In the space of fifty-odd years, the letters had traveled from Shanghai to a labor camp two thousand miles away, only to end up at an antiques shop just two blocks from where they'd been written.

We flipped through the pile, and I gently unfolded one. It was written in Chinese cursive, and I had a hard time making out the characters.

Lei Lei read it out loud: "'I've been busy with housework, so I haven't had time to write. Please forgive me. Our current living conditions are very tough. We can barely get by.'"

"The wife's letters are always updates on their children," Lei Lei paused to say, "but the letters from the husband are more interesting."

We spent the next hour unfolding, discussing, and refolding various letters, fascinating artifacts of a bygone era. Finally, a folded paper without an envelope caught my eye. It appeared to be a hand-written chart.

"What's this?" Rich asked Lei Lei.

"It's a lunar calendar from, let's see, 1958. See here?" she said, pointing to the top. "New Year's Day. That's today."

I looked at the clock: one in the morning. The first hour of the Year of the Snake had slid right by.

LANE 682, STREET OF ETERNAL HAPPINESS. I was familiar with the road's many lane communities by now, and I realized I had been across the street from that very alley earlier in the day, back when it was still the Year of the Dragon.

Because of the holiday, everything was quiet and the *waidi ren*—outsiders—had left for their hometowns. Nearly half the city hailed from somewhere else, and the holiday was a rare moment when Shanghai returned to the Shanghainese. Whether out of guilt from escaping my parenting duties or out of boredom, that afternoon I found myself sitting on a curb with the only other soul in sight: an elderly beggar named Zhang Naisun.

His usual spot was as auspiciously named as you might find in Shanghai: the intersection of the Street of Eternal Happiness and Fumin Lu, literally "Rich People Road."

"Happy New Year," I said to Zhang, placing a hundred-yuan note in his cup.

"Happy New Year and I wish prosperity for you and your family," he dutifully replied.

Zhang had inhabited this corner for years. I'd seen him so often that I had come to ignore him. On the few occasions when pedestrian traffic had thrust me into his domain, I had dug into my pockets and placed coins in his cup. He was always gracious, bowing his head in thanks. He usually wore a green People's Liberation Army coat with a purple scarf furled around his neck, and boots over navy blue trousers. He typically sat atop a black garbage bag of recyclables with a white plastic container placed at his knees for donations. His hair cascaded like a silver waterfall down the middle of his back, wispy strands dancing in the rush of air left behind by passing cars. From a distance, he looked like an old woman until you got close enough to see his sparse snowy beard. He had the calm, patient eyes of a man with all the time in the world—one of the few souls in Shanghai who wasn't in a rush to get somewhere. For Zhang, time was other people's money.

He had carefully chosen this spot. The Street of Eternal

Happiness forms the border between two separate districts in Shanghai. The south side of the street is the district of Xuhui; the north side, the district of Jing'an. This no-man's-land designation meant it was littered with unpatched potholes—both districts left repair to the other, so it was almost never done. Zhang used this lack of oversight to his advantage. Whenever urban management officers from Xuhui threatened to haul him off for panhandling, Zhang would simply walk across the street to resume begging in Jing'an, outside their jurisdiction.

On this New Year's Day, we were seated in Xuhui. When I sat beside him, he seemed unsurprised, as if he expected my arrival. The sun was low above the skyscrapers to the west of us, and a frigid gust blew down the street. I sat upwind from him to avoid being blinded by his hair.

"Where's your family?" I asked.

"My wife's at home on the farm in Henan, and my sons and grandchildren are in Guangdong, working," he said. "It's been twelve years since I spent New Year's with them."

His hometown was nearly five hundred miles away. He leaned back and smiled, resting his elbows on three boxes of oranges, holiday donations from folks in the neighborhood. "It's a good day to be a lonely old man," he said.

After paying rent for a stairwell closet across town and buying a couple meals each day, Zhang said he cleared more than a hundred dollars each month from begging on this corner. That was likely more than he'd make working in his home village. Zhang grew up near the city of Zhoukou, one of China's earliest inhabited regions. The ancient philosopher Laozi—Taoism's founder—was thought to have been born there, and Zhang's flowing white hair and wispy beard conjured up the old philosopher.

Zhang lived solo in Shanghai for part of the year, and wandered home to Henan during summers to escape city rain and heat. He shared another similarity with the great sage: Whether Zhang knew it or not, he was practicing the old Taoist principle of *Wei Wu Wei*: action without action. Taoism is China's only indigenous religion, but its central philosophy seemed to be at odds with everything

China had become. Yet here was its stubborn missionary—like Laozi, an old long-haired hermit from Zhoukou—alone and homeless on the streets of China's wealthiest city on the most sacred Chinese holiday, begging for change.

"You must miss your family," I said, realizing after the words slipped from my mouth how insensitive it must have sounded.

"Nah, I don't miss them," he said matter-of-factly. "I'm so old that I'm nearly dead as it is! What use would it be to miss them?"

Each year his three sons urged Zhang to come back home for the holiday, but he found the mess of relatives to be too much of a hassle. "My grandsons are naughty, my daughters-in-law would reprimand them, and I'd probably get so angry I'd smack the little brats," he told me. "That would create a scene. Why go home?"

More important, he admitted, there wasn't enough food. "According to Chinese tradition, the elder generation must be served rice first," he said. "My sons wouldn't let my grandchildren eat very much if I were there. I couldn't find it in my heart to do that to them."

Plus, he said, he didn't want to miss out on the time of year when the penny-pinchers of Shanghai were most likely to give.

I gathered there were other reasons for Zhang's self-imposed exile at a time when the rest of China migrated home. But it was getting dark, and the distant blasts of fireworks were beginning to interrupt us.

I stood up and bid him a happy new year.

He did the same, collecting his belongings on a portable two-wheeled dolly, rolling his three boxes of oranges down the Street of Eternal Happiness and past the lane where the box of letters had originated, a sky of exploding fireworks lighting his way.

A WEEK LATER IN MY OFFICE, I opened the box of letters again.

Lei Lei had sent them home with me. I wanted to know who wrote them, where they were from, and what they could tell me about the street and its past. In a country where entire swaths of history had been erased from the public record, these letters were rare—unblemished artifacts free from any manipulation of the State.

The lunar calendar we were studying on New Year's Eve was still on top. I looked at the date: 1958.

I unfolded the rice paper. It was written in the meticulous, classical handwriting of China's educated class. A name was scrawled in the corner: Wang Ming.

Nearly all the letters were addressed to Wang. About half were written to him by his wife. The remainder were penned by extended family: Wang's older sister, his twin brother, his father, and a smattering of friends in Shanghai. Wang himself wrote only three letters. I had in my hands, I estimated, only one half of the correspondence between Wang and his family. Where did the rest go? Had they been left behind at the antiques store, or had they been thrown away?

I turned my attention to the aged, crumbling papers in front of me, starting with the calendar.

China's lunar calendar is divided into twenty-four periods of approximately fifteen days each called "solar terms," named after gradual changes in the season. Wang's calendar had listed them all, beginning with Chinese New Year, or *Spring Begins*. After this came:

FEBRUARY 21–GRAIN RAIN
MARCH 8–THE WAKING OF INSECTS
MARCH 23–VERNAL EQUINOX

According to the letters, Wang had been arrested in mid-November of 1957, during *Winter Begins*, and had been transported two thousand miles from the Street of Eternal Happiness to a labor camp in Qinghai province the following September, in the middle of *White Dew*. He traveled across China for weeks, and arrived at the camp during *Autumnal Equinox*. He began hard labor during *Hoar Frost Falls*, and spent his first months toiling through *Light Snow, Heavy Snow, Slight Cold,* and *Great Cold*. There was never a good solar term to be sent to a labor camp in Qinghai province, but these were the worst. The province is a Texas-sized scrubland atop the arid northern Tibetan Plateau. Qinghai winters are among the coldest in China. If you wanted to get rid of someone, you sent him to Qinghai.

Wang was sent there for being a capitalist. He had owned a small factory on the outskirts of Shanghai that recycled silicon steel. He purchased scraps from electrical machinery companies and then melted them down in his factory to build the cores of electrical transformers. He sold them back to the same companies at a profit.

Up until the Communists took control of China in 1949, Shanghai was fueled by capitalism. Wang was one of many who got rich off the city's growth. At a time when China was largely a rural country, Shanghai handled 60 percent of the country's trade with the rest of the world, 80 percent of China's foreign capital, and nearly all the country's international financial transactions. Shanghai alone accounted for more than half of China's industrial output, employing half the country's factory workers.

Wang's success afforded him a three-story cream-colored stucco house tucked into one of the many lanes that branched off of the Street of Eternal Happiness. By 1956, his wife Liu Shuyun had given birth to six children.

I picked up another letter, this one dated 1957. Mother Liu became pregnant with their seventh child that year, and Wang's fortunes began to change for the worse. China's Communist government had worked for years to eliminate private capital, and they had finally seized control of Shanghai's private factories. Two classes—landlords and capitalists—were singled out. Eight hundred thousand landlords were executed, and many others fled to Taiwan or Hong Kong. Wang had tried to hide his class background for years, anxiously standing by as campaign after campaign continued to target men like him.

According to the letter, in 1956, Wang had been forced into a joint venture with a state-owned factory. It was a government takeover of the business he'd spent his entire career building. The Party appointed inexperienced managers to run Wang's factory, and Wang was assigned a job in the supply and marketing department and given a salary of ¥170 a month. It was a fraction of his earnings as a factory owner, but it was still a better wage than most managers under the new Communist regime received. Six months later, Wang's new employer transferred him to another public-private partnership named Mingyun, a company Wang used to supply.

Like many other companies in Shanghai, Mingyun was scrambling to reconstruct its supply chain since the Party's abrupt takeover. It was rapidly losing clients and it teetered near bankruptcy. Wang was enlisted to fix the problem.

Among the letters I found was a two-page essay of self-criticism written in careful script:

How I made mistakes at the public-private partnership of Mingyun Electronic Equipment Factory from 1956 to 1957.

In the essay, Wang explains that his new state-appointed boss had no idea how to source recycled steel and had pressured Wang to find it by any means necessary. "He spoke to me about the difficulties and urged me to solve the problem, mentioning that if the material was of good quality with a normal price, it didn't matter what kind of factory made it, even if it was a private factory," Wang wrote.

Sourcing material from private factories was illegal. But, wrote Wang, he and other employees—all former factory owners—had been forced to sit by and watch supply chains they'd built over years completely unravel during their work shifts. It was too much to bear, and many of them did exactly what Wang had done: reverted to an economic system that worked. "We were in a difficult situation, so I found several private factories to supply us," wrote Wang. "All of them sold the material to us at low prices and we were able to fulfill our clients' orders. I had solved the problem. My managers were satisfied."

It was clear from the letters that he'd sourced the emergency material from the type of private factories that he himself had once owned, and in the months that followed, Mingyun, armed with a new supply chain of Wang's making, became profitable: too profitable. Local authorities paid a visit.

In November 1957, they arrested Wang and his partners for practicing capitalism and labeled them "Rightists," enemies of the people. In Shanghai, one of every ten teachers at Fudan University, the city's top college, was declared a Rightist, along with one of every twenty of the city's industrialists and merchants. Nationwide, half a million businessmen and intellectuals suffered the same fate.

The Shanghai News Daily reported in its December 12, 1957, edition that hundreds of Rightists had been "uncovered" in just a few weeks. These Rightists were "well-versed at deploying all kinds of means and fake masks to deceive the people."

The Daily outlined the "rectification" plan that awaited each Rightist:

> Rightists will become dutiful, accept the supervision from the proletariat, learn from the working class, know how to distinguish the difference between the private and public sectors so that they can accept the leadership from the Party along the socialist path; how to temper oneself through labor, and how to overcome capitalist thoughts and give up the wasteful capitalist lifestyle.

According to court documents, Wang and his bosses were charged with "fraudulently purchasing state-controlled commodities" and "making money in an illegal way."

In another letter I read that Wang had written to a friend, he described what happened to him and his colleagues after their arrest:

> *We were placed into a prison on Sinan Road in Shanghai. On September 9, 1958, the court called up the others in our industry who had also committed this crime and read us its verdict. There were dozens of men. We had all done business with each other for years. Many of us were good friends. We looked at each other in silence, nervous about what was going to happen. We were*

all found guilty. Most of us were sentenced to labor camps in
Qinghai province, me included.

Wang Ming was sent away to a reform-through-labor camp so
that his capitalist thoughts could be eradicated. He was thirty-five
years old. He left his wife and seven children, including a newborn
boy, in Shanghai—three blocks from where I read his letters.

DELINGHA FARM was the first labor camp established in Qinghai
province. It was one of the largest forced labor farms in China. Before the camp was built, it was a desert oasis on a 9,000-foot-high
plateau, sparsely populated by Tibetan nomads. By the time Wang
arrived in 1958, the camp had more than 10,000 prisoners who
spent their days tilling hundreds of acres of wheat and barley.

To the north were the 18,000-foot-high peaks of the Qilian
mountain range. To the south stretched hundreds of miles of desert of the Qaidam Basin. Ancient Chinese considered Qinghai
Lake—an azure body of salt water that is China's largest—to be the
western border of their kingdom, marking the edge of civilization.
Delingha was built two hundred miles beyond that.

There was no need to build a wall around the prison. Those
who made a run for it in any direction would die of dehydration,
their bodies picked apart by vultures.

Camp managers divided prisoners into battalions of approximately a thousand, then further into companies of one hundred,
and finally into working groups of ten. Two prisoners from each
group were selected to be leaders. The Production Leader was in
charge of tracking whether each prisoner met his work quota each
day, and the Study Leader monitored prisoners' socialist thought
progression. Essentially, the Study Leader was charged with ensur-
ing prisoners displayed appropriate knowledge and enthusiasm
for Party campaigns, and with organizing self-criticism sessions
where inmates could identify areas for self-improvement.

The daily regimen was ruthless. Prisoners worked seven days
a week, resting only during blizzards or on one of five days issued

each year for national holidays. Each morning, prisoners woke up, downed a bowl of gruel, and marched outside. A few guards armed with rifles kept watch over each company, placing red flags in four corners of a field, delineating the day's work area. Prisoners were told whoever strayed outside the invisible boundary would be shot.

Harry Wu, a former inmate who runs a museum in Washington, DC, detailing China's labor camp system, told me a day's orders might be "Remove weeds," and each person would be given a target. "When the day was through, Production Leaders would record your work to determine what you got for dinner that night: Good labor, good food; Less labor, less food; No labor, no food."

Nearly all the letters addressed to Wang Ming were sent to his cell at Delingha camp. I wondered what he had endured way out there, past the edge of civilization. In 2013, I tracked down a fellow inmate of Wang's. Professor Wei Xiezhong had been sentenced to five years in a labor camp in 1957 after trying to escape China by swimming to Hong Kong. He later got another ten for keeping a secret diary about his time at the camp. In all, he'd spent twenty-three years imprisoned in Qinghai labor camps, fifteen of them at Delingha. Professor Wei didn't know Wang Ming, but their lives tracked similar paths.

Now seventy-nine, Wei was a balding, retired professor living in the Yangtze Delta city of Nanjing. He was around the same age as Wang. When I met him, I was struck by his quickness. Unlike many men his age, he moved with a certain agility, seeming to escape the deceleration of old age. His mind was sharp, too: he'd authored several books about his experiences in labor camp, but he was careful to label the works fiction. He wrote under a pen name—he had no intention of serving another sentence.

Professor Wei had arrived in Qinghai a few years after Wang had, in the middle of the famine that followed Mao's Great Leap Forward. Tens of millions were dying in the countryside, and now he was, too.

Prisoners at the time were allocated 250 grams of raw wheat if they completed their daily work quota, but they rarely received that.

The only way to survive, he recalled, was to swipe food and quickly eat it before you were caught and shot.

"I stole from the field. Others stole from the warehouse, and some from the kitchen. When we harvested the wheat, we would steal some and bury it underneath the ground."

The squirreling strategy was the only way they would live through the winter. Not all were as lucky as he had been: "I remember one prisoner going out in the morning to bask in the sunlight, leaning on the barracks wall. When the sun went down that day, we found him, dead. That sort of thing happened a lot."

Many new arrivals died within weeks, said Professor Wei. "Our guards were starving, too. After the wheat harvest, I remember men crouching down to eat the remaining grains, but they were hard to digest. So we would sift through our own feces to eat the undigested wheat."

At a camp 150 miles north of Delingha, a little more than 500 of 3,000 inmates survived after subsisting on worms, rats, animal waste, and at the height of the famine, organs from dead inmates. By the end of the famine, Wei estimates a third of the prisoners in his company at Delingha had starved to death. According to the letters, it was clear Wang Ming suffered, too, but by the end of the famine, he had survived.

China had experienced the deadliest famine in recorded history: An estimated 36 million people had died of hunger within the span of just four years—more than the total number of people who had been killed in World War I.

"Westerners don't understand why we Chinese greet each other by asking 'Have you eaten?'" Professor Wei told me, half-joking.

As the country climbed out of famine in the mid-1960s, tens of thousands more inmates arrived at Delingha, more than restoring the ranks lost to starvation. The camp added several departments to absorb the influx, each handling a different industry: livestock, fisheries, farming, even a coal mine.

Wang Ming was assigned to the camp's foundry, forging cast iron and steel. Professor Wei worked in its construction team, responsible for building a hydropower dam on a nearby river. During the 1960s, Professor Wei said, there was a renewed focus on study sessions and self-criticisms, particularly during the frozen winter months when work slowed. I had visited Qinghai in the winter for a reporting trip once, and I could imagine how isolated the prisoners must have felt.

"During 'Winter Training,' we had to offer suggestions for self-improvement and make speeches praising life at the camp," Professor Wei told me, smirking. "We would shout, 'The situation is overwhelmingly good! The economic conditions are great! What can't we afford to buy? We have everything!'"

BACK ON THE STREET OF ETERNAL HAPPINESS, I held in my hands the first letter Mother Liu wrote to her husband, Wang Ming. It is dated July 8, 1958, and she begins by telling him about their new child: "Little Xuesong has been weaned and is eating congee and gruel," she writes.

Xuesong had been born in 1957, only six months before his father was arrested. After six daughters, he was their first son. Like many Chinese families, they had kept having children until they finally had a boy.

The rest of the children, writes Mother Liu, are struggling. Big Sister is falling behind in school, and Liu has sent their two-year-old Baby Sister to live with relatives in the countryside: one less mouth to feed. The sisters in between—whom she identifies as Sister Two, Sister Three, Sister Four, and Sister Five—are also doing poorly.

Mother Liu concludes her brief letter with an admonishment: "I hope you continue to work and study hard and repent your mistakes. Plead to the government to grant you leniency so that you can return home."

Four months later, conditions worsen. "I've been forced to sell our personal belongings and have had to rely on welfare payments from the Bureau of Industry and Commerce in order to survive," writes Liu.

She ends with another reminder of his duties at camp: "Focus on your studies, work hard, and please accept your re-education. It's the only way out."

In the next letter later that year, Mother Liu reports that the Party has assigned her a job making boxes at a state-owned factory. She outlines the family's new routines, highlighting the progress of their only son. "I wake up at four thirty each morning to go to the wet market," she writes, referring to a market north of the Street of Eternal Happiness that still operates along the same block today.

> *When I return, I wash all the vegetables and cook them, and after breakfast I go to work at 7:30. The elder sisters take turns preparing lunch and dinner, and feed Little Xuesong.*
>
> *After a lot of practice, the kids are now capable of arranging what needs to be done and when. They're never late nor do they miss class. They've developed good hygienic habits and are careful about what they eat, so they rarely get sick and are very healthy, especially Little Xuesong, who is very active and healthy. He's starting to talk and sing . . .*
>
> *Lastly, I want to tell you to take care of yourself. Take care of what you eat. Don't miss home. Focus on getting well and recovering. After you recuperate, I hope you can study more political thought and obey all the instructions from your leaders and proactively take the lead in labor. Help others and try to be good and march toward the bright path.*

It was common for letters to and from labor camps to be sprinkled with political encouragement and praise of Chairman Mao and other Party leaders. Every single letter sent to and from prisoners was inspected thoroughly by authorities. Inmates and their families understood that too candid an assessment of conditions at home or at camp would be punished.

Letters between Wang and Liu throughout the 1960s are peppered with praise of either China's economic advancement—despite widespread famine due to Mao's failed campaigns—or the wisdom of Chairman Mao's policies.

In February 1961, Mother Liu learns her husband's re-education is proceeding slowly, potentially lengthening his prison sentence. She employs the propaganda of the times in a single, seething run-on sentence, scolding her husband.

> *You should get the government policies straight and shed the bad habits that remain in you from the old society and you should read beneficial books and newspapers and emphasize your political studies and follow the teaching and guidance from the Party and Chairman Mao, and completely reform yourself and become a new person so that you can return home and reunite with us as soon as possible and share the responsibility along with me to raise these children and contribute to the construction of socialism.*

Nine years pass before Mother Liu writes another letter to her husband. Wang's sister Mei Mei fills the void, explaining that his wife is trying "to save money on stamps. She needs to calculate how to spend even one *fen*."

> *Your wife isn't doing well financially, and she has to raise seven children alone. It's indeed not easy. Whenever she is allocated a food ticket for fish, she gives it away for money or favors. From the welfare subsidies she receives each month from the industry and commerce union, she can only afford to eat basic vegetables and rice. This holiday season, she was given a special gift of eight kuai so the kids will be able to get by on that. After all, some of this food she naturally needs to give away as bribes or gifts.*

Mei Mei later reveals the truth behind his wife's silence. The political environment has grown increasingly hostile in Shanghai. Neighbors, local police, teachers, and classmates have begun targeting her and the children for associating with him, a "bad element" of society. Local police have tried to kick them out of their home, but Mother Liu has been able to fend them off by bribing them with food tickets. Liu decides to cut ties with her imprisoned husband, Mei Mei finally admits, to "draw a clear class boundary" between herself and her capitalist, Rightist husband. Meanwhile, China's Great Famine—the "three-year natural disaster," as Mei Mei writes in Party-approved language—has arrived in China's richest city.

> *It's difficult for the Shanghainese, because we're not used to skipping meals. I hope this year's harvest can improve the situation.*

The first sign that Shanghai has recovered comes a few years later in a letter I read from the summer of 1963. Mother Liu and her six children have made it through the worst years. Little Xuesong will start school in the autumn. "His growth is all due to your wife's hard work. You should also thank the country for taking care of them and preventing them from starving, and for being able to live through their childhood," Mei Mei writes her brother.

Big Sister and Sisters Two and Three are enrolled at an industrial "middle school," where each work inside textile factories making silk or handkerchiefs. After three years of training, they'll be assigned to work at the factories full-time. "They love labor and are thrifty, too," Mei Mei writes.

"Today I write to tell you another thing," continues Mei Mei:

> *Your wife's family could no longer care for your youngest daughter. They've sent Baby Sister further into the countryside as an adopted daughter for a peasant family . . . I don't have the capability to raise her, otherwise I would've done so. It pains to see my niece sent away for adoption to complete strangers. When you receive this letter, please don't worry. You should focus on working hard to receive leniency from the government so you can be released soon.*

In the future, Mei Mei concludes, we will all be reunited.

Mei Mei's letter is written on rice paper that has turned yellow with time. It feels brittle, and my fingers carefully avoid a small tear through the middle, the result of years of folding and unfolding the note. I think of what Wang Ming must have felt when he read this very letter fifty years ago. The news that people he had never met—never even heard of—were raising his youngest daughter must have been devastating. He was reading the letter thousands of miles away, powerless to help. He could only toil in the fields, working hard to smother his capitalist thoughts in the hopes that someday he would be fully re-educated, reformed, and reborn as a true Communist.

"WE WERE BORN at the wrong time," says Professor Wei.

It's a scorching hot spring afternoon in Nanjing, and I've told Professor Wei the story of his fellow Delingha inmate.

"Wang sounds like he was a natural capitalist," he says. "He would've probably struck it rich today in China. He was stuck in the wrong era. We all were."

Professor Wei sighs loudly and says, *"mei banfa."* It's one of the most common Chinese sayings to arrive at the end of a long sigh: *Nothing can be done.*

Professor Wei hands me one of his novels. It's titled *Chan Deng (Temple Light)*. On the cover, a woman with a voluptuous figure and long flowing hair tucked under a beret stands in a white dress gazing across a blazing orange desert. I read the book jacket description. The novel is about an intellectual who is labeled a Rightist and spends the next twenty years at a labor camp. After his release, the copy proclaims, "he becomes a university professor and later starts to do business. His entangled relationships with several women turn his heart into a cauldron of love and hate."

It's clearly autobiographical, although I wonder about the romantic encounters. I don't prod for details. He's spent two decades in a labor camp. Why not cast yourself as a Don Juan in the book version of your life? I thank him for the gift.

"I'm seventy-nine years old," Professor Wei says. "There aren't many people left who were sent to the camps. Pretty soon we'll all be gone. I feel like it's my responsibility to write about what I could."

Even so, Professor Wei believes young people would prefer to remain ignorant about any uncomfortable period in China's recent history. "Isn't it nicer to sit back and watch a Korean soap opera?" he asks me.

It's certainly safer. History of the Great Famine—still known fifty years later as a "natural disaster" or "three years of difficulties"—remains tightly censored by China's government. School textbooks avoid using the term "famine" to describe the period, and people who lived through it aren't allowed to publish anything about it. Later this year, former Xinhua reporter Yang Jisheng's meticulously reported book about the Great Famine, *Tombstone,* will be released. Based on fifteen years of poring through official archives, it will be hailed by historians as one of the most exhaustive and accurate accounts of the famine.

No one in China will be allowed to publish it.

Professor Wei shakes his head. "Mao had a famous saying: '*Hao bu li ji, zhuanmen li ren,*'" he tells me—*Devote yourself to others without any thought for yourself.*

"It's clear now that it was Mao who was the most selfish," Wei says. "After he died, everyone began to behave in direct opposition to what he'd always said. What do people care about these days? A good job, a healthy family, enough money to buy a house and a car. Who actually cares about the country and the people anymore? Very few."

After years of living and traveling throughout the country, I had met only a handful of Chinese who truly, deep down, believed in the Party. It was foolish to have faith in a government that, time and time again since the beginning of its rule, had proven it wasn't trustworthy. The Party's principles—broadcast in flowery catchphrases—might sound nice, but after so many years of authoritarian rule, the Chinese had become pragmatists. Inside of a political system that provided little real benefit, you were left only to rely on your family and, ultimately, yourself. *Mei banfa.*

The new government under Xi Jinping seemed to understand this lack of faith. Xi had become China's ruler in early 2013. In the first speech of his presidency, he told his countrymen they should strive to realize "the Chinese dream." Its meaning was yet to be clearly defined. "The great rejuvenation of the Chinese nation is a dream of the whole nation, as well as of every individual," Xi said.

Corralling people's dreams—one of a human being's most personal, individual posessions—to serve the nation and the Party sounded an awful lot like the Communist directives of the Mao era. I thought about Wang, his wife, and their seven children, who were likely adults now. How would they see the Chinese dream? How devoted would they be to a government that had robbed them of their father? Would they dream of the Party's "great rejuvenation" of the Chinese nation? What were their dreams?

Professor Wei has heard about the Chinese dream, too.

"The sound of it is very inspiring, but first the Chinese people need to rejuvenate their trust in this country. There is no patriotism anymore. There is no trust. There is no love," he says. "China is on a path without a soul."

6

Auntie Fu's Get-Rich-Quick Plan

长乐路169号

Street of Eternal Happiness, No. 169

Visit Gatewang and you can buy nearly anything, says Mr. Huang, his nose tilted toward the ceiling. He points his inch-long pinkie nail to the offerings on his computer screen: a cicada made of green jade, a shiny golden carry-on suitcase, or an air filter that promises to remove every particulate of city smog from your apartment. Gatewang has it all, Mr. Huang insists, and it will soon be a household name.

We're five miles north of the Street of Eternal Happiness in an office overlooking Shanghai's train station. Auntie Fu sits beside me on a leather sofa. Neither of us has ever visited Gatewang. It's a virtual place, not a physical one. Auntie Fu has come to Mr. Huang's office before, though, and this is the second time she's heard his sales pitch. The company's tagline: *Whatever you can't find on Taobao—China's largest online retail site—you can find on Gatewang.*

The shopping experience begins with the Gatewang terminal, Mr. Huang tells us. It's a machine that resembles a 1980s-era arcade game. "Pretty soon, you'll find these machines in most public places," he promises.

Once stationed in front of the terminal, shoppers log in, browse through wares on the secure Gatewang site, select items for purchase, and pay with special Gatewang money. It's so easy, Mr. Huang assures us.

"But I can buy whatever I need over Taobao on my phone," I say. "Why should I leave the comfort of my home in search of a shopping supercomputer?"

Huang bows his head and holds up his finger, its curved nail high in the air, dismissing a line of reasoning he's heard before. He lifts his head and looks me in the eyes. "On Gatewang, you can buy anything," he repeats slowly, pausing to add: "except for human beings and weapons."

Mr. Huang's business card lists several occupations: Painter, Calligrapher, traditional Chinese medicine vendor, Gatewang representative. It's been three days since I attended the illegal church service with Auntie Fu, and she's already convinced me to attend this investor meeting. I'm skeptical of Mr. Huang's sales pitch, but that doesn't faze Auntie, who's already given him more than five thousand dollars—months' worth of her retirement savings—to buy Gatewang shares.

Huang hopes I'll eventually do the same. The gleam from his freshly shined black loafers match the glare of his slick shoulder-length hair, dyed jet black. A mole the size of a five-jiao coin protrudes from his left cheek, and his smile reveals a missing front tooth. He holds his head with his chin tilted upward and his eyes half closed when he shakes my hand. I see a man ready to pounce.

But Auntie, well, she only saw opportunity.

There were three of us. Auntie Fu had brought a church friend named Xia, a middle-aged dark-skinned peasant from the countryside of Jiangsu province. The women addressed each other as *zimei*—sister. When we met outside, Xia looked me up and down suspiciously, turned to Auntie, and proclaimed: "He's a foreigner."

"Yes, I'm a foreigner," I repeated back to her, my voice muffled by an air mask.

Auntie broke the ice. "He's a *dixiong*, a brother. He's Catholic. He's a believer, just like us. He speaks Chinese, too!"

Xia looked up at me and smiled, giving me a thumbs-up.

Xia and I were there for the same reason: we were both too polite to turn down Auntie's invitation to an information session about a vague but "lucrative" investment opportunity.

Mr. Huang greeted us in the doorway of his ninth-floor office. It was difficult to look at him without feeling hypnotized: he was covered in stripes. Navy blue ones on his pin-striped suit, royal blue and white ones on his shirt, and diagonal red ones on a tie that hung loosely from his long, thin neck.

The walls of Huang's office were four panes of dirty glass. Inside, particleboard desks and cabinets were covered by rice paper watercolors depicting various songbirds perched on trees. Huang had painted them in the morning and set them out to dry in the hazy sunlight streaming through floor-to-ceiling windows, which looked out onto a landscape of dozens of identical white and gray high-rises stretching as far as Shanghai's smog allowed us to see.

Auntie Fu sat close to me, folding and unfolding her fingers. "I've told them the company will be listed on the London exchange in January," she announced, pointing to Xia and me, "and that they've only got two months to invest, so they've got to make their minds up fast."

Mr. Huang nodded slowly, his fingers clasped.

"I've told them there is no risk," Auntie added.

"*Zero* risk," interrupted Mr. Huang calmly.

"That's right! *Zero* risk!" she repeated, as if waking from a dream. "And that's because this is not just a private company, but a company with national support behind it, so the listing must happen. I told them our company would service all of China and the rest of the world. It will enter foreign markets and eventually allow the renminbi to flow freely around the world!"

Mr. Huang nodded majestically, pleased his loyal pupil had spread the good news so thoroughly. He leaned forward and began to speak. "China's exports have slowed and the government needs to boost consumption," he said matter-of-factly. "A week ago, Taobao announced sales of nineteen billion renminbi. That was a big boost to consumption. But the majority of the profit goes to Japan, not China. Eighty-seven percent of Taobao shares belong to the Japanese. That means we're working for the Japanese."

Taobao belonged to Alibaba, a company started by Jack Ma, China's most successful entrepreneur. Japan's SoftBank had been an early investor in the company, but Mr. Huang was wildly exaggerating the firm's stake in Alibaba. SoftBank owned 37 percent of Alibaba, not 87 percent. He made it sound as if Chinese shoppers who make purchases on Taobao funneled their money directly into the coffers of the enemy.

"Due to these circumstances, China helped create *Gatewang*," said Mr. Huang, pointing to the name of the company printed on the wall behind him.

Mr. Huang turned back to us and smiled, the gap in his teeth exposed, as he challenged his pupils. "What's the difference between Gatewang and Taobao?"

Xia stared blankly at him. She had never been online, much less on Taobao. Auntie gave me an encouraging smile. I played along, shrugging my shoulders.

Mr. Huang wagged his fingernail in the air. "Gatewang is a *super* Taobao!"

He waited for my reaction. Seeing none, he turned to his wife. "Mrs. Shao will tell you how it's done."

Mrs. Shao was younger than him—in her forties—and had curled her hair and dyed it auburn. She wore a black jacket, tight jeans, and a red scarf. Hearing her cue, she walked from the side of the room, her high-heeled shoes making a loud clopping sound upon the Pergo floor. She stopped beside a bookcase and positioned a computer screen toward us.

"Don't turn it on yet," said Mr. Huang softly.

"Don't turn it on!" yelled Auntie Fu.

Mrs. Shao glared at her. "I'm not turning anything on," she spat back.

My presence seemed to make Auntie anxious. She had hand-delivered two potential investors, one of them a foreigner. I assumed there was something in it for her should we decide to invest. Mrs. Shao regained her composure and ordered Auntie to go and find a mouse pad. She fired up the monitor. It showed a picture of a refrigerator-sized computer terminal with "Gatewang" emblazoned on its side. It looked like what I used to play Pac-Man on at the arcade.

Mrs. Shao explained that Taobao required an online transaction to buy products, but Gatewang's customers could instead buy credits offline. They could spend these credits at standing terminals located at convenience stores, restaurants, and barbershops throughout China.

Mr. Huang cut in. "We already have fifty-two thousand types of products available on Gatewang: you can even buy a house, gold bars, and luxury cars such as BMW or Mercedes-Benz. In developed countries, shopping this way is very popular, but Gatewang is the first of its kind here in China."

I thought of saying: In developed countries, shopping this way is unheard of because buying a house or a car with credits at a terminal inside a barbershop is a terrible idea. But I held my tongue.

Mrs. Shao turned to me. "If you're interested, the initial price is just two yuan per share, and you'll get free credits with that," she said. "The listing price on the London exchange will be at least five pounds per share. That's equal to fifty yuan. If you buy ten thousand shares, it'll be worth at least twenty-five times more when Gatewang lists!"

Auntie Fu had heard the pitch before, but this part still made her excited. "Now's the time for us Chinese to make money off of foreigners!" she shouted, forgetting who was sitting a few inches to her left.

I had a lot of questions about Gatewang. Who owned it? A man in Guangzhou, replied Mrs. Shao. Who set the price of the stock? The man in Guangzhou, answered Mrs. Shao. When was the listing date? January 31, but that was up to the man in Guangzhou, said Mrs. Shao.

Gatewang hadn't listed anywhere else. Why start with the London exchange? Mr. Huang took that one: The UK market was the world's most regulated, he claimed, and the man in Guangzhou determined it to be the best place to list.

"Who is this 'Man in Guangzhou'?" I asked.

Mr. Huang showed me a photo on his phone. The Man in Guangzhou was stout, had a full head of hair, and stared at the camera with beady eyes. His right hand appeared to be in midshake with that of a distinguished-looking foreigner wearing a suit. Behind them on the wall was Gatewang's company seal. "Look who visited our office," said Mr. Huang, "the British consul general of Guangzhou!"

This raised even more questions. Sensing I would ask another one, Mr. Huang chose the distraction strategy. "Look at this," he said, directing my attention to a book on the coffee table. It was bound in leather and bore a nonsensical title in Chinglish:

CAPITAL INVESTMENT OF NEW THINKING CONSUMER BUSINESS

It was written by someone named Pang Bofu, who was identified as a researcher at the Chinese Academy of Social Sciences in Sichuan province. "Our company philosophy is based on this book," he said, reaching across the table to caress the cover.

The book had been placed on the table so that it lay precisely in the middle, allowing nothing else to touch it. The entire volume—all 148 pages—was about the Gatewang machine, Mr. Huang explained.

Back at my office, a quick online search revealed that Pang Bofu makes a living giving talks at investment conferences and is a strong advocate of Amway, an American company accused of being a pyramid scheme. An Internet forum devoted to Gatewang was filled with posts alleging the company was a scam, and its founder, Mr. Li—the Man in Guangzhou—had operated several pyramid schemes throughout China and was already moving his assets overseas. But sitting on the sofa staring at the Gatewang bible, I didn't know any of this. I only knew that investing in the company seemed like a very bad idea.

Mr. Huang could sense I was skeptical. But he was a salesman. "I sell Chinese medicine, too," he said, his voice trailing off.

He reached around me—I shifted sideways in surprise—to produce a tiny brown bottle from a box that had been resting behind the sofa. "If you are drunk and you drink two bottles of this, you immediately become sober," he claimed.

He opened the bottle and offered me a taste.

"I'm not drunk," I said.

"Drinking this can also help you lose weight. A friend of mine said his son lost five kilograms after a few bottles."

"Then I'll buy some!" said Auntie.

She took a sip and then offered the bottle to Xia and me. I took a swig. It tasted sweet, like prune juice.

"You can give these bottles as gifts to your Chinese friends if you don't like the taste," suggested Mr. Huang. "They will be grateful. The market price for a bottle is sixty-eight yuan, but the price among friends is only ten."

I politely declined. I asked the couple how they had met Auntie Fu.

"We met at the Gatewang meeting in Shanghai a couple of months ago," said Mrs. Shao. "Since then, we've recruited a couple dozen friends to invest, too. You get credits for each new investor you find."

I asked Mrs. Shao why I had never seen a Gatewang terminal in Shanghai. "Oh, people from Shanghai are very suspicious of this type of business," she said. "They don't believe they can actually make money from this. But in Wenzhou, these machines are everywhere. People in Wenzhou are very advanced."

AUNTIE FU SEEMED surrounded by people from Wenzhou. The city was three hundred miles down the Pacific coast from Shanghai. The leaders of the underground church she attended were from

Wenzhou, as were many investors in Gatewang. This wasn't a coincidence. Wherever in China I traveled as a reporter, the people from Wenzhou—*Wenzhou ren*—were usually characterized as the worst kind of capitalist, running Ponzi schemes and get-rich-quick scams throughout the country. It was *Wenzhou ren,* the reasoning went, who had pooled money to buy up urban homes, driving up property prices to bubble-sized proportions. It was *Wenzhou ren* who swindled seniors desperate to get a piece of China's fast-moving economy. And it was *Wenzhou ren* who made up a dense web of informal networks of lenders who charged outrageous interest rates for off-the-books loans to family businesses too small to obtain legitimate credit from state banks. They were greedy fiends, those *Wenzhou ren,* and apart from Auntie Fu, my neighbors on the Street of Eternal Happiness didn't have anything nice to say about them.

"They call us the Jews of the Orient!" Huang Fajing told me proudly during a visit to his Wenzhou factory.

I met Huang in the autumn of 2013 while reporting a story on China's underground lending networks. He had made a fortune exporting lighters to Europe and the United States. He was the chairman of Wenzhou Rifeng Lighter Company, and for years his company dominated the global market. If you used a lighter in the 1990s, the odds were it came from his factory. *Wenzhou ren* called him *Dahuo Wang*—the Lighter King. He had a gentle, sincere face, a raspy voice from using his product too many times to smoke cigarettes, and he dressed casually in a polo shirt and track pants. Strands of long, black hair caressed his eyebrows, and his soft hands were well manicured down to the tips of his inch-long pinkie nails—high fashion among former peasants, proof they were no longer working with their hands. I asked His Excellency how *Wenzhou ren* had earned a reputation for excelling at business.

The Lighter King didn't mince words. "Geography," he said with authority.

The city of Wenzhou had always been isolated from the rest of China, surrounded by forested mountains on three sides. Its coastline along the East China Sea was historically the only way out. Because of its proximity to Taiwan, China's government had viewed the city as a potential target for a bombing campaign or invasion from Taiwan. As a result, Beijing didn't bother to invest in the city's infrastructure. Wenzhou would have to fend for itself as a *luohou* backwater, forgotten by the motherland.

For *Wenzhou ren*, this was a blessing. It meant the city was spared much of the economic and spiritual destruction from decades of violent Maoist campaigns spreading like cancer through the rest of China. "They left us alone," the Lighter King told me, "and we made money. It's as simple as that."

By the time Deng Xiaoping's economic reforms surfaced, Wenzhou already had tens of thousands of small businesses built on capital raised through mutual help foundations called *chenghui*. Each member of a *chenghui* was required to invest the same amount. Then the group would take turns withdrawing money to fund their business, returning more capital to the pool after they made a profit. The system helped *Wenzhou ren* develop their own economy built on a credit system that predated banks, harkening back to a time when a loan was simply a pile of cash pooled together by friends and family. "I began making cigarette lighters twenty years ago," the Lighter King told me, smiling. "Four of my family members each put in fifteen hundred dollars and lent it to me without interest. That's what we call a Wenzhou loan."

The city's economy raced ahead, and Wenzhou businessmen began showing up in other parts of the world. In Europe, they ran garment or shoe factories in the industrial suburbs of cities such as Milan and Barcelona. China's government even seized on the "Wenzhou Economic Model," drawing on the coastal metropolis's entrepreneurial spirit to inspire the rest of the country, but conveniently ignoring how these businesses were financed. As more money flowed into the city, the Wenzhou loan evolved into a more complex and less innocent line of credit. Loans were no longer limited to just family and friends. "Bigger groups of lenders began to form," explained the Lighter King. "They began lending money with very high interest rates. And they lent it to strangers."

In the past year, two Wenzhou businesswomen had been arrested for conning investors out of tens of millions. According to court documents, Lin Haiyin promised low risk and high returns to friends and friends-of-friends if they let her invest their money in stock offerings. It was an arrangement not dissimilar to Auntie Fu's investment in Gatewang. Lin instead used the money to speculate in stocks, losing everything. The previous year, businesswoman Wu Ying—nicknamed "Rich Sister" in Chinese—had persuaded her investors to pour $122 million into her hair salon, foot-massage parlor, and later, copper and real estate investments, enabling her to buy one hundred properties and forty luxury vehicles, including a Ferrari worth half a million dollars. It was a Ponzi scheme of epic proportions that left her investors with nothing. In the end, the intermediate court in Wenzhou sentenced both "Rich Sister" and Lin Haiyin to death, sending a shudder through China's home of investment scams, shadow banking, and all sorts of pyramid and Ponzi schemes.

"This recent financial crisis has sparked a loss of social trust in Wenzhou," lamented the Lighter King inside his office. "If things don't get under control soon, this will spur a fair amount of social instability."

He pressed a button on a cut-glass stationary lighter on his desk, igniting a tiny cylindrical stream of blue flame that gushed straight up to the cigarette dangling from his mouth. I mentioned to him how, in so many interviews in other parts of China, people had placed the blame for China's economic woes on the shenanigans of Wenzhou businessmen. Where had Wenzhou's lending practices gone afoul?

"I think one point should be made crystal clear about what's going on," he said, pointing the burning tip of his cigarette at me. "A key reason behind all of this chaos is the global financial meltdown. If it weren't for the subprime loan crisis in your country, China wouldn't have had to issue hundreds of billions in stimulus and the country's financial situation wouldn't be like this."

I had pushed the Lighter King into a corner, and he did what any *Wenzhou ren* does when blamed for a monumental problem: he pointed a long-nailed finger to another scapegoat with an even worse reputation.

A FEW DAYS AFTER the Gatewang meeting, I stopped by Auntie Fu's home to tell her about my online sleuthing: the accusations of fraud, the background of the Man from Guangzhou, the Ponzi schemes he was accused of running.

It was the first day of December and it was freezing outside. The sun was obscured by thick smog. The air quality index hovered around 300: HAZARDOUS proclaimed my phone in big purple letters. When the air got this bad, the local government recommended that residents stay indoors. Lenora and I kept our boys inside with all three of our refrigerator-sized air filters set on high.

When I arrived at Uncle Feng and Auntie Fu's, the door to their kitchen was wide open. I let myself in, and Uncle got up and brought me a chair and a fried turnip cake. The cold weather had been good for business, he said, beaming. He had made ¥160 the day before—close to $30. "Have a turnip cake!" he yelled to people passing by the window. "Turnip cakes! Scallion pancakes! They smell so good!"

Auntie emerged from the back door to help her husband serve a group of customers who had formed a line along the sidewalk. "Hey there," she said to me, realizing she had a referee standing in her kitchen. "Which one tastes better? Turnip cakes or scallion pancakes?"

"Both," I said carefully.

Uncle handed over a bag of turnip cakes to a customer and peered over at me. "She thinks my scallion pancakes are too tough."

"You should serve pancakes while they're hot," Auntie lectured. "I met an old lady a few days ago who said your pancakes were luke-warm and had become tough and less tasty than before."

"You'll always find one or two complainers out of a hundred," Uncle responded.

Auntie had spent the previous evening at Central Church, and she had saved a seat for me for the Christmas Eve service. I protested, telling her I needed to stay at home with my children that night.

She was undeterred. "Bring your kids, then!"

"Our tradition is to stay at home and attend church on Christmas Day," I explained.

"All right, I'll bring someone else. But you should come this Saturday," she said. "Yesterday we had a preacher from Henan province. His sermon was very good," said Auntie Fu.

"Was he a reformed gangster, too?" I asked.

"No. He used to be a very bad student," Auntie said. "The teacher put him in the back row because he never did any homework. But he was a prodigy, and he began to preach in the countryside to the poor. People brought him chickens, ducks, and eggs. They even brought pigs as their offerings!"

Genius move, I thought: spinning tales of the generosity of China's peasantry to guilt the urbanites into giving a tenth of their salaries. He sounded like a good follow-up to Preacher Jiang.

"It was packed," continued Auntie. "Not an empty seat in the church. Wenzhou churches always find the top preachers."

"Fancy a pancake?" Uncle yelled to passersby. "How many do you need? Here. Take the hot ones first."

Auntie turned to me with a question. "Does Ecuador belong to the United States?"

"No, it's in South America."

She handed me a pamphlet. The Chinese on the cover said:

PREPARE TO MEET YOUR GOD!
HEAVEN, HELL, AND THE RETURN OF CHRIST

The first page had images of Jesus weeping, Pope John Paul II with his arms in the air, and a woman engulfed in flames. A map of Ecuador was farther down the page.

"Where did you get this?" I asked.

"A Sister gave me this. I'll make a copy for you. This little girl from Ecuador died and returned to life after twenty-three hours!" Auntie said. "Do you know Mai Ke Er Jie Ke Xun?"

I sounded out the name until phonetics took over: Mi-chael Jack-son.

"She saw Michael Jackson in hell!" Auntie said. "Have you heard of him? He died. He danced like this."

She stood up and shook her ample hips, pointing her chubby fingers in the air. It was as good a Michael Jackson impersonation as a sixty-four-year-old Chinese auntie could muster. I paged through the brochure. A photo of Jackson was on page 9, holding a microphone and dancing on stage.

"He's in hell now," Auntie said matter-of-factly. "He was just like those Hong Kong celebrities who had too much plastic surgery. All of it finally killed him."

The pamphlet was twenty-two pages. It told the story of an Ecuadorean girl named Angelica Zambrano who said she died and met Jesus. She claimed the two traveled to hell, where Jesus showed her deceased celebrities like Selena, Michael Jackson, and even Pope John Paul II consumed in flames, tortured by demons. Departed children who had watched too many cartoons in their lifetimes were stuck in hell, too. Jesus gave the girl a tour of heaven and showed her a preview of the Rapture on a movie screen. After all this, Jesus ordered the girl back to the land of the living. Her job was to spread the news about what she had seen.

"I'll make a copy for you. See here. She saw many kids in heaven," Auntie said, taking the pamphlet from me and beginning to read it out loud. " 'Jesus said: Daughter, yes, heaven belongs to the children. The children must come to me. Anyone who comes to me, I won't abandon him.' Look. God said that."

Auntie and Uncle had two children. I asked her if they were believers.

"I brought them to church, but they didn't believe. We have a seventeen-year-old granddaughter. I saw her yesterday. How old are your kids?"

Five and two, I said, showing her a photo on my phone.

"One boy and one girl?"

"No. Both are boys."

Auntie smiled. "Boys are good. You are blessed. Girls suffer."

Uncle stopped shredding carrots and flashed a look of annoyance at his wife.

"What nonsense are you talking about?"

"Boys are the best," said Auntie, looking away. "I could only hope all my descendants were boys. If you're a girl, your only hope is to find a good husband so that you might have a chance at a good life. If you don't, you'll be miserable forever."

"If everyone's like you, they won't be able to feed themselves," said Uncle, returning to his cutting board.

I had stopped by his kitchen in the past week when Auntie was gone, and Uncle Feng had told me he was tiring of his wife's investment "opportunities" and all the time she was spending at that Wenzhou-run church of hers.

"There are few good men in this world and plenty of bad men," Auntie continued, looking at her husband. "Very few who show real love. I was incredibly unlucky to end up with you."

Uncle dropped the vegetable peeler, wiping his hands on his apron, irritated. "You're not doing too badly. You've got a home, don't you? Many people don't even have a roof. You don't even work! There's something wrong with your head."

"Why do I need to work?" she asked.

Uncle turned to me. "She hasn't been working for twelve years. And she hasn't bothered to take care of our children, either."

"And he nearly killed me," Auntie said, facing me. "I told you that story, right? I almost lost my life."

Uncle studied both of us for a moment, realizing his wife had told the foreigner the story of their first pregnancy and going through labor in the middle of the desert. For a moment, he flashed a look of betrayal, but he quickly regained composure. His wife was the type of person who told everything to anyone who would listen. I looked at the floor, uncomfortable to be drawn into the middle of a fight that appeared to have been going on for years. Uncle turned away from us and stared out the window. Outside, it was growing dark. "You nearly died because you don't have a brain," he said.

"My body's never been the same, and the only one there for me was God!" Auntie shouted.

"Then go and live in church!" Uncle shouted back.

He dried his hands on a towel, unplugged the griddle, and stormed out of the kitchen to their bedroom.

Auntie was unfazed. She immediately took advantage of his absence, asking me in a hushed voice what I thought about Gatewang. "They're listing in January! If you want to invest, now's the time."

Her friend Xia, it turned out, had decided against Gatewang. I asked if she had found anyone else to invest.

"I got my neighbor to put in twenty thousand," she whispered. "She wanted to invest fifty, but she didn't have enough money. This really is a good opportunity. At the investment conference, the author of the Gatewang book, remember Mr. Pang? He told everyone that if Gatewang couldn't get listed, he'd kneel down and take out his right eye! Everyone stood up and applauded. I never saw anything that great before!"

"Have you invested more money?" I asked.

"I just got my retirement salary today—two thousand—I'll go back to their office tomorrow to invest that. If I could borrow a hundred thousand from someone, I'd write a guarantee note saying, 'If the project loses money, I'll give you back half! If it makes money, I'll take just one-third!'," Auntie Fu said. "I wouldn't ask for a fifty-fifty split. It doesn't matter. I'm that confident."

I hesitated, trying to process the math behind what she had just told me. All her retirement funds were being funneled into Gatewang, but it still wasn't enough. It was clear she had done a lot of thinking about borrowing even more. I doubted Auntie knew anyone with access to ¥100,000—except for me.

She seemed to be waiting for me to respond. I squirmed in my seat. She was a good person who was making bad choices. It was hard to watch her throw her money away like this, and now she was trying to pull me into this mess, too.

"Auntie, I think you should be careful about putting your savings into this," I said measuredly. "I searched on the Internet and there were a lot of people who said Gatewang is a scam."

She shook her head vigorously. "The people who invested ¥100,000 months ago already earned twice that! Just wait until

Gatewang lists in London," she said. "You'll probably never have another chance to make this much money again!"

"Auntie, don't invest any more money," I said. "I don't think you should trust them."

"Don't worry!" she said. "Jack Ma made a bet and he became rich, right?"

"I think this is different," I said.

I noticed Uncle Feng's silhouette in the doorway connecting the kitchen to their bedroom, quietly listening to our conversation. It was likely he had heard everything. Auntie noticed him, too.

"There were government officials at the investment conference. This is a sure thing," Auntie insisted, glancing toward a movement in the darkness.

Finally, Uncle emerged from the shadows. "She doesn't have any money to invest!" he yelled. "Since we returned from Xinjiang twenty years ago, she hasn't earned one *fen*."

"I'd like to invest more, but I can't," she said, ignoring her husband.

"Auntie, these types of scams are everywhere in China. They're designed to target older people like you," I said.

Uncle had heard enough. He was already angry about the accusations his wife had been tossing his way earlier, and here was confirmation of his worst fears: his unemployed wife was plotting to pour even more money into yet another flimsy scheme.

"She hasn't even returned the fifty thousand I lent to her!" Uncle shouted. "And now you want to invest *more* money? Where's the house you supposedly bought?"

Auntie didn't answer. She slowly let her head drop forward, as if it were too heavy for her neck to carry. Outside, a young man and woman walked by the window, hand in hand, the woman giggling at a story her lover was recounting, their voices melding into the subdued din of the city at night as they continued down the block. A car sounded its horn in the distance, then a return honk.

Auntie stared at the floor as she spoke. "Sometimes you meet bad people and you can't help it. There are a lot of bad people in Shanghai," she said slowly, quietly.

"Auntie, you're right," I said. "There are a lot of people in Shanghai that will cheat you. I think the people at Gatewang might be bad, too."

"*Aiya!* Something's wrong with your brain!" Uncle yelled.

Auntie held her gaze on the floor and repeated what I had said. "Yes, there are a lot of people in Shanghai that will cheat you . . ."

Uncle propped both of his hands onto the edge of the kitchen sink and stared out onto the street in his usual position. He murmured something angry in Shanghai dialect meant for Auntie's ears, not mine. She stared hard at the floor, her face cast with total defeat. She picked up the Ecuadorean religious brochure from the chair, mindlessly thumbing through its pages.

"This girl," Auntie said with a sad smile, "after she reached heaven, she didn't want to return."

Uncle turned his head toward her, sneering. "Heaven? What was heaven like? I'd love to hear about it! Ha! Heaven!"

Auntie gently placed the pamphlet back on the chair.

Uncle grinned and shook his head. "China's sending rockets up to the moon and *they* haven't even seen heaven yet!"

That very hour in the city of Xichang, just miles away from Auntie's hometown in Sichuan, China had launched the country's first lunar rover into space. Uncle had just caught the launch live on state television in his bedroom. The rover's name was *Yutu*, "Jade Rabbit." It was named after a Chinese folk tale about a woman who stole the pill of immortality from her husband. The husband then banished his wife to the moon along with her pet rabbit. As the story goes, the woman became a goddess, and the rabbit's dark outline was forever etched into the illuminated topography of each full moon.

Tonight above the frigid haze of Shanghai, though, was a new moon. The rabbit was nowhere to be seen. Instead, its tiny namesake was racing toward it, a symbol of China's global ambitions. Before saying goodbye to *Yutu*, the director of the Xichang Launch Center declared China's space dream as "part of the Chinese dream of national rejuvenation."

But below, in the city of Shanghai, inside a grimy open window overlooking the Street of Eternal Happiness, lavish dreams and visions of immortality were in doubt.

"Don't leave tonight without a pancake," said Auntie Fu, fetching one from the bottom of a pile that was still warm. "It's cold out. This will warm you up for the ride home."

She placed it in a plastic bag, handing it to me. "Are you sure you don't want to invest in the company?" she asked one last time, unwilling to let go of her dream. "Zero risk!"

Uncle Feng guffawed at her persistence. I smiled and shook my head.

"Okay," she said, accompanying me to the door. "Let's wait after I make my money, and maybe you can invest later on."

"And if you make anything more than a *fen*," Uncle said with a chuckle, "then you should return all the money I lent you."

Auntie turned around and gave her husband a long, cold stare. "Just wait until January," she replied.

7

Bride Price

长乐路109号
Street of Eternal Happiness, No. 109

There were few places in China where the price of a bride was higher than it was in Shanghai. In 2013, Sina, China's largest Web portal, and Vanke, the country's largest real estate developer, combined their data to construct a map of bride prices around China. To make a match in Shanghai, a man typically offered the family of his intended the equivalent of $16,000 and a certificate of home ownership. In Inner Mongolia, the damage was about a tenth that: an auspicious ¥8,888—1,500 USD—plus 9 head of livestock and 3 pieces of gold jewelry. The coastal province of Fujian notched somewhere in the middle: $7,000, a set of gold headpieces, and a gold tiara.

In comparison, rural Shandong seemed like a bargain. Zhao, the owner of my favorite flower shop, spent the equivalent of $3,000 for her younger son's wife there. As insurance, she dipped into her earnings to buy apartments back in her hometown for both sons. Little Sun—the younger one—seemed set after he married Zhang Min, the daughter of a farm family from Zhao's hometown. In typical Chinese fashion, though, Zhao thought he could have done better.

"If my son were as tall as you are," Zhao told me once, "he wouldn't have settled for her. She's not that pretty."

I stopped by Zhao's shop on a freezing Sunday afternoon in January to find her wearing a down jacket zipped over two sweaters and three pairs of thermal underwear. The puffy layers matched her round cheeks, turned rosy from the chill. Zhao didn't heat her shop; in fact, she was one of the few whose electricity bills crept downward in the wintertime. Shanghai's damp, freezing air created ideal conditions for her merchandise.

"Perfect timing!" she said when she hobbled over to her door. "I could use some help."

I looked down at her right foot. It was encased in a brace that looked like a black ski boot. She hopped back to her stool, gently resting the foot atop a plush brown teddy bear pillow on her foldout table. The remnants of hours' worth of sunflower seed eating were scattered on the floor. A dating show blared on television.

She'd broken her ankle while carrying her grandson down the stairs. Luckily, the boy—the family's prized jewel—was undamaged.

"I slipped, and I held him up in the air so that he wouldn't get hurt. But I'm a mess. I'm so clumsy! Thank the heavens he's fine."

The boy's name was Shuo Shuo. He was the son of Little Sun, Zhao's younger boy who had come to Shanghai straight from the county seat's school for autistic children. Ever since Little Sun's wife had given birth a year and a half ago, Zhao had taken charge of feeding and caring for her grandson at night, waking up to tend the flower shop by day. Shuo Shuo was the same age as my younger son, Landon, who was now learning to walk, though Shuo Shuo still hadn't achieved that milestone. Zhao, like many Chinese grandparents, insisted on carrying him everywhere, fussing over the boy's every move. His grandmother temporarily crippled, Shuo Shuo would finally be given the freedom to take his first steps.

"Things aren't going well for me this year," Zhao told me. "There's a saying in my hometown: 'After your parents die, you'll have bad luck for three years.' Now I have to wear this brace. It looks awful. Whenever I go outside, I lose face."

Her father had died from esophageal cancer a few months ago. Her daughter-in-law's grandmother had also just passed. Her son, daughter-in-law, and little Shuo Shuo were out of town for the weekend to attend the funeral, leaving her alone in her shop. I told Zhao my father had just died of cancer, too.

"How old was he?"

"Sixty-eight," I said.

"*Wah!* Too young! What a shame. My father was eighty-two, so we were expecting it. Did you see him before he died?"

I told her that my family and I had taken care of him at his lake home in northern Minnesota, where he chose to spend his last days.

"What did you do with his body after he died?" she asked.

It seemed like an insensitive question, but Zhao knew my father lived in the country, far from any city, and she had a business owner's mind. She was curious about logistics.

"We called a mortuary to come and take his body to town," I explained.

"Did you bury him?"

"No, we had him cremated."

She beamed. "That's how we do it in China!"

Knowing death rites were the same on the opposite side of the planet seemed to cheer her up. Zhao shifted her body and leaned forward, gingerly moving her leg. "When my father died, it cost five thousand yuan for the wooden coffin and five thousand for the tombstone and cemetery plot. My dad's work unit paid for it all, though, so it was okay. Did you have to pay for all of that?"

My father's union benefits covered much of the cost of his funeral. I thought for a moment about how to phrase it in a way she would understand. "My father's work unit also paid for these things," I finally said.

Zhao smiled. "You see? America and China are so much alike! Who would've thought?"

She opened a thermos to take a sip of tea. Steam gushed forth, swirling in the freezing room. Winter was my least favorite season in Shanghai. The wet, frosty air penetrated clothes, gradually dampening each layer until your skin was clammy and frigid. It felt like being trapped inside an icy sponge. Retreating indoors didn't improve things much. Nearly all buildings lacked insulation and only the swankiest residences in town had central air. Our apartment's heat came from air conditioner units in each room. Their location—mounted high up on the wall—meant the hot air pumping out of them flowed straight up into the ceiling. By our second winter in Shanghai, we had purchased space heaters that traveled like rolling IV stands to whichever room we happened to be freezing in.

Air pollution was at its worst in winter. Hundreds of millions of people heating their homes at once meant coal-fired power plants worked overtime to provide electricity. Their emissions hovered over much of the eastern half of the country for weeks, pushing smog to dangerous levels. Those who could afford air filtration systems stayed inside and cranked them to high, which used more electricity, requiring the burning of even more coal.

I wasn't one to sit inside, hiding from the elements, and I often went biking wearing a helmet and an air mask to keep warm. My typical route took me through the tiny alleyways in the southern part of the Concession. Then I usually traveled north, turning right onto the Street of Eternal Happiness. I would stop in to see CK at his sandwich shop, pause again three blocks east at Auntie Fu and Uncle Feng's kitchen, and typically finish a block farther at Zhao's flower shop.

Today, I had worked up an appetite. Zhao reached for a pear, sliced it, and offered me the bigger half.

"I need some advice," Zhao said while I ate. "It's about my cousin back home, the one who is a year younger than me. I think I told you about the problems with her husband, the official from the Tax Bureau, right?"

Zhao's gossip about relatives back in her village was the stuff of legend. There were family feuds settled with knife fights, cousins losing control of multiple mistresses, and tragic suicides over unrequited love. Life in her hometown was like a telenovela she watched from her perch in civilized Shanghai. Occasionally she was pulled back into the drama when someone pleaded for help. I couldn't recall the story about the government official, but if there was one place in the world where a bureaucrat from the Tax Bureau could be immortalized, it was Zhao's village.

"Well, he had a mistress and he divorced my cousin, but he still beats her. She just called me this afternoon after he beat her up again. What do you think she should do?" she asked me. "Are you allowed to continue to beat your wife even after divorce?"

This was a question that I had never considered before. I was trying to figure out how to respond when I was saved by a knock on the door. A neighbor appeared with a box of lunch. "Ah, thank you! I'll eat this for dinner," Zhao said, placing the box on top of a pile of produce donated by other neighbors. When a shop owner on the Street of Eternal Happiness was injured, the entire block helped with meals and small chores.

"I didn't have any advice for her either," Zhao continued. "It was terrible. He pushed her head into the ground and whipped her with a belt. They have three kids, all grown up. They all know. They allow it because their dad's the one who makes all the money. He's bribed them all."

I told her that he sounded a lot like other government officials I had reported on in China.

"Even his mistress came over to beat her! Nobody can help her now. She told me today, 'If you can become independent, I can, too.' I said, 'No, you can't. Your husband works for the taxation bureau!'"

Zhao was right. Tax Bureau employees were some of the most powerful local officials in China. They were charged with collecting fees from businesses, and bribes were a big perk of the job. In some ways, it was the perfect position: not so high on the Party totem pole that it attracted investigations during central government anti-corruption crackdowns, but high enough to afford a couple of homes, a luxury car, and at least one mistress maintained with whatever funds could be skimmed off the top.

"What if she comes to Shanghai like you did?" I asked.

"She ended up with a few of his homes after the divorce. She's used to the lifestyle there. She wouldn't be able to start over and eat bitter here," Zhao explained. "It's hopeless. Last year she drank a bucket of pesticide, but they pumped her stomach and she didn't die. In my hometown, drinking pesticide is the most common way to solve problems."

I thought about what Zhao had said earlier: America and China are so much alike. I was touched Zhao considered me close enough of a friend to ask me for advice on a matter like this, but any guidance I could offer would seem naïve. This was a thorny rural Chinese problem rooted in cultural tradition, endemic political corruption, and centuries of poverty no foreigner from America could hope to solve. All I could do was sit silently beside Zhao, thinking how sometimes our two countries seemed so far apart.

I asked about Big Sun, Zhao's eldest son. A few months ago, he had quit his job at the golf course to work as a hairdresser in Hangzhou, a city a little over an hour away by high-speed train. It seemed strange he wasn't here, helping his disabled mother run the shop while Little Sun and his wife were away.

Zhao scrunched her nose in disappointment. "I asked him to take a few days off and come to Shanghai to help me, but he didn't come," she said. "He said it was the busy season for hairdressers. I lost my temper and told him he shouldn't bother coming home for Chinese New Year."

This was probably one of the worst things a Chinese mother could say to her son. But refusing to help your crippled mother was a serious violation of filial duty. This situation was becoming more common in China. Young adults of working age faced too much pressure in their jobs or lived too far from home to fulfill the traditional role of caregiver for their parents. The new reality posed a threat to two millennia of Confucian custom—one of the most distinctive elements of being Chinese—and it worried leaders enough to issue a national statute requiring family members to attend to the spiritual needs of the elderly and visit them "often" if they live apart.

The law had only been in effect for a few months, yet elderly parents across China were already winning lawsuits against their children for neglect. What seemed like lighthearted news fodder for Western media was a grave issue for China's government. Demographers predicted that a third of the country—nearly half a billion people—would be seniors by mid-century. If economic growth depended on moving hundreds of millions of young workers to the cities in the next dozen years, who would take care of the parents back home? As if left-behind children weren't a big enough problem, China now had left-behind grandparents, too.

Zhao wasn't finished complaining about Big Sun. "He wants to save enough money to get married," she said. "Where's he going to get it?"

Zhao knew her eldest son didn't have enough money to become a husband and that she'd have to foot the bill, but it felt good to vent. "A couple of years ago, he rejected girls I helped find for him. Back then, finding a girl for your son cost around twenty thousand kuai"—around $3,500—"now the price has doubled."

Zhao's daughter-in-law Zhang Min had been purchased at a good price for her younger son, but the girl's family was poor and couldn't offer much of a dowry in return. Zhang Min was built like a farm girl: strong and big-boned. Her face resembled those of peasant girls I had seen in Party propaganda posters from the 1960s: high cheekbones, glowing skin, and a perpetual look of confidence. In many ways, she looked and behaved a lot like Zhao must have when she was younger. She was beginning to help Zhao in significant ways at the shop. She was in charge of purchases from the wholesale markets, and she cooked for the entire family.

"She sure is smart," said Zhao. "She works hard. She knows how to take charge."

Zhang Min was a natural. She had Zhao's booming voice and her open smile made customers feel at ease. Her husband, Little Sun, on the other hand, often kept to himself and was slow to learn.

"I tell him he's like mud that can't even be used to build a wall,"

Zhao said. "He answered, 'If you think I'm no better than mud, then you must be right.' Isn't that aggravating? He has no brain, you know? He turns all his earnings over to his wife. He prefers not to handle money. Last time my daughter-in-law put two hundred yuan into his pocket he returned it to her. What are you supposed to do with a son like that?"

IT WAS NEVER EASY for young Chinese men and women to please their parents. This is especially true today, with the country's economy growing by hundreds of billions of dollars each year. Zhao had always felt her sons would be denied their piece of China's bulging economic pie because she had failed to steer them on the path to college.

But many college graduates I knew seemed worse off. The previous year, seven million Chinese had earned university degrees. A year later, nearly a third of them were still looking for work. With more and more opportunities arising from China's growing economy, the numbers didn't make sense.

In the spring I visited a job fair a few miles west of the Street of Eternal Happiness on the outskirts of downtown Shanghai. Thousands of young graduates milled around the floor of a sports arena, hopping between booths from hundreds of companies throughout China. The arena hosted a fair like this every Friday.

I met a petite young graduate with oversized eyeglasses that made her look birdlike. She was from Guizhou, one of the poorest provinces in China. She'd completed her student teaching at a local kindergarten, yet she didn't want to work as a teacher. "After taxes, I'd only make two thousand renminbi," she said with a pout. "I'd rather be a wedding planner."

The only problem was she had no capital to start a wedding business, and no experience to speak of. "Well, I've helped plan a friend's wedding," she told me.

"What kind of job are you seeking?" I asked her.

I hadn't seen any booths from the wedding industry at the fair.

"*Bu zhi dao* . . ." she said, lazily drawing out the last word of "I don't know" as if she were a little girl. "Most of the jobs here aren't really interesting. I'm looking for a company that'll give me a high salary, money for meals, and rent. A place where the working hours aren't too long."

"Aren't you being a little unrealistic?" I asked politely.

"Yeah, probably," she said through giggles.

Chinese born in the 1990s had never experienced an economic downturn. In the four years this young woman had spent at college in Shanghai, the city had added six subway lines and the country had completed the world's most extensive high-speed rail network, reducing the time it took to ride a train from Shanghai to Beijing by nine hours. No civilization on the planet had ever grown this quickly. But as far as she and her peers were concerned, this was normal, and it had come to influence what they wanted from the world. It was at job fairs like this where these outsized expectations came to die.

A human resources manager I met at the job fair summed up the problem neatly. "We need technicians to fix software problems, but college graduates don't have these skills," she complained. "We need people for exhibitions who can do presentations in English, but they can't do that, either."

The manager showed me a pile of a few dozen applications dropped off that day from graduating students.

"How many are qualified?" I asked her.

She held up her hand, touching her finger to her thumb: zero. "They're all spoiled. Their parents probably give them five thousand yuan a month. Our jobs pay around three thousand a month. We're not interested in them and they're not interested in us."

It made for a miserable job fair: thousands of prospective employees and employers gathered together in one place, only to be disappointed in one another. The predicament made me wonder if Big Sun and Little Sun—two high school dropouts—might be better off than their college graduate peers. They weren't picky about the type of job they had, their parents had low expectations, and they were both charging forward, gaining skills that might help them later on in their careers. In times like this, people seemed better off skipping college altogether.

BIG SUN was a lousy flower salesman.

First, he overdressed for the job, wearing black slacks, black dress shoes, a black polyester V-neck shirt, and over that, a black sport jacket. He looked like a shadow standing in front of a window full of bright spring flowers.

Secondly, he was easy to anger, and didn't like pandering to strangers.

I had biked to the flower shop on a breezy, sunny afternoon in late March and saw mother and son arranging bouquets together on the sidewalk. The two had made up, and he was in Shanghai to help his mother. Zhao was out of her brace, but she still walked with a limp and leaned on a cane.

Big Sun was tall, thin, and handsome. He had dark skin, an aquiline nose, and calm eyes shaped like almonds that stretched to the ends of his face. He spoke confidently and was naturally curious, asking lots of questions. He was nothing like his younger brother.

A Shanghainese woman in her sixties stepped into the tiny shop moments after I arrived. "What's this?" she asked, pointing to a potted flower.

"Western peony," said Zhao from her position on the sidewalk.

"Really? I don't think so. It looks like a *Chinese* peony. Western ones don't have this many petals."

"It's a Western peony," said Zhao.

"That can't be right," huffed the woman.

Big Sun jumped in. "If you say it's a Chinese peony, then it's a Chinese peony. Would you like to buy some? They're twenty yuan."

The woman ignored Big Sun. "Can you lower the price if I buy two pots?"

"Two pots for thirty-five. I normally don't haggle," Zhao said.

"I'll give you thirty," said the woman.

"Fine. Thirty," said Zhao, reaching over to wrap the pot.

Big Sun seemed irritated. "You can search online to learn more about peonies," he said.

The woman looked at him, her jaw tight. "I don't think a Western peony looks like this," the woman said stubbornly.

"I don't think a Chinese peony looks like this, either," replied Big Sun with a smile, looking her in the eye.

The woman stormed out of the shop. Zhao burst into laughter at her son's defiance. I watched the two together, doting mother and rebellious son.

"What happened to your job at the golf course?" I asked him.

"Sheer exploitation of cheap labor," he responded. "It was terrible. The salary was low and the food was lousy."

His bosses had lured him with the promise of becoming a golf coach and possibly a manager someday, but he gradually realized they had been lying. Eventually, he and his colleagues left. "A lot of Chinese companies behave this way—they promise you a great future, but it's hopeless."

Zhao clipped white rose stems, listening intently.

I thought about Zhao's first factory job making televisions. Her bosses certainly didn't promise management positions. They just expected her to work hard, and she did. Twenty years later, inside the flower shop she had worked so hard to establish, here was her firstborn complaining about his job at a golf course. Flowers had also been unworthy. *"I don't want to deliver flowers in the rain,"* he'd said. Big Sun's generation felt more pressure to find jobs that conveyed status than working on an assembly line or at a construction site—jobs typical of their parents' generation. In doing so, they were limiting their options. In Big Sun's case, he had followed a *shifu*—a master—to Hangzhou to learn how to become a hairdresser. He didn't have many customers yet, he admitted, but he was still studying the craft.

Zhao broke her silence. "Big Sun argues with me a lot. He places a lot of hope in our new president. He tells me he's a good leader. I said, 'How good is he if I'm losing business because of him? Is he your grandfather? Is he filling your stomach?' "

Zhao laughed, but it was a serious topic among the street's shop owners. Xi Jinping had only been in power for a year, but he was already clamping down on endemic corruption within Party ranks. He issued a steady stream of new rules for local officials: no more gifts, no more alcohol, and no more lavish banquets.

Xi was born in 1953, four years after the Communists had taken control of China. His father was a revolutionary leader, and Xi grew up surrounded by other revolutionary "princelings" in Beijing's exclusive residential compounds, groomed to one day become China's ruling elite. In the years leading up to the Cultural Revolution, Mao purged Xi's father from the Communist Party, and Xi was sent to rural Shaanxi province, where he lived in a cave, worked alongside farmers, and studied Marx. A professor who grew up with Xi told U.S. diplomats in a WikiLeaks cable that while he and his friends "descended into the pursuit of romantic relationships, drink, movies, and Western literature as a release of the hardships of the time, Xi Jinping, by contrast, chose to survive by becoming redder than red," choosing to "join the system to get ahead."

By contrast, Xi Jinping's predecessor, Hu Jintao, was the son of a tea trader and was trained as an engineer. During Hu's ten years in power, China's economy grew at a double-digit rate, but the flood of investment led to unchecked corruption. When Xi Jinping became president in 2013, he set his sights on cleaning up the Communist Party. Within two years, his anti-corruption campaign led to disciplinary action against more than 400,000 Party officials.

The Party's party was over. Up and down the Street of Eternal Happiness, shops were closing, and Zhao was steadily losing business. The Pine City Hotel had just called: the district government's annual banquet had been canceled. Each year the hotel had paid her a thousand dollars—half her month's salary—to arrange flowers for the event.

Big Sun defended the new president. "This will impact the economy in the short run, because public spending drives China's economy," he told his mother. "But from a long-term perspective, if the welfare of the people can be secure—for example, better medical insurance coverage, and things like that—the situation will get better."

As a reporter covering China's economy, I couldn't have said it better.

"Regardless of how good he is, does he feed you?" Zhao retorted.

"If the leader is good, then the country will improve and the people's lives will naturally become better. *Bing xiong xiong yi ge, Jiang xiong xiong yi wo,*" recited Big Sun. *An incompetent soldier only hurts himself. An incompetent general hurts everyone.*

Zhao's generation of Chinese were born into poverty in the 1960s and '70s before riding a wave of economic growth during their working years. They tended to focus on short-term gain in a system where corruption was an everyday reality. Those in Big Sun's generation, however, were worried about the long-term sustainability of China's economic system, especially now that the economy was slowing down. How would they provide better lives for their children?

Big Sun turned to me. "I think America seems very different from China," he said. "Chinese people think the U.S. is a great place, very democratic and free."

"You're free to buy guns in America!" said Zhao.

"Yeah," I said, "but guns can also become a problem."

Big Sun thought about this for a moment. "But if you own guns, no matter how strong you are, you have the same attack power. If you don't have guns, then the powerful will take advantage of the weak."

Reciting ancient Chinese war proverbs, making eloquent arguments for the arming of the working class, Big Sun reminded me of a young Communist leader. He was intelligent, well read, and had spent a good amount of time thinking about China's problems. I thought about what his future would have been like had he finished his schooling at the top of his class in Shanghai. With the grades he was getting and with a mind like his, he might have ended up in one of China's elite schools. Instead, he was drifting from one menial service job to another, working as a hairdresser-philosopher.

The wind picked up, and the bare branches of the plane trees rattled against each other, sounding like a band of castanets. Light green leaves were emerging from their buds, but it would be a month until the signature canopy of the neighborhood returned.

I asked Zhao if she was happy about her son's career change.

"I'm not satisfied at all," Zhao said sternly, "but what can I do? In the end, being safe and sound is good enough. Don't aim for anything too high. His father will retire in two years, his younger brother is married, and once he's married, my mind will finally be quiet."

Big Sun stared at the floor, dejected. I reminded Zhao that Big Sun was doing exactly what she had done: quit a job, find a master, and try to make money for himself.

"Right," she said, "he's doing his own thing and learning skills so that he can start his own business. That's exactly how I started. I knew nothing."

Zhao laughed, looking over at Big Sun. "But I had pretty high hopes for him. I didn't expect much from his younger brother, but from him, I expected a lot," she said. "Once when he was a little boy, we went out to eat crabs. He noticed that other people's crabs had ovaries and fat. Why didn't his have that? He realized the others were eating female crabs. He's always liked using his brain. He likes reading. He's smarter than most everyone his age in my hometown, and now he's a hairstylist."

Chinese typically saw male stylists as lazy waifs. There was a lot of downtime working as an apprentice hairdresser in China. I had noticed this at the barbershop I had frequented in Shanghai. Whenever I arrived for a cut, I sat behind customers who all wanted their hair done by the shop owner, not by his flamboyant-looking posse of young apprentices. The trainees—dropouts with hair dyed a rainbow of colors—often sat around gossiping, watching television, or styling each other's hair, posing in front of the mirrors.

Big Sun was different, though. He used this downtime to read books by George Soros and Warren Buffett. His fascination with the markets went beyond the typical investment scams like Auntie

Fu's Gatewang. Zhao told me that when he bought stocks for her, she usually made money. "One time he made thirty-six thousand yuan in one afternoon!" she said excitedly. "People at the VIP trading lounge were all asking him for tips."

Big Sun perked up. "At first I didn't understand, so I learned by figuring out how to compare price trends. Now I'm starting to do some trading."

Excited he had someone apart from his slack-jawed coworkers to talk with about this, he continued. "When the stock price dips below the company's net assets, the real value of the company will be revealed. But here in China, what we know of many companies' financial performance is usually fake, so then I turn to company financial reports, the book value per share, and the earnings per share. I look at the growth rate of its net assets, the scale of the investment, and occasionally I take a look at the candlestick chart."

Zhao beamed at her son's handle on all these foreign terms. "See how thoroughly he's studied the stock market? He just keeps talking!"

Big Sun smiled shyly and Zhao paused to take a sip of her tea before turning on her son again. "He is smart, but he's out of words when he's dating a girl."

The change of topic silenced Big Sun.

"He doesn't understand a girl's heart. He's not good at dating."

I turned to Big Sun. "Any prospects?"

"Mom's introduced some girls from our hometown, and one of them seems nice. I'll go back in two months and have a look and meet her parents," he mumbled.

"We're all going back home in May!" said Zhao excitedly; her nephew was getting married. "You should come, too. It's only three hours by high-speed train. You can see how people in the countryside celebrate a wedding!"

"Do you have a photo of her?" I asked Big Sun. He showed me the girl's WeChat profile photo.

She had pretty brown eyes. The rest of her face was covered with a Hello Kitty surgical mask—the type worn to protect against air pollution.

"This is the only photo I have of her," said Big Sun glumly, nodding at his phone.

He'd spent five minutes talking to the girl at a cousin's wedding the previous summer. The meeting was orchestrated by Zhao, her cousin who had married the tax official, and the girl's parents. Big Sun and the girl didn't object to a second meeting, so all parties involved put the couple on the marriage track.

"She's very good at saving money," Zhao jumped in, excitedly. "She'll say, 'I bought a turnip for half a yuan and that was enough for today.' She gets by on soup each day—she only buys cheap stuff. A Shanghainese girl can't compare with her."

I looked at Big Sun for a reaction—thriftiness wasn't exactly romantic, but it was a prized trait in China—yet his face revealed nothing. He was on a path to marry a frugal hometown girl he had spent five minutes with months ago. He had gotten to know her a little more over WeChat, scrutinizing her masked profile each time they texted.

In just a couple of months, Big Sun would return home and bring gifts to the girl's parents. If they approved, the marriage of Zhao's firstborn son would be sealed. Dowries would be exchanged, then the wedding, and Zhao could await her second grandchild. Her motherly duties fulfilled, she could finally stop worrying and be at peace. But there was still work to be done, and Zhao worried that Big Sun's inexperience with matters of the heart threatened to unravel the whole arrangement.

Outside, a warm southerly breeze swept through the neighborhood, and the branches of the plane trees swayed back and forth in the afternoon sun, shadows dancing on the flower shop's floor. Zhao leaned back on her chair and smiled, closing her eyes. Big Sun stepped outside to bask in the day's remaining sunlight, looking pensive. It was the first day of spring. Big Sun would soon be married.

8

Cultured Youth

长乐路810号

Street of Eternal Happiness, No. 810

It was late afternoon. CK and I sat inside *2nd Floor Your Sandwich*, staring out the window overlooking the Street of Eternal Happiness. Young office workers spilled out of the skyscraper across the street, set free from their cubicles for the evening. "I've never wanted to chase a stable life," CK said, watching his peers jostling each other as they fought their way to the subway station, another workday complete.

CK observed them quietly. He was after something else. "I don't know what, actually. Recently, I've had a problem. I mean, it's not a big problem. I feel like I've always wanted to explore myself more and more, go deeper and deeper, and recently I've gotten a little bit . . . I just feel like I'm stuck."

Whether it was from too much navel gazing or for other reasons, his sandwich shop hadn't turned a profit since it opened. On days like this, CK didn't seem to mind. He was selling enough accordions to pull in around 50,000 U.S. dollars a year. It was a comfortable salary that gave him the freedom to try out other endeavors, such as running an unprofitable second-floor sandwich shop, or sitting in the empty unprofitable second-floor sandwich shop, pondering the meaning of life. None of my older Chinese friends had the time to think about these things, but that's why I enjoyed spending time with CK.

"It's like when I play my accordion and something new comes out," he said. "It's a distinctive feeling. I call it 'strength of breath.' It's like when you breathe, but you can't catch a full breath."

After wheezing through a winter during which the concentration of air pollution was twenty times higher than the level experts say is unsafe, I told CK I could relate to that.

"Dating is, well, I think there are a lot of interesting girls, but after I talk to them a couple of times, I quickly lose interest. I don't know. Then I keep asking myself: what's wrong? Because every time I feel something is wrong in my life, that means the real me is telling myself that it's time to take one more step to improve myself."

"So you've felt like this before?" I asked him.

"Yeah. And it's always the same. My feelings go flat."

"Like you've run out of desire or you're not happy?"

"It's like I could feel things before, but now I just feel numb. I can feel that something is going to happen inside of me soon."

"Like what?" I asked.

"I don't know. It's like when you play a videogame, right? And you've killed all the monsters, shot your way through all the levels, but now you have to fight with the big boss. And the big boss is powerful and you'll have to dodge all his bullets. He's got a lot of life and you'll have to fight with him for a long time. I think now's the time in my life when I have to face the boss. I have to fight him, kill him, and enter the next level."

CK took a sip of his coffee while I thought about this.

"So," I said slowly, "in real life, who's the big boss?"

"Myself," he said, staring into the sea of nine-to-fivers walking along the Street of Eternal Happiness below. "It's always myself."

GENERATIONS OF CHINESE had relied on family or the state to guide them through life. The men and women of CK's cohort were the first to make life decisions on their own. They held the key to a future when individuals, with all their differences, would be given greater value in Chinese society.

The previous winter, I'd met a man named Li Zixing at CK's café. The thirty-three-year-old had an intense gaze and was a fast talker, as if he were continually late for an appointment. Li promoted young Chinese writers through his website, China30s, and his work stirred the attention of retailers that market products to his generation. He was on the public speaking circuit, too. He started each event with a question: If you were to change your career, would you consult anyone in your family? "People who raise their hands to answer 'yes' were born in the 1960s," Li told me, "but those born in the eighties hardly ever raise their hands."

The 240 million people born in 1980s China are the country's first generation born after China's reform and opening, the first to adjust to double-digit economic growth, and the first born under the country's planned-birth policy. Without siblings, their lives are the center of orbit for their two parents and four grandparents.

Despite being outnumbered six to one, they tend to ignore their elders' guidance. Their parents and grandparents toiled most of their lives through Mao's political campaigns without much of an education. Like Auntie Fu and Uncle Feng, they now struggle to cope with the free-market realities of modern China and they usually give lousy advice. "In many cases, we can't explain simple ideas and decisions to our parents," Li told me. "They just don't get it."

That's why young Chinese like CK often make career decisions for themselves before giving their elders face. "We'll usually discuss them later with our parents in a respectful tone that sounds like we're seeking their advice," Li said.

The generation gap is obvious up and down the Street of Eternal Happiness. Fu and Feng spent their working years tossed around by the state: first to Xinjiang, then back to Shanghai. The two have been struggling to adjust ever since: Feng, relegated to selling scallion pancakes; Fu, confounded by the wealth surrounding her, desperate to get rich quick, yet without the skills to do so. Compared to CK or Zhao, the couple seemed lost in a labyrinth of capitalism, relics of much simpler economic times when you did whatever the Party told you. "They're the generation who never learned to swim," Li told me, waxing metaphorical. "It was all a terrible memory for them. But what they don't realize is that their children's generation enjoys the freedom of swimming, and we don't need life jackets."

Li's sense of freedom sounded a little naïve to me. Sure, his generation feels free to take a plunge now and then, but the waters of China's economy can make for dangerous swimming. Many Chinese in their thirties are the sole source of income for their low-skilled parents and their own children. They're under immense pressure to make money, and while they're free to make their own decisions, their individualism has limits.

MUCH OF THE REAL ESTATE inside the blue-tinted glass skyscraper across the street from CK's café—the building he sometimes stared at while thousands of his white-collar peers poured out each afternoon—is devoted to marketing to young people like him. Chinese millennials outnumber the entire population of the United States, and in 2012, companies spent more than 35 billion dollars advertising to them. The office tower stands forty-five stories, the tallest building along the Street of Eternal Happiness, dwarfing the tiny shops and eateries below.

From a corner office on the twenty-fifth floor, I could barely make out the glass roof of CK's sandwich shop below. I was in the workspace of Tom Doctoroff, who manages a staff of two hundred hipsters at the China headquarters of J. Walter Thompson, one of the oldest advertising agencies in the world. For fifteen years, he has helped drive the golden era of advertising in China, endlessly trying to figure out what makes young Chinese like CK tick.

There are conflicting goals, Doctoroff believes, inside every Chinese. "It's a tension between upward mobility and ambition on one hand," he explained to me, "and on the other hand, a need to master a system, as opposed to rebel against it; a need to navigate a mandated order to climb the hierarchy of success."

Doctoroff is a plain-speaking Midwesterner. He lit up a cigarette after his succinct summary of what was inside every Chinese heart. I thought about how his theory applied to the people I knew along the Street of Eternal Happiness. Across the street at the sandwich shop, CK's struggle with *the system* was not a longing to defeat it, but to control and master it, navigating it successfully on his terms so that he could use it for his own means. Farther down the street, Zhao had left her home village and had astutely navigated China's constant economic shifts all the way to her corner flower shop. She had made sacrifices along the way, but with each step she gained a greater understanding of the system that she would pass on to her sons. In the end, the risks were worth it: Her family was better off, and her grandson was beginning his life in a much better place than a run-down coal-mining town.

Doctoroff believes the priority on safety, for yourself and your family, marks the main difference between Chinese and Americans. "As Americans, we're raised to believe that self-expression is good," he explained. "It's not dangerous."

Americans are encouraged to define themselves independent of society. The basic economic unit in the United States is the individual, and American institutions are built to harness and develop the economic power of the individual. In China, on the other hand, the basic economic unit has traditionally been the clan, whether it's the family or the Party itself. Individual Chinese often don't feel like they're in complete control of their own destinies, and they don't necessarily believe the future is going to be safe.

The ads Doctoroff's team develops for Chinese millennials high above the Street of Eternal Happiness are produced to convey a sense of risk, rebellion, and self-expression, but the end result is always the same. In a television commercial his team developed for the Ford Focus, a group of young artists paints a mural in a parking lot. Their friend drives up in a Focus, a girl standing on the scaffolding turns to admire the car, and she accidentally knocks over a can of paint that topples over other cans, making a rainbow of a mess below. Their friend puts the car in gear and takes a joyride through the spilled paint, splashing it onto his friends as he speeds by, showing off the features of the car. The camera pans out and you realize all of this rebellion wasn't wasted: with help from his new Ford Focus, he's made a mural of his own: a colorful painting of an eye.

"At the end, it beautifies the parking lot," said Doctoroff as we watched the commercial together, pausing at several points to discuss it. "It's not a rebellion against the system. They've created something that's worthy of admiration. Part of the challenge of doing communications in China is knowing how to balance the aspiration for individualism over the fear of rebellion, and that line is always moving forward in terms of how it can be expressed, but it has never turned from solid to dotted. So the idea that there is true individualism in China is something that I don't agree with."

Nearly all of Doctoroff's employees were bright, young members of the post-'80s generation who graduated from the country's top universities. They wandered in and out of his office as we discussed the commercials, curious about our conversation. Some of them didn't share their foreign boss's theory about individualism in China, and I found their insights on their Chinese peers just as interesting as Doctoroff's.

The director of the agency's planning department was one of them. Henry Chen grew up in Shanghai and had studied philosophy at Fudan, Shanghai's top university. His hair was an inch longer than a buzz cut, and he wore stylish tortoise-colored eyeglasses. He stood at least a foot shorter than his boss, and he dressed in loose khakis with a tight-fitting cardigan over a T-shirt. He listened to our conversation while leaning against the doorframe to the office, one leg in front of the other, sternly looking at the floor.

At a break in the conversation, I asked for his opinion. Henry agreed with his boss that true individualism was hard to find in much of China, but that in the country's wealthiest cities, things were changing fast. His take boiled down to simple economics. It wasn't Chinese culture that was holding back true individuality and rebellion. It was a lack of money and opportunity. This was something CK believed, too.

I asked Henry what he thought about Han Han, China's most popular blogger at the time. Han Han was born in Shanghai in 1982 and was far and away the most influential member of the post-'80s generation. He was a professional racecar driver with a talent for writing. His novel *Triple Door*, on life in a Shanghai junior high, was China's bestselling literary work in two decades. His online critiques of China's government often ventured into dangerous territory, and Party censors removed many of his blogs from the Internet inside of China. CK enjoyed reading Han Han's posts, but there was something about the Internet celebrity that didn't sit well with him.

"I think Han Han is an opportunist," Henry said. "He sells a dream of rebellion, but he is a typical Chinese. He was married at a proper age, he has a mistress who he is very proud of; he himself is not very rebellious from others. I just think he's not very honest about himself. He just talks, talks, talks. He never *does* anything."

Doctoroff listened to his employee with the grin of a proud father. "I think Henry is not a typical young Chinese," he said. "I think he's a romantic and a dreamer at heart. Henry believes more than I do that Chinese youth are becoming more individualistic in a Western way. The words he uses to describe Han Han are very interesting, because Han Han has disappointed him personally. I think that romantic dream of what individuals can be in China is still in Henry's heart."

Henry looked slighted. "I'm not that extreme. But I still think we are moving in a direction that has huge potential," he said, speaking for Chinese youth.

I asked Henry if China's hundreds of millions of young people would someday influence Western culture. This was something CK believed.

The question seemed to excite him. "We can, definitely through our talent, because for so many cultural and political reasons, our talents have been repressed," he said. "And no matter what it is, technological innovation or whether it's literature or philosophy and thinking, there will be a renaissance and it will come. Maybe that's the dreamer part of me," Henry said, smiling bashfully.

"When do you think that'll happen?" I asked.

"Soon," he answered.

"Will other cultures look to Chinese youth culture to define their own generational identity?" Henry's boss asked him.

Henry nodded. "I think so. We have the potential. Everything is in the seed and we have a potential to go very far. I have a firm belief in the root of Chinese culture and that it still has value in a global perspective. And if we can leverage our roots and heritage, we will be invincible in the future."

There was a pause in the room. Doctoroff and I looked at him. Did he just say young Chinese would become "invincible"? He sounded like China's Darth Vader. Doctoroff broke the silence, attempting to restore face to his young colleague. "Henry is very exceptional, but usually you have, in my observation of young Chinese, a dream phase before they enter the system. I can't tell you how many young Chinese women say, 'I want to go to France and study cooking,' but ultimately, the system and structure pull them back to conformity."

Henry smiled calmly, and with a soft voice, he corrected his boss: "I was never outside the system."

WHILE DREAMERS on one side of the Street of Eternal Happiness marketed tennis shoes and imported cars, a dreamer on the opposite side sold accordions. But business was slipping. Years ago CK helped build Polverini's supply chain to keep up with demand in the European market. Now with the EU in the midst of an economic crisis, accordion orders were down. What's worse, the instruments that CK managed to sell were marred with problems. CK had signed contracts with his suppliers and had paid them an initial price to begin production, but after the assembly was finished, the accordions didn't sound right.

The previous year, CK had spent an entire month at a factory in Jiangsu province rebuilding thousands of accordions. But after the instruments were exported, the problems multiplied. More than two thousand customers in Europe had returned defective Polverinis that had fallen apart after a few months of use. It turned out the Jiangsu factory had used the wrong type of glue. Polverini's Chinese suppliers were required by contract to compensate customers in cases like this, but when CK traveled to the factory to collect the money, the factory boss laughed at him. "He told me to fuck off. He said it had been over half a year and it wasn't their problem anymore," CK told me, shaking his head. "He said, 'You came here and checked them one by one! It was your fault that they were shipped to Europe! It's not my problem, it's your problem!'"

That's when Polverini stopped making accordions in China.

Instead, the company retained CK to sell its Italian-made accordions to middle-class Chinese. Chinese factories may not have treasured the craftsmanship of a Polverini, but China's rising middle class did. At first it was refreshing for CK to be on the opposite end of the global supply chain. He had traveled throughout China establishing a promising network of distributors. Soon enough, though, another typical Chinese problem arose: a competitor appeared online claiming to sell Polverini accordions at nearly half the retail price. CK called the number on the site and a man with a northern accent answered. "He told me he was selling Polverinis in all sorts of colors, colors like dark blue, which we don't even make. I told him, 'Really? You have a dark blue Polverini? Could you send me a photo of that?'"

CK had to train Polverini's legitimate distributors how to deal with customers who had fallen for the ruse. "The copyright problems in China, it's just horrible," CK sighed.

Managing *2nd Floor Your Sandwich* was adding to the headaches. Now whenever I stopped by the café, there didn't seem to be anyone working in the kitchen. I asked CK if he and Max had downsized. "No! Everyone just quit!" he said.

CK had fired his chef, and nearly everyone else resigned in solidarity. They were left with two waitstaff and one kitchen helper, a gangly, lost-looking young man who was promptly promoted to chef. A month later, they still hadn't found anyone to replace the rest of the workers.

And just when the *Your Sandwich* sign facing the Street of Eternal Happiness couldn't seem to get any smaller, CK said they were eliminating most of the sandwiches from the menu to make room for breakfast and brunch items. "Nobody wants fancy sandwiches," CK told me, "but they'll spend a lot on a pancake which costs next to nothing to make."

He was also thinking about removing the wall of books and obscure record albums in the restaurant's sunroom, décor that made the place feel cozy. "All of this gives people the impression that they can stay here all day and read," CK complained. "People like busier places where you come in and out very quickly. People like *renao*, hot and noisy."

CK lit a cigarette and exhaled. His eyes were developing bags under them from a lack of sleep. He was working seven days a week from ten in the morning to one in the morning, dividing his time between selling Polverinis and doing whatever it took to save his restaurant. "I guess we're putting aside our dream of a sandwich shop for a bit," he said.

After failing at his first business idea, he was entering a familiar phase of the Chinese entrepreneur: throwing everything onto the wall in the hopes that something will stick. Down the street, I noticed Uncle Feng's electric griddle was producing an expanding offering of fried snacks. When flower sales were down, Zhao Shiling dabbled in prepaid phone cards. A block down the street from CK was a tiny Kodak shop that sold silk pajamas. The place hadn't developed a roll of film in years. In a place like Shanghai, consumer fads came and went like a typhoon rolling in off the East China Sea. A good businessman adjusted quickly to the changing winds.

Some of the changes CK had made to his shop were inspired by a trip he had made to Seoul for Polverini. "Koreans care about how a place looks and feels and how things are built and designed," he said, marveling at everything from the architecture in Seoul to the minutiae of the handles on some of the city's subways. "They're not clunky like the ones here in China with plastic ads for telephone companies on them. These are made of steel and they're round and they fit in your hand, and each of them has a different color: orange, yellow, red, brown.

"Before I went to South Korea, I thought it would be full of people getting plastic surgery and all caught up in how they looked," CK observed. "But I was wrong. They're not fake. They're interesting. You know why? Because they don't have a government like ours who lies to them and forces them to be uncreative. Their system is different."

It was a predictably sweeping judgment based on a short trip to a developed Asian country. The South Korean government wasn't a perfectly transparent model of governance and all 1.3 billion Chinese were certainly not all uncreative drones, but CK was tired and angry, and he felt like ranting. "It's our education system," he griped. "It lacks two very important lessons for students: creativity and the ability to love others. If you're creative, you begin to question things and you see deeper ideas into everything. But we are very shallow and we are unable to do that. We just come out of school very selfish and unable to love others. We only care about serving ourselves. We're all shallow and selfish."

YOUNG CULTURE CONNOISSEURS like CK labeled themselves *Wenyi Qingnian,* literally "Cultured Youth," or *Wenqing* for short. The term was often translated as "Hipster," but *Wenqing* evoked a love of art, culture, and living life to its fullest without the snobbery and cynicism associated with the hipster label in the West. Another difference was that hipsters were often born into the cozy suburban middle class of a developed economy. *Wenqing* were not, and they had to work hard to find their way through a competitive and intricate system to earn money to support their interests. CK's generation grew up in a China that was emerging from decades of economic hibernation. They were China's first generation in nearly fifty years who had opportunities to work for the time and the means to do things like study existentialism, watch independent films, and visit art galleries. *Wenqing* were those who incorporated these new ideas into the way they lived, altering their value systems and making life decisions based on these fresh—oftentimes global—perspectives.

A popular Beijing arts magazine listed profiles of *Wenqing* in a 2014 article: "An advertising employee who writes critiques of plays and goes to the Philippines for diving trips. In her spare time, she translates cookbooks. Another works at a multinational and is in charge of public relations. She goes to work on a bus and listens to classical music. She copies poems into a tiny notebook each night and has translated three romantic novels from English into Chinese . . . They want a comfortable life, but also a rich spiritual existence. They appreciate the poetry of Rilke and they go to Europe for fun."

Sometimes they didn't come back. *Wenqing* were known to quit high-paid, unfulfilling office jobs in the big city to search for beatific enlightenment elsewhere, like CK had. In 2013, a young couple who worked corporate jobs in Beijing abruptly quit their jobs and drove their orange Volkswagen Polo station wagon across China to resettle in Dali, an ancient walled town along the banks of a scenic alpine lake in Southwestern China more than fifteen hundred miles away from Shanghai. The blog they wrote about their new life went viral. It was circulated among millions of post-'80s office workers who longed for a similar escape from the pressures of city life.

"We're not looking for business opportunities," wrote Shi Xuxia in a blog post; "we only want to live in a small town near the mountains and the water, to pursue a peaceful life, a breath of fresh air, a pot of tea made with snow water, and a meal made with natural ingredients. Many people back home admire us or are jealous of us. All I'll say is you can do it, too."

Her final blog before arriving at Dali ended with a farewell to China's smoggy, pressure-ridden capital:

GOODBYE, BEIJING.
GOODBYE, PM2.5
GOODBYE, UPS AND DOWNS OF LIFE IN THE CITY.
GOODBYE.

A book deal followed. *Leaving Beijing for Dali: Do What You Like with Whom You Like* was in stores two years later, the ultimate *Wenqing* experience, neatly packaged and sold through one of China's largest state-owned publishers.

The book was a hit among young urbanites. Dali was everything cities like Beijing and Shanghai weren't: the pace of life was slow, wages low, and the air and water were clean, the locally grown food safe to eat. The lake town was completely surrounded by snowcapped mountains. It was an ideal place for idealists: more and more *Wenqing* from the cities were arriving to town to stay, in search of a better life.

On a reporting trip I took to Dali in 2013, I met several people CK's age who had dropped everything and had moved there from the big city. "We've met more friends here in a year and a half than we did in our fourteen years in the city," one urban transplant boasted to me.

She had moved there with her husband and three-year-old daughter from Guangzhou, where the two adults had worked long hours in the import/export business. The urban refugees lived in a traditional courtyard home at the foot of the mountains above town, offering a panorama of the water and mountains. Each morning they biked downhill to the old town to drop off their daughter at preschool and to open their wine-tasting gallery among the cobblestone lanes of the old town. Just like CK, the couple had established their shop in hopes of attracting like-minded people.

"There are more interesting people here from all walks of life," she told me as I enjoyed the view. "We're friends with film directors, journalists, writers. We get together and talk about how life should be lived and our ideals. That's the last topic urban dwellers in China want to talk about. Back in Guangzhou, people were only interested in talking about buying new apartments or new cars. All of urban China has been engulfed in a whirlpool of consumption. Everyone is helpless," she told me.

I asked them about the downsides of living in Dali. Healthcare was bad, they said, the schools weren't the best, and they were far away from family—the same downsides to being a foreigner in Shanghai. But the biggest disadvantage seemed to be money. None of the *Wenqing* I had met there was independently wealthy, and between conversations about the evils of materialism, several of them quietly admitted they weren't making enough. They had traveled more than a thousand miles to sell wine, psychological advice, books, or coffee to people who were just like they used to be: tourists and transplants from the city who had money to spend. Their customers were daily reminders of a time when they were part of the consumer class.

What's worse, they were now competing with each other to serve these tourists. Even the *Wenqing* married couple from Beijing with the book deal ran into these problems. In September of 2014, Shi Xuxia stunned her devoted blog followers with the news that she and her husband were packing up and returning to Beijing. She wrote that she had received a "sudden job opportunity" that required her to start working after that year's National Day Holiday. No other explanation was given. Her final post from Dali was accompanied by a photo of her dressed in a hemp blouse longingly gazing toward the sun descending behind the mountains, radiant clouds hovering overhead.

> It's the last day in Dali. The sky cleared up after a few days of drizzle. I walked up to our terrace on the second floor and stared into a sky full of stars. I spent over five hundred nights in Dali like this. The dream has been achieved, so it's time to chase the next one. I think that's life. We are about to start a new life. In fact, every day is a new life. Every day is a beautiful day, isn't it?
>
> Goodbye, dear Dali. I will return to see you someday.
> Dali, Dali . . .

CK ONCE REFERRED to himself as a *Wenqing*. But in true *Wenqing* fashion, he immediately qualified the label, explaining he was more of an engineer by nature. It was his engineer's mind that had helped him secure the job at Polverini and paid the bills, but it was hard to overlook the *Wenqing* parts of CK: he was a musician, he read Nietzsche, he dabbled in drugs, and before establishing his sandwich shop, he worked in a store that specialized in Lomography, an obscure art movement dedicated to a Russian camera that devotees used to take colorful lo-fi images of everyday objects.

But there was also a *Fenqing* side to CK. The term was short for *Fennu Qingnian*, literally "Angry Youth." It described young patriotic Chinese who were suspicious of foreign intentions in China but who also didn't completely trust China's own leadership. *Fenqing* were deeply proud of the country's long history and cultural traditions, and they channeled that passion into fighting for a stronger Chinese role in global affairs. Apart from the generational groupings, the term was yet another categorical box young Chinese neatly sorted themselves into, making introductions a fatiguing exercise in pigeonholing: Are you a post-'80s or a post-'90s generation? Cultured Youth or Angry Youth? *Wenqing* or *Fenqing*? After a while, the classifications seemed meaningless. To me they were all simply *Qing*—young. They were trying to make sense of their world. And they were doing what came naturally to young people everywhere. They were searching for happiness.

WHEN I RETURNED from Dali that spring, I stopped by *2nd Floor Your Sandwich*. It was lunchtime, and the place was empty. CK was sitting behind the bar counter deep inside the café, doing the books on his computer. "I'll be out in five minutes!" he yelled.

He wore a forest green scarf around his neck and a beige sport coat over a button-down shirt sprinkled with flowers. His wrists were covered in Buddhist beads and he was dabbing an open cold sore on the left side of his mouth with a tissue. While I waited, a young foreign girl with bright pink hair wearing a trench coat sauntered in. "Hello, darling," CK greeted her in British-accented English.

It was sunny but chilly outside. Buds on the plane trees outside the windows showed spring was on its way, but warm temperatures were still a ways off.

The British girl ordered a cup of tea, and while CK made it, he used the downtime to grill her about the different types of English tea. "Proper tea would start with English Breakfast," she said, the lecture becoming drowned out by R&B playing over the stereo.

CK listened carefully and took notes, her tea came, and she took it to go, mouthing "Ciao, sweetie," over her shoulder as she descended the spiral staircase to the sidewalk.

CK sat down next to me and I asked him about girls. "I'm just playing around," he said, "seeing girls here and there, but I'm getting tired of it. I'd like to get serious about someone. I just haven't found her yet."

CK had met his last serious girlfriend over WeChat. She was from the coastal city of Qingdao. Her frequent posts, written in the same breathless style as the blog written by the couple who had moved to Dali, were forwarded to him by some of his friends. It was standard *Wenqing* material: her dream was to go to Cuba, but her parents wouldn't let her. So she entered an essay contest to win a free year's worth of sailing lessons. She won, moved to England, and learned how to sail. After she completed the training, she sailed all the way to Cuba. "She sailed across the Atlantic for eighteen days without showering or anything," CK said, marveling at the thought that such a woman existed.

Now that sailing to Cuba was out of the way, she was trying to start a café in her hometown, and CK had become friends with her on WeChat after he offered to share his own experiences doing the same. Following a few months of trading stories from the front lines of the food-and-beverage industry, she flew to Shanghai to see him, and a romance blossomed.

"But then she went back to Qingdao. She didn't want to put aside her dream to start a café," he told me wistfully, looking like he respected her more for that anyway. That's what he would've done.

I glanced around the empty restaurant and noticed some

changes from a few weeks before. There were purple placards on the tables advertising "Free Tarot." If a customer spent more than one hundred yuan, they could make an appointment for a tarot card reading, free of charge—limited to a single question. The consultation had to take place at 2nd Floor Your Sandwich. "The type of people who come here are curious about this sort of thing, and it ensures they come back to eat here. It's a win-win," CK explained.

That wasn't the only change. CK handed me 2nd Floor Your Sandwich's new menu. He had sold off the touchscreens, and before me was a completely revamped list of options: Boston Lobster, Grilled Sea Bass, 280-Gram Australian Rib Eye Steak. "I guess you're no longer a sandwich shop," I said, scanning the new offerings.

"We've changed to brunch during the day and high-end French food at night," he announced. "We've never made money at night—nobody wants to eat sandwiches for dinner. I thought we should offer more upscale food."

I thought about the sign outside. How much tinier could Your Sandwich get?

CK seemed excited about the changes. "We offered these things to foreigners on Valentine's Day, and they said it was good!"

I pointed to the lobster. "Is this really from Boston?"

"Yes!"

"Fresh or frozen?"

CK gave me a look that seemed to say: Do I look like I can afford a lobster tank?

"What about this?" I asked, pointing to the Australian Rib Eye.

"We actually don't have that. I tried a few suppliers, but the quality was terrible."

"So what happens if a customer orders it?" I asked.

CK shrugged. "We just tell them we're out of it. Then we point them to the Alfredo! It's a dinner menu! I have to have steak on it. People would think, 'What the fuck is up with this menu? I thought this was French food!' It's got to be on there."

CK told me the new menu was his last stand. 2nd Floor Your Sandwich had never been profitable, and he and Max had poured hundreds of thousands of their own yuan into the business. If they weren't making money by the end of the year, they would shut it down. "If we can't accomplish that, then our dream is over."

I thought about the dreams of those I had met in Dali, and the dreams for China that Henry had shared with me across the street, high above the city. I thought about Xi Jinping's politically charged Chinese Dream, a dream the Party hoped all Chinese could share.

It was the era of big dreams in China, and it didn't seem to matter much if those dreams came true. The husband and wife who dreamed of moving to Dali and had now returned to Beijing weren't failures, nor did their readers treat them as such. They had gotten a book deal out of the whole affair, and for them, it was time to make money, start a family, and move on to the next dream.

The state's dreams, however, often stood in the way of individual dreams. I thought about those whom I had met in Maggie Lane—Old Kang, Mayor Chen and his wife—whose simple dreams to live peacefully at home were brutally overpowered by the visions of prosperity from powerful local officials. It would be a while before all 1.3 billion Chinese would feel equal in their pursuit of happiness. But when I considered what China had gone through in the twentieth century, I found it hard to be pessimistic. I thought about the Wang family's letters of survival in the 1950s and Auntie Fu and Uncle Feng's stories about building Xinjiang in the 1960s. Who would've thought that, fifty years after such violent revolution and catastrophic famine, the Chinese would have enough spirit left in them to be able to dream, much less have the means and freedom to try to pursue them?

When I returned to CK's a month later, a wet southern wind was blowing through the city; a soft, warm rain cleansed the air of pollutants. It smelled like flowers outside. Pink peach blossom petals covered the surface of the pond in the courtyard at my complex. Inside *2nd Floor Your Sandwich*, thousands of small green leaves began to obscure the view of the street, restoring the tree house effect. The place was empty, the lights were off, and the sliding glass windows were wide open, the *whoosh!* of cars barreling through soaked asphalt punctuated the soothing soundtrack of steady rain.

Below, along the Street of Eternal Happiness, dozens of umbrellas scurried by, looking like brightly colored blood cells bouncing off one another on their way to a pulsing heart. CK greeted me with a smile and some good news: after two years, he and Max had finally had a profitable month. The dream was still alive.

Dreams, Seized

麦琪里

Maggie Lane

A map of the street from the 1940s, brown with age, shows a string of little shops along the block where CK's sandwich shop now stands. A magnifying glass is needed to make out the intricate strokes of the traditional Chinese characters that fill the tiny squares: "Prosperity Rice Shop," "Scholar Pen Factory," "Auspicious Health Soy Sauce Shop." Their customers lived a block away, inside a labyrinth of alleyways winding around dozens of numbered plots on the map: red-and-gray-brick *shikumen* homes of the wealthy class. Hardly any of these places—the old shops, the stone-gated homes, the alleyways—have survived. They're dreams from a forgotten time. Yet a block away from today's sandwich shops, bars, and cafés, inside an abandoned lot of burned-out homes surrounded by a wall, Mayor Chen remembers.

THE CHEN FAMILY'S DREAM was purchased for ten bars of gold.

The *shikumen*-style brick house was inside a new neighborhood under construction inside the French Concession. It had an exotic-sounding name: Maggie Lane. Tucked away from the bustle of Peaceful Happiness Road down a quiet alley, it was a burgeoning community of three-story homes, each with a courtyard where children could play.

The father had longed to live in a new development a block away on the more affluent Street of Eternal Happiness. But he only had thirteen gold bars weighing four kilograms, worth around $70,000 at the time, barely enough for a small apartment. So in 1933, the elder Chen and his family settled for a spacious house in Maggie Lane, happy he had three gold bars to spare.

Thirty-three years later, there was a loud knock on the door. His twenty-one-year-old son Chen Zhongdao darted upstairs to help his mother hide the three bars. He stuffed one in his pants pocket, and his mother hurriedly hid the others in the back of a wardrobe underneath some clothes. The knocking turned to steady pounding. He rushed downstairs and opened the door.

It was 1966. China's economy was in tatters and Mao had launched the Cultural Revolution. Red Guards had just raided the home of Chen's neighbor, who had converted his *shikumen* into a small sewing machine factory. The group of gangly teens confiscated jewelry, cash, deposit books, any evidence of capitalist activity. When Chen opened the door that summer afternoon, he was surprised to see such a ragtag group of adolescents conducting state-sponsored home raids.

"We've come to help you destroy the Four Olds," one of them announced: Old Customs, Old Culture, Old Habits, and Old Ideas.

Young Red Guard regiments across the country seized classical Chinese literature, paintings, jewelry, religious icons, and furniture from residents, declaring them anti-proletarian objects that had poisoned the minds of the people.

Chen Zhongdao suppressed a smirk and let them inside, wondering how these ten youngsters would determine what in their house would fit into these four puzzling categories. The guards, some as young as middle school children, awkwardly rifled through his family's belongings for hours, a little unsure of what they were looking for. By early morning, they had settled on a few articles of clothing and his mother's silver jewelry. They had missed the gold bars stuffed inside the wardrobe, and Chen said they were too nervous to ask him to empty his pockets. They clumsily marched to the next home down the lane.

Families who had originally bought homes in Maggie Lane were used to this sort of harassment. Many of them had bought their own homes in pre-Communist times and belonged to the upper class. They had spent almost two decades trying to pad their Communist résumés, carefully dodging labels like "landlord," "counterrevolutionary," "capitalist," "bad element," or a host of other commonly used names that marked someone an enemy of the state.

Just six years after the Party had "liberated" China in 1949, it owned nearly all the land, becoming the de facto landlord to hundreds of millions. Chen's father was required to pay the new government rent on a house he had purchased with his life's savings. In the following years, he was overcome with anxiety. Up to then, he had run a textile plant and made three hundred renminbi a month, a good salary at the time. The elder Chen worried that it was a matter of time before he would be labeled a Rightist or a capitalist and sent away to a labor camp. The younger Chen says his father was so convinced of this outcome that when his mill was taken over by the state several years later, he took a 75 percent pay cut and worked as hard as he could, plowing through multiple shifts, refusing to sleep, and skipping meals, ultimately earning a "model worker" award from local Party officials for his efforts. In 1959, while his work unit was melting down metal to make steel to support Mao's Great Leap Forward campaign, Chen collapsed and died from exhaustion just months short of his fiftieth birthday. He left behind his wife and eight children in his beloved Maggie Lane home that no longer belonged to them—a family's dream, seized.

A few days after the Red Guard raid, young Chen Zhongdao pedaled his bicycle to the textile factory where he worked. He hid the gold bars in his dirty corduroy work uniform he left inside a shared dorm room. When he returned home that evening, his older siblings and his mother discussed what to do next. Possessing large quantities of gold was illegal, and with all the Red Guard raids it was a matter of time before they checked Chen's workplace and he was caught and imprisoned or executed. A gang of clumsy teenagers raiding the family home may have bordered on the comical, but others in the lane who couldn't hide their connections to the Four Olds were shaken up. A famous Shanghai opera singer who lived in Maggie Lane, a woman named Xiao Aiqin, was relentlessly targeted by the Red Guards and repeatedly humiliated in public. After two years of this, she reportedly drowned herself in the Huangpu River.

Chen's mother sent him to the State Industrial and Commerce Bank ten blocks away at Jing'an Temple. It was a hot summer afternoon, and he stood in line holding the three gold bars wrapped neatly in newspaper. When it came his turn, Chen nervously handed over the gold, the bank teller weighed them one by one, and he remembers the teller giving him a receipt and telling him he could come back to retrieve the bars anytime.

Three years later, the campaigns of the Cultural Revolution had quieted down and Chen's family thought it would be a good time to visit the bank again. Chen rode his bike to the State Industrial and Commerce Bank, receipt in hand. He walked up to the counter. "I'm sorry," he remembers the teller saying, "but we can't give you your gold back. Possessing gold is against the law."

The teller gave Chen 2,900 RMB, the bank's assessment of the gold's value. It was a sixth of what the gold was worth on global markets. Chen didn't raise a fuss. It was still a lot of money at the time, he was at a state-owned bank, and he had just been told that he had broken the law. He thought about his neighbors who had been sent away, punished, and died for less. Chen put the cash in his pocket, bit his lip, and walked out the bank's front door, glumly riding his bicycle back to Maggie Lane.

"I WAS SO NAÏVE," Mayor Chen told me, thinking about the gold. "I was young and naïve."

We sat in the reading room of a community center across the street from what was left of Maggie Lane. My first visit had gotten the security guard in trouble and I was now barred from entering the lot. It didn't matter; I had a clear view of daily goings-on there from my bedroom.

The wall surrounding Maggie Lane had been stripped of dozens of "Better City, Better Life" posters from the Shanghai world's fair. At the event's closing ceremony in October of 2010, Vice Premier Wang Qishan told the audience the motto of the event would be carried forward from generation to generation. "I am convinced that the vision of 'Better City, Better Life' will become reality," he announced confidently.

The following morning, Shanghai was engulfed in a toxic cloud of smog. Skyscrapers a kilometer away from our bedroom window at the Summit had suddenly disappeared behind a thick haze. During the fair, construction sites had been closed, farmers upwind from Shanghai were prohibited from burning rice husks, and there were clampdowns on heavy vehicles entering the city. Shanghai's air quality was recorded as "good" for 90 percent of the duration of the six-month event. Now all of these rules had expired, and the air in Shanghai was back to its gritty, polluted self.

At Maggie Lane, a demolition crew visited Mayor Chen, his wife, Xie Guozhen, and the four other families who remained living in partially destroyed homes—a dozen people in all. It had been five years since their last visit had ended with arson, murder, and prison time. This crew came better prepared. The Xuhui District government had sent them notices, and they carried an official-looking relocation order signed by a local court.

By now, Chen had become an expert on laws pertaining to forced relocations. He was, after all, the lane's unofficial mayor. He knew that in order for a document like this to be legally enforceable, it had to be issued and sent to individual residents, not through a demolition crew.

The crew—a group of hardened middle-aged men used to dealing with stubborn residents—were not swayed by Mayor Chen's interpretation. They returned one day with sledgehammers. The Mayor had dealt with this before. He retrieved a propane gas tank from his kitchen and called down to the men from his balcony. "I told them that if they try to take me from my home, I'll strap the gas canister to myself and we'll all die together," Chen told me. "I told them, 'I'm in my sixties, and you guys are in your forties. You've got families, you've got kids, and you have your lives ahead of you. I'm not afraid to die.'"

The crew didn't come back.

Xuhui District officials had rezoned Maggie Lane as "public" land. The designation meant it could be used later as a park, school, hospital, or government building—anything serving the public— but not for commercial or residential purposes.

Nobody in the neighborhood put much stock in this designation, though. Maggie Lane was likely the most valuable piece of undeveloped land in Shanghai. As one developer told me, there was just too much money to be made to allow the land to become a park or a school. And the district could afford to wait: between 2003 and 2013, property prices in the city had climbed an average of 14 percent a year, with the most luxurious condominiums in the neighborhood selling for the equivalent of millions of U.S. dollars each.

All Mayor Chen cared about was that officials either made good on their original promise to return him to the land or to compensate him with enough money to be able to afford to live somewhere else in the neighborhood. "Allowing the land to be resold is technically illegal," the Mayor told me, showing me copies of the legal code governing his rights. "This policy states we have the right to move back, but that's obviously nonexistent now. These officials are sitting back and watching the housing prices soar, so they're reluctant to do anything for the time being."

I looked through Chen's files spread across a knee-high table in the community center's reading room. Most of the police reports were ten years old: "Resident complains of rocks being thrown through windows," "Resident complains of electricity being cut off to building," and so on.

It was a well-documented history of harassment by demolition crews. Then it dawned on me: the Summit was built ten years ago. When I visited Maggie Lane, I had told Mayor Chen and Old Kang I lived across the street and had a clear view of their homes from my window. "You can thank us for such a nice view!" Old Kang had said, laughing.

"What was on the land of the Summit before it was built?" I asked Chen.

"There were just lanes of ordinary homes. They weren't part of Maggie Lane and the houses weren't as nice as ours," Mayor Chen told me. "One of the residents was killed during the relocation there, too."

"What happened?"

"I heard the guy had a house next to the street where he ran a small business. When the demolition crew came to take his house, he poured gasoline over himself, held himself tightly to a guy from the crew, and then lit a match."

Mayor Chen told me it was the same crew that had harassed him and had set his neighbors on fire.

"I forget the dead man's name, but I've got the number of his widow at home. I'll find it for you. She's still trying to petition the government now," Chen told me. "Our neighborhood is full of stories like this."

THE CHINESE GOVERNMENT still owns all the land in China. Since the death of Mao, the Party has gradually given individual Chinese more rights to its property. Today, they can "buy" seventy-year leases to homes. The Party officially designates them as "owners," even though the state is the ultimate landlord.

With this ownership come legal rights that are becoming stronger each year. In 2011, China's State Council issued a ruling stating that local governments could no longer force people out of their homes unless the land was going to be used to serve the public interest. The same government body later laid out clear rules regarding compensation in the event of a forced demolition, requiring the government to pay property owners the market value for whatever was seized by the state.

The ruling came after decades of violent standoffs between property owners and local governments. China's economy was growing at a historic pace, and local officials had become de facto land brokers, seizing property from residents and selling it to developers to turn a profit. By 2013, local governments in China made, on average, more than a third of their operating revenue from these types of land sales.

"In a normal system, the government is not supposed to be benefiting from the land transaction process," Wang Cailiang, a prominent Shanghai property rights lawyer, once told me. "The government should only be responsible for managing the land. They are not businessmen."

Over the years, though, local officials had become some of China's shrewdest capitalists. When they weren't taking residents' land and selling it to the highest-bidding developer, they were commonly seen driving around in black Audi sedans and shopping at luxury outlets like Coach or Louis Vuitton to buy handbags for their spouses or mistresses. It was a spectacle of greed and corruption, and whenever I covered land seizure stories, residents blamed their predicaments on these local officials while, on the other hand, maintaining their belief that China's central government remained a benevolent one. "If Party leaders in Beijing only knew what was really going on down here," I was often told, "they'd put a stop to this whole mess."

The corruption among China's top leadership, though, made land seizures seem like stealing candy from a corner store. For years, the elite ruling families of China had accumulated billions of dollars' worth of company shares and real estate by leveraging their positions of power. News of this, however, was blocked from the Internet inside of China. Instead, local reports of China's leaders were often accompanied by photo ops of leaders checking in on rural schools and hospitals, making sure all was well. To the common folk of Maggie Lane, it was clear who the good guys and bad guys were. The truth, though, wasn't always so black and white.

The leadership in Beijing not only knew about these rampant land seizures, they had created and maintained the system that had perpetuated the practice. Li Ping, a lawyer for the international property rights advocacy group Landesa in Beijing, laid it out simply: "Most taxes that are collected—more than seventy percent typically—go straight to the central government, leaving local governments with no other way to generate revenue," he said.

Li was one of the country's most prominent property rights experts. China's State Council sought his advice when drafting new laws. Li believed that local governments had become addicted to seizing land because it was the only way to generate enough revenue to fulfill its mandate of providing services to its residents. He thought the best solution would be a combination of allowing local governments to start collecting property taxes—unlike most homeowners in the West, most Chinese aren't required to pay taxes on their property—and implementing market-style reforms by giving governments the freedom to issue municipal bonds, a measure some Chinese cities began taking in 2014.

With the current pace of local government land seizures, it was clear something had to be done. Li estimated that up to 2013, local officials had illegally seized land belonging to at least 40 million Chinese. "According to the current pace of land expropriation, that will add three million people every year," Li said. "If compensation is not adequate, you basically add three million more dissidents in China each and every year."

XI GUOZHEN (no relation to Mayor Chen's wife Xie Guozhen) was one of them. Mayor Chen had told me the story of how Xi's husband had burned to death fighting the same demolition crew that had bullied Maggie Lane's residents. His horrific final moments took place across the street from Maggie Lane on the plot of land where I now lived.

Xi's name was pronounced "She." The day I met her, she had just stepped off a high-speed train from Beijing. Early the same morning, she was released from a Beijing jail after being arrested for petitioning China's leaders. She had served her sentence at Majialou, a former police station that had been reopened to detain people who had come to the capital from all over China to complain to the central government. Their grievances—anything from land seizures to higher-level corruption—had been ignored by courts run by the very people they were complaining about. After arriving in Beijing, they had been apprehended by "interceptors," thugs hired by their hometown governments.

Majialou was like a second home for Xi. "I've been in and out of there for half a year now," she said.

"One time I spent fourteen days there, one time nine days, one time six days, the time before this thirty-eight days, and this time six days again. Whenever they let me out, I go straight back to Zhongnanhai," she said, referring to the central headquarters for China's Communist Party along Tian'anmen Square.

At Zhongnanhai, Xi would unfurl a banner or throw leaflets about her case right in front of security guards. Within seconds, they would tackle her, arrest her, and throw her in a van headed back to Majialou. "My life is on repeat," she told me.

The harsh cycle of Xi's life had taken a toll on her body. In the past six months, the sixty-one-year-old said she had been dragged across the prison by her hair, beaten up by her captors several times; on one occasion they had broken a few of her ribs. She had become overweight and bags were beginning to form underneath her brown eyes.

Xi once owned an apartment on the second floor of a house inside a small lane off the Street of Eternal Happiness, several stories below where my own home now stood. She grew up in the apartment and, later as an adult, she lived there with her husband, a thin man with a boyish face and glasses named Zhu Jianzhong.

The couple had a son and they ran a tailor shop from home. "My husband would measure the clothes, and I'd do all the stitching," she told me. "We were quite famous in the neighborhood."

Hundreds of families lived in their single-square-block neighborhood. Their apartments weren't as nice as those across the street in Maggie Lane; a typical family lived in a space of a few hundred square feet with a simple kitchen. The public bathrooms were a quick stroll down the lane.

In 1992, the Xuhui District government auctioned off the land to a Hong Kong developer owned by Li Ka-shing, the richest man in Asia, to build what would later become the Summit—the complex I lived in—and an office building called the Center, the forty-five-story tower across the street from CK's sandwich shop. Li's company worked with a crew from Chengkai Group to negotiate resettlement with the lane's residents, the same group of men, in fact, that would later botch the Maggie Lane demolition by murdering an elderly couple.

The developer offered residents a modest resettlement sum and tiny apartments in a new complex bordering farmland an hour away from Shanghai. Most residents accepted the deal and Chengkai began to demolish the vacated homes, but Xi and her husband stayed put. She was born here, grew up here, and now she and her husband ran a neighborhood business here, she told the crew. Everyone who was important to them lived within a few blocks. If you want us to move, she told them, resettle us nearby. By 1996, they were one of the last remaining families in their lane.

On the morning of October 17, 1996, Xi was walking home from the market when she saw them: six men and women from the demolition crew propping a ladder up against their balcony. She screamed for her husband, and someone tackled her. A woman and two men forced her into a car, breaking her fingers. Hearing the scuffle outside, her husband came onto the balcony, but it was too late. A few men had already climbed the ladder to his apartment. They shoved him inside as Xi watched, still wrestling with the crew below. From inside came yelling and a loud crash, and after a few minutes, a cloud of smoke rose from the balcony window. The crew emerged from the building, but Zhu did not. Within minutes, the building was engulfed in flames, leaving a trail of black smoke high above a crowd of onlookers along the Street of Eternal Happiness.

The police report alleged Xi's husband had poured banana oil—used for removing stains from customers' clothes—over himself and set himself on fire, injuring men from the demolition crew in the process. Xi refused to believe this. "He didn't want to die. My theory is that this group of men beat my husband up and they had severely injured him or had killed him," she said, "and they set him on fire to cover up what had happened."

After the fire, she was taken to a hotel and locked in a dark room. In the evening, a tall man from Chengkai Group opened the door. "He said, 'It took seconds for your husband to die.'"

Xi screamed at the man, accusing his crew of murdering someone like them: a common person, a *laobaixing*.

"Then he interrupted me," she said, "and he asked me, 'Does your family have a special background? Are you friends with anyone in the Party? Killing a *laobaixing* is like killing an ant.'"

Xi discovered later that Yang Sunqin, the man from Chengkai's demolition crew who coordinated the demolition of their home, had been promoted for removing them from their property. Nine years later, a court would sentence Yang to death for burning the elderly couple alive in their beds across the street in Maggie Lane.

In return for the loss of her home and her husband, the Xuhui government gave Xi a small apartment several blocks away and a shop space across the Huangpu River in Pudong that she could rent out for income. Later, police officers asked her to sign a document confirming she had received compensation, but she refused. Doing so would be akin to confirming the police account of what had happened. She told the officers she wouldn't give up until they conducted a proper investigation.

Xi estimated she'd visited the police station more than a hundred times since then to request an investigation into her husband's death, but none was ever authorized. As a result, she's spent the last ten years petitioning officials in Beijing and has been imprisoned more times than she can remember.

Her perseverance was impressive, but it also seemed pointless. Why continue to seek justice from an unjust legal system? She had heard this rationale before, and she didn't pause to think. "My husband's soul is still there. If I give up, the Communist Party wins, and they can laugh at us. I'm fighting for his soul."

"What do you think your husband would think about what you are doing?" I asked.

Xi thought for a moment. "If he were here, he'd try to persuade me to stop," she admitted. "Sometimes at night I dream of him pleading for me to stop. But I won't. I don't want to disappoint him."

This type of determination was typical among petitioners. After years of reporting in China, I had interviewed several of them. When I mentioned their stories to my Chinese friends in Shanghai, they often shook their heads as if these people were an embarrassment to the whole nation. They saw petitioners as desperate, penniless, and uneducated commoners who were all slightly out of touch with reality. China's state-run media had helped push this idea, and petitioners' fearlessness—repeatedly getting beat up and thrown into prison—was baffling to many in a culture that emphasized a pragmatic approach to settling problems.

It seemed like a harsh criticism of people whose lives had suffered terrible damage from people in power, but I sometimes found myself agreeing with the stereotype. Though their causes were usually just from a moral standpoint, many of the petitioners I knew seemed dysfunctional and unbalanced. Their quests to right society's wrongs often seemed unreasonable given the harsh system they were up against. Fighting China's system almost never produced good results. It was like trying to swim against a powerful rip current: You would likely drown. My neighbors along the street who successfully navigated this system—people like CK and Zhao—refused to allow it to drag them to unknown depths. Instead, they swam with careful strokes at an angle that followed the current but took them to the edge of it, carving their own way while ceding control to its raw power.

XI'S SON WEIQI was ten years old when his father burned to death. When he found out what happened, he stopped speaking. Xi remembers him staring out into space. The day after his father's death, she found Weiqi with his forehead against the wall of the hotel room where they were detained, hitting it with closed fists. "He just pounded the walls over and over," Xi told me. "*Peng. Peng. Peng.* He wouldn't stop. His knuckles were a bloody mess."

Xi said her son's personality took a permanent turn. Before his father's death, the child had been outgoing, talkative, a natural leader. Among the children in the lane, it was Weiqi who had always organized games of marbles or tag after school. When his father died, he became shy, serious, and intense. The boy preferred to spend time alone.

That was eighteen years ago. I was almost scared to ask what had become of him. "Oh, he's studying in the U.S.," Xi said. "He's finishing his doctorate at *Kang Nai Er.*"

I didn't recognize the name, so she said it again: *Kang Nai Er.* I repeated it a few times, waiting for the phonological synapse to fire, and then it hit me: Cornell.

THE LONGER I LIVED in China the more I realized that for every dreadful story that dragged my pessimism for the country's future to a new low, there was someone like Weiqi who could restore my hope. Weiqi's story alone encompassed opposite poles of this duality.

Weiqi's name is pronounced "Way-chee." I met him over Skype. It was eight in the evening on a weekday night and he spoke to me from inside his office at a bank in Hong Kong. He had taken a job there to be closer to his mother while he finished writing his doctoral thesis. The poor Internet connection frequently froze the image of his face on my screen: a little pudgy, with eyebrows that were fixed close together. They framed narrow eyes with lids that seemed perpetually tightened, as if he were scrutinizing everything he heard. We spoke in English, and he chose his words carefully, speaking in a slow and deliberate cadence. He was rational and curious, asking me just as many questions as I asked him, and he was never emotional. He reminded me a little of Mr. Spock from *Star Trek*.

Weiqi told me that growing up in his quiet lane off the Street of Eternal Happiness was like being brought up in a village. Your entire life unfolded within two blocks where everyone knew everything about your family. He was eight years old when he first left this nest. It was 1994 and Shanghai's first subway line had just opened. A station had appeared just a block away. For Weiqi, a single word summed up his memory of that first ride: "People," he said. "I had never seen that many people before in one small space."

Weiqi had spent his short life tucked away inside a lane in the heart of the most populated city of the most populated country on the planet, and it was the first time he had come into contact with Shanghai's enormity. "I grabbed tightly onto my father's hand. I was so scared of getting lost," he said.

When the subway first opened, there were two types of tickets. For one yuan, you could experience what it was like to ride in a subway, but you had to return to the same station you started from. Weiqi's parents bought the two-yuan tickets, which allowed them to get off somewhere else.

They took a trip to Xinzhuang, the place where they were told they would be relocated. It was the last station of a forty-minute trip to the end of the subway line. "When we got out of the station, there wasn't anything there—no homes, no shops, nothing," Weiqi told me. "The roads were just being paved for the first time, and there were farm fields all around. We knew right away we didn't want to move there."

Weiqi said life in the lane was simple and happy. They were poor, but so was everyone else. It was the early '90s, and China's economy had yet to take off, but there was optimism in the air. "It wasn't so hierarchical like it is today. Everyone was looking ahead."

Weiqi said one of the reasons for his success was that he had grown up in a place where he never felt any pressure. He was a leader of the kids in his lane, staying up late into the evening not to study, but to play hide-and-seek in the alleys. His father worked hard, but he wasn't strict with his son. "We Chinese have a saying:

'*Cimu, Yanfu*'—mothers are kind to their children, and fathers are strict—this is a typical Chinese family," Weiqi told me over Skype. "But my parents were the opposite. My mother held me to high standards. My father was more like a friend. Most parents of people in my generation weren't like that. They were more like coaches to their children."

Weiqi used to watch the U.S. sitcom *Growing Pains* with his dad, one of the few American programs on television back in those days. "My father was kind of like the dad in that series," he told me. "His parenting style was similar to how a foreigner would raise their children."

Weiqi worked at UBS Bank in Hong Kong, analyzing secondary markets. "Very boring work, but the pay is high," he said.

Weiqi's uncle and aunt—both wealthy businesspeople in Shanghai—lent him money to attend an Ivy League university in the United States. His doctoral dissertation focused on how people respond to economic crises. Weiqi had mapped out statistical models based on how people had behaved in the wake of the 1984 and 2008 economic disasters in the United States. The behavioral finance models might someday prove useful in the wake of future crises.

His mother told me that ever since Weiqi's father died, her son had concentrated on his studies. "He wanted to work hard. He would cry when I dragged him to go petition the government with me, so I stopped. He preferred to study. He told me, 'Mom, I can change my fate with the power of knowledge.' He was very precocious."

Back then, Weiqi's mother shuttled back and forth to Beijing on her petitioning trips, while he spent nights studying alone in the tiny Shanghai apartment the government had relocated them to, making his own meals and waking himself up to go to school in the morning. His grandparents on his father's side were angry with his mother for her stubbornness and for leaving Weiqi at home alone, but Weiqi never seemed frustrated. "I pretty much have always agreed with her, because first and foremost I think what she's doing is right," Weiqi told me. "I think it's the most basic pursuit of a human being. It's become her life's task, her only goal, almost like a religion. If I try to stop her or even express a different opinion about what she's doing, she'll feel really, really lost and sad. I'm her only son, and if I don't support her, I can't imagine what it would do to her."

Weiqi was more worried about his mother's health and her life-style. "She might be healthy now, but what if she's still doing this in five years? There needs to be a time when she should stop and go back to a normal life."

Because of her political activity, Xi wasn't allowed to visit her son in Hong Kong. She told me she hoped to live with her son in the United States someday, but this, too, seemed doubtful for some-one who made a habit of protesting in front of the headquarters of China's leadership.

All Weiqi could do was hope she would come to peace with his father's death in her own way and move on. But in the meantime, Weiqi would do what he could to make sure she was safe, and he would support her. "I read a story once about an airplane crash," Weiqi told me. "A Japanese man; his wife was on the plane, and it crashed into the ocean and after he lost his wife, the man spent years learning how to dive. Even though he knew he had no chance of finding her, every weekend he dove where they think the plane crashed to look for her. He said he would never give up. My moth-er's story is similar."

I asked him if he had ever returned to the Street of Eternal Happiness. "No. Too much happened there," he told me.

He asked me what it was like now. I told him about the empty lot across the street where Maggie Lane once stood and how every month or so there was a new restaurant on the street catering to foreign expats and wealthy Chinese. I told him about the shop own-ers I knew: CK, Zhao, and Uncle Feng.

"It sounds like the neighborhood has changed a lot," Weiqi said, sounding distant. "There aren't many local residents left, are there?"

"Not too many," I said.

The same could be said for much of urban China. Within twenty years, neighborhoods that once functioned like villages had transformed into impersonal condominium towers like the Summit where nobody knew their neighbors and where a runaway economy had generated enough money to enjoy a meal at the new tapas bar down the street, but it also put more pressure on people, often making them grumpy and wary of others.

"My honest feeling as one of the old residents of the neighborhood is that I feel detached from my old home," Weiqi told me. "The old people, the old stores, the old memories are no longer there. It's been replaced by a neighborhood where foreigners live. All of it is a bit sad, I'd say."

I was one of those foreigners. I tucked my sons into bed each night several stories above where Weiqi's parents used to tuck him in. I was speaking to him from the very site where he lost his home and his father, the place my own children now called home. "Yes," I said, speaking to the digital image of Weiqi on my computer screen. "It is pretty sad."

WE MET IN PERSON a month later on the Street of Eternal Happiness. It was a blustery, sunny day. The wind blew from the south: gusts of warm, unpolluted air marking the start of spring.

Weiqi wore a black cashmere sweater and khakis. We sat on a bench in front of the Center, the office building across the street from CK's café, behind my home at the Summit.

It was a holiday weekend. Locals had left town, leaving few cars on the street. The whistling of songbirds taking a rest from their northbound migration filled the trees. The bench was just ten feet away from the site of Weiqi's old home.

Weiqi rested one foot on the opposing knee, unconsciously fiddling with his shoelaces while he stared up at the glass and steel Center building, and then at the Summit complex, trying to get his bearings.

"The only thing I recognize is the China Merchants Bank

building over there," he said, pointing behind us to a dusty building over there," he said, pointing behind us to a dusty building covered in purple and white bathroom tiles, the trademark architectural style of 1990s China. "They had just built that before we left. Everything else is different."

It was the day after *Qingming*, "Pure Brightness," when Chinese honor their deceased ancestors. Weiqi had flown in from Hong Kong to spend the holiday with his mother. They had taken a half-hour train ride to Suzhou to visit the grave of his mother's grandparents. They spent the afternoon arranging food on the gravesite, and then they burned phony paper money so that their ancestors had something to spend in the afterworld.

Earlier that morning, they had done the same for Weiqi's father on the sidewalk below their Shanghai apartment. It was a slightly more awkward ritual. His father's ashes remain in a wooden box kept inside his mother's apartment. His mother refuses to bury them until police investigate his father's death. "We just burned two candles on either side of the box and propped up a framed picture of him in the middle," Weiqi told me.

The box of ashes was delivered to Weiqi's mother a few days after his father died in 1996. Police didn't allow them to see his remains. Instead, the day after the fire, an officer visited the boy and his mother and showed them a picture of what was left of his body. "It was completely terrible," Weiqi said. "I couldn't believe it was my father. All I could imagine was that the fire must have been huge. You couldn't make out the head, not even the skeleton. It was completely black. A little green, too, I don't know why. You could see a little blue from the eyes, and that was it."

Xuhui District officials detained Weiqi and his mom in a government hotel on the southern edge of the district for ten months. They didn't allow him to go back to school and he missed nearly the entire fourth grade. That year, he suffered from insomnia. When he did sleep, he had a recurring nightmare. "I was on a track. A railway. It was endless. And I was running. Then something—I don't know what it was—but something black and horrible would chase me. It was very, very abstract."

Nearly a year later, district authorities allowed him to return to school and begin the fifth grade, escorting him with an official vehicle each morning and afternoon to and from the hotel where they were being detained.

"That first day back, my classmates stood in two groups, in two lines," he said. "And they all clapped in unison to welcome my return."

Weiqi returned to school a quiet and morose boy, a year behind his peers and struggling to catch up. By the end of junior high, though, Weiqi had surpassed his classmates academically and he was confident again. His mother had recovered, too, even though she was frequently in Beijing to continue to seek an investigation into her husband's death.

One night, when he was in junior high, the police knocked on the door of Weiqi's apartment. He was home alone; his mother had been gone for weeks. He had just cooked noodles for himself and he figured the matter had something to do with his mother, so he ignored the knocks and began to eat. The police knocked harder. No response. They finally smashed through the door, ripping it off its hinges. They found a startled Weiqi at his table. They handed him a document that stated his mother had been detained in Beijing. They demanded he sign it. "My mother told me never to sign anything from the police, so I refused," Weiqi said.

Their mission thwarted, the officers stormed off, leaving the boy inside an apartment without a door. At fourteen years old, Weiqi had lost his father, his home, and now his mother would be away for a while, too. Hardly anything scared him anymore. He stepped over the splintered mess, walked through the naked entryway, down the stairs, and out onto the street where he found a handyman. A new door was in place before he tucked himself into bed that evening.

SINCE THE DEATH of Mao in 1976, the leaders of China's Communist Party have been big on slogans to define their guiding principles.

Deng Xiaoping preached the Four Modernizations, Jiang Zemin the Three Represents, and Hu Jintao envisioned a Harmonious Socialist Society. Propaganda signs at train stations, airports, along highways, and everywhere in between advertised the clunky mantras, big red Chinese characters defining the rule of one leader eventually making way for those of the next.

For the 1.274 billion Chinese who weren't members of the Party, these slogans were about as meaningful as they are to the average American, unless they've studied and absorbed the finer points of Socialism with Chinese Characteristics. For most, the phrases were mysterious and nonsensical, and for the few *laobaixing* who had time to stop and consider them, they served little purpose except to remind them that there was a very large gap between them and their leaders.

So when Xi Jinping was formally approved as China's leader in March of 2013, there couldn't have been lower expectations for what would replace Harmonious Socialist Society.

The mild-mannered son of a revolutionary aimed high, restoring faith among the masses with a guiding principle that people wouldn't forget within seconds of hearing it: 中国梦, *Zhongguo Meng*, the Chinese Dream. It was simple, evocative, and immediately understandable by anyone. Finally, here was a slogan the Chinese could stand behind.

That is, until Xi Jinping attempted to explain what it meant in his first speech as president in March of 2013:

> The Chinese Dream fundamentally is the dream of the Chinese people, the realization of the Chinese Dream closely relies on the people's effort and in return benefiting the people. In order to build a moderately prosperous society, a prosperous, democratic, civilized, and harmonious modern socialist country and to achieve the Chinese Dream that will see the great rejuvenation of the nation, we need to achieve national prosperity and the revitalization as well as the happiness of the people. These things profoundly reflect the dreams of the people of China today and they are in accord with our glorious traditions.

In a carefully executed career from low-level bureaucrat to local leader to provincial leader to national leader, Comrade Xi had consumed decades of vague and clumsy Party catchphrases, and he was now regurgitating them, restoring what seemed to be an intriguing slogan to the familiar Communist drivel people had grown accustomed to.

It didn't take long for scholars to offer a concise explanation of Xi's long-winded definition. Sinologist Geremie R. Barmé summed up the above portion of the speech in seventy-seven fewer words than its official English version: "The Chinese can realize their individual dreams only if they also accept the common national goals derived by the Chinese Communist Party."

Most of my neighbors didn't hear Xi's speech. But the people I knew along the Street of Eternal Happiness had heard of the slogan, and the consensus was that the Chinese Dream had a good ring to it, whether they understood it or not.

"It sounds nice," Zhao Shiling told me one day while preparing flowers at her shop, "but I don't pay attention to politics, so I'm not sure what it means."

Inside Maggie Lane, Mayor Chen saw the Chinese Dream as a positive development. "Xi Jinping has been in power for a very short time, but it seems like he's already accomplishing a lot of practical tasks," he said with a smile.

China's new property laws encouraged Chen, and he was especially impressed with the new president's promise to root out corrupt officials. "I like that President Xi says he's going after the tigers and flies," Chen said, referring to the nicknames of crooked powerful leaders and local officials. "We've certainly got a lot of flies buzzing around here."

One morning in the spring of 2013, I looked out my bedroom window and noticed a couple dozen men in hard hats digging ditches alongside the remaining homes in Maggie Lane. Later that day, Chen brushed aside the activity over the phone. "Oh, they're just installing new gas lines for us," he said. "The old ones had been damaged by the demolition crew and they were all leaking."

He seemed encouraged by this, optimistic that change was

afoot not only in Beijing, but that the new edicts from on high had filtered down to China's local officials, scaring the flies into making amends for their past transgressions.

The days of big-spending Party officials appeared to be numbered, and decades after the rule of a megalomaniac who demanded a kind of loyalty among the masses that often transcended worship, here was a Chinese leader asking his people to corral their dreams into a single national dream where the Party, not the individual, was the chief consideration. Yet in today's China, where people had money to spend and more options than ever, state propaganda became easier to tune out.

THE MORNING OF SEPTEMBER 24, 2013, started like any other inside Maggie Lane. Mayor Chen brushed his teeth and washed his face in his bedroom while his wife, Xie Guozhen, used the toilet upstairs. It was a gorgeous autumn day: blue skies and a slight breeze blew from the east, pushing clean air from the ocean into the city. A pleasant draft wafted through the open windows of their home.

That's when Chen heard a loud slam downstairs. Before he could make it to the stairwell, six men emerged from around the corner. Three of them rushed toward him, taking him by the arms and forcing him to the floor. They tied his wrists together with rope as he yelled for help. The other three ran up the stairs and forced open the bathroom door where Xie was using the toilet.

"I was only wearing underwear. I screamed, 'This house is mine! My father-in-law bought it with gold! You can't rob our house like this!'" said Xie. "They looked like migrant workers and they didn't understand. One of them punched me and then gagged my mouth to prevent me from screaming. I tried to fight, but they twisted my arms so far behind my back I thought they were going to break."

The men ordered Xie to get dressed, and then dragged the couple downstairs and out their front door into the morning sunlight to where a van was parked. They pushed the couple inside, rolled the door shut, and drove past the security guard onto the street. It was the last time the couple saw their home. By the end of the day, Maggie Lane would be destroyed.

I MISSED THE DEMOLITION. I was in the United States on a business trip. When I woke up, I read an email from my assistant describing what had taken place. It was a well-coordinated blitz, she wrote. The demolition crew had removed Chen, his wife, and his neighbors from their homes and detained them in a courtyard complex a few blocks away for eight hours while excavators demolished their homes. The same day, *Marketplace*'s account on Weibo—China's version of Twitter—was shut down for the first time ever, preventing us from posting news about the demolition. I was the only journalist keeping tabs on the story, and Chen suspected the district had waited until they were sure I would be gone to go ahead with the demolition.

When I returned home a few days later, I looked out my bedroom window. What once looked like an abandoned lot sprinkled with several homes was now just an abandoned lot. *Shikumen*-house-sized piles of rubble littered the landscape, each of them underneath bright green netting. The portion of the wall that had been destroyed to allow the large equipment inside had already been rebuilt, and there was little sign that just a week ago, there had been people living here.

The next day I met Chen and Xie at a run-down hotel a few blocks away. They wore identical blue shirts, looking like prison inmates. Their son had given them his official work uniforms because they no longer had any clothes. They looked terrible. Neither of them had slept much, and bags were forming under their eyes. After being detained, Xie was taken to the hospital. She had already been suffering from colon cancer, and the stress of what had happened that morning had caused her to vomit and then faint. When she came to, she had shown signs of a heart attack. The demolition crew had paid her hospital bill and was covering their hotel stay, too.

I sat on the edge of their bed and took out my notebook. It

had been several days since the incident, but when I began to ask questions, the two spoke over each other, angrily yelling their accounts of what had happened as if it had occurred minutes ago. "In my seventy-three years, I have never lived a more undignified day," Xie told me. "I was no longer a human being. They kidnapped me! They kept us hostage. It was unimaginable. It was what the Mafia would do. They were like thieves. And this is supposed to be a socialist country!"

Xie wiped her eyes. She showed me purple bruises around her biceps where the men had grabbed her that morning. Chen told me they'd been kept inside a courtyard the entire day, allowed to leave only when their son showed up with a lawyer.

It was early evening when they returned to Maggie Lane. Security guards wouldn't let them inside. One guard was resting on the couple's bed, which had been deposited on the sidewalk. Another was lounging on an antique mahogany chair that had been salvaged from their home. The rest of their belongings were nowhere to be seen. The demolition crew told Chen some of their stuff had been taken to a warehouse, and other things had gone down with the house. What about our cash and our jewelry? Chen asked them. He had thousands of dollars in cash and gold and silver jewelry, as well as family heirlooms that were stored inside their bedroom. The workers said they didn't know what happened to any of it.

It was unclear whether the demolition was legal or not. An official with the Xuhui government told the couple the land would be used for the public good, which would make a forced relocation permissible under Chinese law. However, it was clear the tactics the demolition crew used to clear the land—abducting residents and detaining them—were illegal. In the case of a forced demolition, a local court is required to personally notify residents in advance so that they have time to move their belongings. No such notification was given to them. "They stormed the lane like Nazis," Chen told me.

Legal or not, Maggie Lane was now gone. It was another piece of Shanghai's history to be redeveloped. "Shanghai brags that it's an international metropolis, but it's a city without any culture," Xie said. "It only has skyscrapers. The property prices are too high for *laobaixing* to afford. Xuhui just sold a piece of land for a record amount. Our land is five times as big as the one that was just sold. How much will our land sell for?"

Chen had gone to the Xuhui government office and asked the same question the day after he had lost his home. "I told them that the Japanese didn't steal our house in the 1930s, the Nationalists didn't take the house in the forties, and it survived the Cultural Revolution. But now a gang of outlaws has taken it from us."

Xie took out a letter the couple had written to the Xuhui government and read it aloud to me. " 'As long as you have power, you can trample the constitution and insult and humiliate people, as well as violate your people's human rights. We've been overly naïve to believe in the reports in the newspapers and television about the government's propaganda and false promises to the people. You can take the people's land, but what you lose is our trust, the cornerstone of this Republic.' "

I thought about my last meeting with Chen before I had left for the United States. He was upbeat about his prospects of getting a fair settlement, confident the new president was finally rooting out corruption. It had been six months since the unveiling of the Chinese Dream, and now here he was, homeless.

He looked out the tiny hotel room window and began to cry. "My wife has lost her dignity. We've both lost any sense of security we've ever had," he said through tears. "It's all gone. The government talks about the Chinese Dream. Whose dream is that?"

It is rare to see a Chinese man cry, and it was clear from the way Xie looked at her husband that he was no exception. After a decade of fighting, he had finally lost everything he owned. Xie put her hand on her husband's shoulder.

"They just want us to keep dreaming," she told him softly.

10

Escape

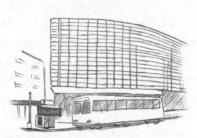

长乐682弄70号

Street of Eternal Happiness, Lane 682, No. 70

It's a Friday night at the intersection of the Street of Eternal Happiness and Rich People Road. This summer evening, both live up to their names. Affluent foreigners and Chinese stumble out of dance clubs onto the hot and noisy sidewalk. Uighur men pursue with whispered catcalls: "Hashish! Marijuana!"

Steps away, people throw coins at a monkey performing tricks, while his master, a disheveled fat man with a beard, scoops up the renminbi and shoves it into his pocket.

Perched upon the curb on the Xuhui side of the street is my homeless Chinese New Year companion Zhang Naisun. He sits atop a bag of recyclables sipping the remaining Heineken from a bottle a foreigner just donated. I stop to chat. It's late August, he tells me he just returned from his annual summer vacation to

Henan, and he's back to being dressed in tatters with a donation box in front of him. It's bursting with coins and notes.

The rest of the Street of Eternal Happiness settles in for the evening. Six blocks down, Zhao Shiling has closed up for the night and is turning in. She'll wake up early tomorrow to manage the morning shipment from the flower wholesaler. Four blocks away in their tiny room behind their streetside kitchen, Uncle Feng and Auntie Fu are fast asleep. Just a block away, CK is upstairs at *2nd Floor Your Sandwich* drinking imported beer and discussing tantric Buddhism with friends.

But here on this neon-lit corner, the night is young, and the scene is already coming close to conjuring Ringling Brothers. Moments later, the circus is complete: the motorcycle gang arrives. A thunderous rumble of two dozen Harley-Davidsons reverberates through the muggy evening, the earsplitting firing of pistons rising and falling as they slowly make their way down the street. The machines climb single file up onto the sidewalk. The monkey scurries out of the way. They ride past Old Zhang, who raises his fist in greeting, hoping for a few coins in return.

The group park their bikes in a row, a few of them revving up their engines one last time to announce their arrival to the hard-of-hearing. If there were any corner on the Street of Eternal Happiness that could attract the Hells Angels, this would be it: there's a row of bars and a Mexican-themed cantina with outdoor seating. But this group struts past all of these establishments, earning stares, and instead turns into the Coffee Bean and Tea Leaf. They emerge with foamy lattes and frothy cappuccinos, sipping them around outdoor tables.

This is a motorcycle gang of Chinese executives and self-made millionaires. They meet for coffee here every Friday night to discuss business and plan road trips together. "Between us, we probably know everyone in town," one of them boasts.

The gang takes up five outdoor tables. Their gear—helmets and leather jackets—takes up a sixth. They chat and laugh, keeping an eye on crowds of young Chinese who hold their phones up to take photos of their machines. "One Friday night we got rained out and everybody drove their cars," the group leader tells me, motioning to their bikes, lined up neatly in a row. "This area was full of Bentleys, Ferraris, and Land Rovers."

These men were born in a humbler time. The country was rising from the ashes of Mao when a diminutive leader named Deng told his subjects to go out and make money. An old quote of Deng's from the 1960s—a pragmatic proverb from his native Sichuan— was resurrected to clear up any contradictions between socialism and capitalism: "It doesn't matter whether a cat is black or white, as long as it catches mice."

These leather-clad tycoons have caught a lot of mice. Chen Jun's factory makes designer clothes. Tony Tang is a diamond wholesaler. Frank Zhu owns a cashmere sweater company. Winston's company ships coal, and a Taiwanese guy named Sa owns a gold mine in Zimbabwe. Their motorcycles, lined up along Rich People Road, display their status. In the United States, Harley-Davidsons start at eight thousand dollars. The same machines in China start at twenty thousand dollars and work their way up past fifty thousand, with an additional ten grand for a license plate.

Frank Zhu, a fifty-two-year-old man under a mop of curly black hair who can't seem to stop smiling, shows me pictures on his phone from a Harley tour he had just completed across Tibet and Xinjiang, two of China's most remote and unforgiving regions. Others show me photos of rides to Mongolia, Southeast Asia, and beyond. China has paved 32,000 miles of highways in the past eight years. It is the world's most expansive road-building campaign since the United States built its interstate system fifty years ago. For the first time, hundreds of millions of middle-class Chinese are driving their first cars cross-country, exploring this vast land, deepening their understanding of their nation.

This age of exploration carries with it a newfound sense of freedom. "Life in the city can be very depressing," Harley rider Jerry Gong tells me over an espresso. "You're stuck inside all the time in a confined space. A motorcycle doesn't have a roof or a window or any doors. It gives me freedom. It lets me indulge my passion for life."

I think about my friends down the street who have never

known what it's like to indulge in a passion for life. I wonder if they ever will. I think about Wang Ming and the family he left behind along this very stretch of the street four decades earlier, a time when capitalism was punished with a labor camp sentence instead of rewarded with high-end toys.

I study Jerry as he sips from his tiny cup. He has watchful eyes and a slightly uneasy smile, but among his leather-clad friends here, he seems at peace. I ask him what he does for a living. His mouth curls into a nervous grin.

"I build prisons," he says.

IN 1957 ON THIS BLOCK, they arrested a capitalist. Police marched past red propaganda banners urging neighbors to root out Rightists and arrived at the home of factory manager Wang Ming. The letters in a shoebox on my desk tell the rest of the story: Police seized Wang from his wife, six daughters, and unborn son. Months later, a judge sentenced him to fifteen years in a labor camp two thousand miles away on the edge of Tibet. He was charged with practicing capitalism.

I fumble through the stack of letters and select one with the return address *Delingha Camp*. It's a letter from Wang to his wife, Liu Shuyun.

I open it. It's dated March 14, 1968. In the upper-right-hand corner of the browned sheet of rice paper is a printed box outlined in red. It's filled with simplified Chinese characters:

CHAIRMAN MAO'S WORDS

We should be humble and careful. Avoid pride. Be patient. Serve whole-heartedly the Chinese people.

—"The Two Fates of China"

The letter is scrawled in tiny black traditional Chinese characters. The penmanship is impeccable.

Liu's husband, Wang Ming, has survived ten years inside the camp and has five years left of his prison sentence. Liu had stopped writing her husband seven years earlier. Corresponding with a "bad element" has gotten her in trouble with local police. At school, classmates and even teachers bully her children for having the wrong background.

Yet Wang's letters continue to arrive. The letter in my hands is written to his father. The first line contains an error that violates the code of the times: Wang addresses his dad as *Fuqin Daren,* an honorific title permissible in any other time save for that of the Cultural Revolution. In a return letter dated May 24, 1968, Wang's father takes his son to task:

> *You referred to me with the honorific "Da Ren." It is now the era of the Cultural Revolution and it is time to smash the Four Olds. Next time you write, simply call us Father or Mother. You should study hard and learn how to think correctly and study Chairman Mao's words more often.*

Quotations from Chairman Mao Tse-Tung—known in the West as the *Little Red Book*—is quickly becoming one of the most printed books in history. Elderly Chinese and schoolchildren alike commit its passages to memory.

At the family home on the Street of Eternal Happiness, Mother Liu has little time to memorize quotes. Apart from managing six children, she works full-time at a neighborhood box factory.

By 1968 the famine has passed, and Big Sister and Sister Two have both dropped out of high school to work at textile factories. Sisters Three, Four, and Five and their little brother Xuesong have the luxury of attending school.

"They are all positive inheritors of socialism," writes Wang's sister later that year. "They study hard and they love labor."

The children have overcome malnourishment and now look "nice and fat."

Little Xuesong, she writes, is old enough to read his father's letters.

More than a thousand miles away at Delingha Labor Camp, Wang Ming attends study sessions of Mao Zedong Thought followed by self-criticism sessions. Inmates are trained in the habit of searching their own thoughts to suss out counterrevolutionary ideas.

Other thought purification methods are employed, too. In a letter dated January 14, 1969, Wang Ming complains of suffering from repeated bouts of the flu and a bloated stomach, a sign of malnourishment. His close-cropped hair is turning gray and the sturdy physique of his younger years has been reduced to skin and bones. Instead of treating his physical ailments, the camp doctor gives him narcotics.

"I later learned this old doctor was treating me for having 'thought problems,'" writes Wang. "I continued to have stomach problems. Sometimes on Sundays I play poker. I recently won the price of a stamp. I ate very happily that day, and I didn't have any stomach problems. That was a good day."

Eventually, he discovers the root cause of his stomach ailment and treats it himself—with "Chairman Mao Thought": "First, I diligently studied 'Fight Privatization, Criticize Revisionism,' a reading issued last year . . ."

Wang tops it off with Mao's writings on the role of the family in Communist China. "Before we raised children to take care of the elderly," observes Wang in a letter to his uncle. "But now we raise them to prevent revisionist thinking. In the past I became overly obsessed with the traditional idea of a 'happy family,' and I became mired deeper and deeper until I couldn't relieve myself from its grasp.

"Once I tasted the sweetness of the great works of Chairman Mao," concludes Wang, "my stomach problems haven't returned!

"But are the Chairman's thoughts embedded firmly enough in my head?" Wang asks himself in the letter. "Not necessarily yet. Old thoughts sometimes return uninvited. So I must further my studies in order to embed these thoughts more firmly."

Reading this made me wonder what was going on inside Wang's head. Was he writing this to please authorities who would be inspecting the letter? Or was it the drugs talking? Did he really think "Mao Zedong Thought" was curing his illness?

Harry Wu, who spent decades inside a Chinese labor camp near Delingha at the time, explained it this way: prisoners of that era endured so many study and self-criticism sessions that most of them believed Mao was God. Wu talked to me over the phone from his home in Washington, DC. It was a gradual transformation, he said, and it evolved alongside emotional deprivation, hunger, fatigue, and isolation.

"Today you say, 'Long Live Chairman Mao!' and I say, 'Bullshit,'" Wu explained. "Tomorrow you say, 'Long Live Chairman Mao!' and I say, 'I'm tired.' The third day you say 'Long Live Chairman Mao!' and I don't respond. The day after that you say, 'Long Live Chairman Mao!' and I ask 'Why?' The fifth day you say, 'Long Live Chairman Mao!' and I'm interested. The sixth day you say, 'Long Live Chairman Mao!' and I repeat it.

"And then when Chairman Mao dies," concluded Wu, "I weep."

ON APRIL 17, 1970, after nine years of silence, Liu Shuyun finally writes a letter to her husband. She offers no explanation for the gap in writing, and it begins the way all of her letters do: "Your letter has been received."

In it, she advises her husband to get a second opinion about his illness. "Don't procrastinate," she writes. "It should be treated as soon as possible and you should properly diagnose the cause."

There's good news. The children are all grown, Mother Liu writes, and they're helping put food on the table. The couple's little brood has grown up and they're all taller than she is. Three of them have started working. Big Sister makes thirty-six yuan a month. Sisters Two and Three are apprentices, making eighteen yuan a month each. Sister Four was just assigned to work in the countryside in Anhui after graduating from middle school.

Baby Sister, the child they gave up, is doing well in the countryside, writes Mother Liu. And their little boy is now in middle school, earning 100 percent on all his exams. Liu includes six photos of the children.

Wang hasn't seen his children in twelve years. He's waited nearly a decade for a letter, for news of their health, for anything. His response to Mother Liu is grateful, and filled with questions. It's the only letter in which Wang apologizes to his wife for how everything turned out.

April 26, 1970

Shuyun:

I received your letter yesterday with the photos. I was so happy. At the same time, it brought thoughts and feelings to the surface. I didn't sleep last night and luckily today is a day of rest here. The children are all grown up and they are all well. This is a result of your hard work. All of this has had an impact on your health. You look older. It's all my fault. I escaped the responsibility I was supposed to fulfill and I left you alone to shoulder everything. I can only wait until I get a new life to make up for my ways.

I keep looking at the photos of the children. Their faces still retain the same shape from when they were young. Only Sister Two and Sister Three have completely changed. It's probably the same for Baby Sister. When I look at these children—my own flesh and blood—I feel like I'm looking at strangers. Our family has transformed. Everything has changed for the better. We have changed from a family that exploited others like parasites to a family that makes their livings through honest work.

As long as you can write me a letter each month, that's my biggest comfort. If indeed you have difficulty or trouble to write, please ask the children to write instead. If you have Baby Sister's photo, please send it. Please also send one or two photos from the past, such as our family photo when I was still there. When I'm depressed, I read your letters over and over and carefully study the photos. This is good for my health. I hope you understand.

Wang Ming

From the surge of letters that follows, it's clear the dynamics between husband and wife have changed. Mother Liu now writes to her husband with the self-assurance of a mother who has raised six children, alone, through famine and constant intimidation. The children are on career paths, and their only son is on the track to a higher education.

The Party's Cultural Revolution demanded people smash Confucian traditions, but the reality of Mother Liu's situation left no alternative. The mother was in charge here, and her children were growing to resent their father.

Dozens of letters in the early 1970s show Mother Liu repeatedly pulling rank on her husband in family matters. The oldest girls are approaching marrying age, a time when a Chinese father would typically oversee an appropriate match for his adult children. In a letter in 1971, Mother Liu assures her husband, "As for the marriage matters of the kids you're concerned about, they should be able to choose for themselves. Besides, the government is now promoting marrying late. Stop worrying about that."

Later, when Liu's second and third daughters apply to become Communist Party members, managers from their factory first check on their father's progress at Delingha. In a letter to her husband, Liu writes that her greatest fears are confirmed:

> Several months ago, the leaders from our daughters' factory went to your labor camp to check on your behavior and your progress. The feedback was bad. According to your file, you routinely violate the rules of the camp and are not dedicated to labor. They said that sometimes you have even skipped work to go out and trade cigarettes that I've sent you for other things from locals in the nearby village. Apart from that, they heard that you often talk about returning to Shanghai and living on government subsidies meant for the ill and disabled.
>
> I was so heartbroken to hear this. You should behave yourself, not only for your own good, but also for the future of our children. They all have worked very hard and are consistently praised by

their colleagues. It hurts them so much to hear how their father has
failed them. I hope you will take real action to make a change for
your children and for me. Next time, think twice before you speak.
I will never send you cigarettes again.

The final year of Wang's prison sentence was 1973. His release
proved to be incredibly short-lived. Just a little over a week after
he returned home, police escorted him to the Shanghai Railway
Station and put him on a train that would take him two thousand
miles back to Qinghai. They'd denied his application for a Shanghai *hukou*. Without a residency permit, his presence in his own
hometown was illegal.

After a brief taste of freedom, Wang returned to the place of
his *hukou*: Delingha labor camp. He continued to labor. He had
finished serving his sentence, but he had no other choice but to
continue to serve time, work hard, and study Mao Zedong Thought.

That is, until Mao Zedong died.

I WALKED SLOWLY along a curved section of the Street of Eternal Happiness, my eyes fixed on the green number plates. I didn't expect to
find the Wang family home. It was inside an old lane community,
and my experience with Maggie Lane had taught me what usually
happened to old lane communities.

I passed 640 . . . 662 . . . then I saw it on a bright green plac-
ard: Street of Eternal Happiness, Lane 682. I stepped into the alley.
It was lined with cobblestones, filled with the dancing shadows of
clothes hanging three stories above. I walked inside and searched
for house number 70.

For the past three months, I had pored over the letters, one by
one, translating them and putting them into chronological order.
I delayed looking for their home on the street until I had finished
reading through the letters. My goal was to piece together what happened to the family from what was just one side of a decades-long
correspondence between husband and wife.

The crinkled, yellowed letters spanned thirty-two years, beginning in 1958 with Liu's news that their youngest son was weaned, and ending in 1990 with a letter addressed from a cousin in Taiwan: "I heard from the news that the Communist Party intends to shape Shanghai into a prosperous Oriental city!" the cousin wrote. "I figure this might be good news, regardless of which party is in power. After all, as long as the Chinese people have the freedom to become rich and powerful, I am optimistic about their success."

That's it. The box of letters was now empty. An inauspicious beginning had turned into an auspiciously abrupt end.

What had happened to the Wang family? Were they still living at Lane 682?

I knocked for what seemed like a minute before I heard a movement inside. A woman with short gray hair opened the door.

"Sorry to bother you, Auntie," I said, "but I'm looking for Wang Ming. Do you happen to know if he lives here?"

"Who?" the woman asked, a little startled.

"Wang. Wang Ming. He's probably in his eighties now. I'm not sure . . ."

"Wang?" she interrupted. "Sure, I know the family. They're my landlords. They're not here now. They left the country," she said in staccato bursts of Shanghai dialect.

"Left the country? Where?"

"New York! You're talking about Wang Xuesong, right?"

"Yes. He was the youngest son," I said.

"Wang Xuesong lives in New York City. He moved there a few years ago with his mother. What business is it of yours?"

"I'VE NEVER READ those letters. I don't know anything about them," Wang Xuesong told me over the phone from New York City. I had found Wang's number by entering his mother's name into a city directory. He spoke in Mandarin with a slow, gentle voice that stuttered a little when trying to recall past events. He patiently listened to my story of how I had come to read his parents' letters. He was now fifty-six years old and baffled by how his parents' letters had ended up in an antiques store. "I was the last to be born in the family, so I'm afraid I'm not going to be much help," he warned me.

I asked Wang about his father. "He-he passed away," Wang said. "I think it was a few years ago. I c-c-can't remember when. I'd need to ask my older sisters."

It seemed like an odd response, but Wang's stutter signaled I shouldn't pursue the matter further. Wang told me after his father served his full term at Delingha, he stayed on for another six years before finally coming home in 1979.

I asked him when he first saw his father: 1973, Wang said, when his father returned home briefly before being sent back to the labor camp. "I was a teenager," Wang recalled. "I went with Big Sister to Shanghai Station to meet his train from Qinghai. I didn't know who I was looking for. I was just a baby when he left, and after the Cultural Revolution started in the 1960s, my mother had burned all of his photos. It was a time when people were being investigated for their family backgrounds, and ours wasn't good, so we were afraid of having any evidence of him around. I had no idea what he looked like. Big Sister was nine years old when he left home, so she had a vague memory of his face, but that was when he was in his thirties.

"When the train arrived, people scrambled this way and that, and we stopped an older man who we thought might be him, but it wasn't. In the end, we missed him completely. Neither of us knew what the other looked like. When we got home, there he was—my father had taken a public bus, alone," said Wang.

It was a vivid memory and his recollection of it was stutter-free.

"His hair was gray; about seventy percent of it had turned white. His skin was dark from working outside for years," he said. "But he had returned empty-handed. He had no job, no income."

By then, Wang's older sisters had already started working in textile factories, quadrupling the family income. Each month, they would hand over their salaries to their mother so that she could manage the family finances. Wang said his mother knew how to save money and spend carefully. "Each night when she returned home from the factory, she'd patch up sweaters for a few fen [1/100th of a renminbi] each. Most nights after all of us children fell asleep, she would drag the lamp low and sit on a high stool, stitching sweaters into the early hours of the morning. Then she'd leave for work. She barely slept," Wang recalled.

Wang told me by the time his father made his first return trip home from prison, the worst had passed. "My mother was someone who would submit meekly to maltreatment yet shoulder all the responsibilities herself to raise her children," Wang told me. "She strongly believed that sooner or later, life would get better, bit by bit. She was a very traditional Chinese woman. She was only thirty-one when my father left, and she could have easily remarried, but she refused. There's an old Chinese saying: 'A heroic woman doesn't marry twice.' My mother believed my father would 'improve his thoughts' after he returned from Qinghai."

"Did he?" I asked.

"Not really," he said. "He stayed with us at home for a while and then he began feeling restless because he wasn't making any money."

I thought about the letters I had read from Wang Ming. They were filled with Communist propaganda, railing against his old capitalist ways. Two decades of laboring in the fields and a nightly brainwashing in Marxist, Leninist, and Mao Zedong thought had convinced Wang he had been right all along. All of these ideas may have sounded nice from the miserable confines of a labor camp in a forgotten corner of the Tibetan Plateau. But back in civilization among the busy streets of Shanghai, they proved no match for capitalism.

I had read several drafts of letters dating back to when Wang Ming was still in prison that showed he was eager to get back to business. In a letter dated April 30, 1981, Wang wrote to leaders in Shanghai's Department of Commerce and Industry in an attempt to help them reestablish the city's silicon steel recycling industry. "There are so many unemployed young men these days who we can hire to set up factories in the city's suburban areas. These types of factories are labor intensive, low investment, and they produce high yields. We can build them anywhere," he wrote the officials, mentioning Deng Xiaoping's campaign to revive China's economy before posing a final question: "Can I play an active role in contributing my energy and wisdom to the 'Four Modernizations'?"

A year later, Wang Ming managed to find work through some old friends in the industry, paid on commission to help find new business for metal-recycling enterprises in his rural ancestral home outside Shanghai. He was fifty-seven years old, three years away from being eligible to collect retirement benefits. In order to do so, though, he first had to submit a petition to a local court to rectify his name, clearing himself of his crime. The petition was his final self-criticism, the last remnants of Wang's submission to the Party:

> *If you examine the root cause of my actions, it's clearly because my worldview had yet to be reformed. That is to say, I didn't study enough at the time; I didn't stand firm and I was too obsessed with my own selfish needs. I can only blame myself. If only I could have used my experience in recycling silicon steel and devoted myself wholeheartedly to the socialist cause after the public-private partnerships were formed, if only I could have built wealth for the country rather than for myself, then even if I were arrested, I could have explained my actions in the firm belief that I would be treated fairly.*

"The court rejected his petition," Wang Xuesong told me over the phone. "His original crimes still stand today."

I asked Wang if he thought the government had treated his father unfairly. I expected Wang to blame China's government, the system, or the chaotic political atmosphere for what happened.

"Of course *he* didn't think it was fair," Wang said slowly, "but during each unique period of time, China's government has unique rules. My father opened an underground factory. Underground factories were banned after the Communist Party took power. The government wanted tight control over raw materials, and forbade individuals from controlling them. That was the rule of the game. My father's sentence wasn't unfair. He was breaking the rules of that time. When you violate a rule, you'll be punished."

There was silence over the phone line. I didn't know what to say. The Anti-Rightist campaign was madness, and his family suffered terribly because of it. How could he believe his father's sentence was just?

Wang paused a moment and continued. "From my own perspective, my father had a clear choice," he said. "He shouldn't have done what he did. His life was good; his life was stable. He-he didn't need to run an underground factory. He was earning one hundred and seventy renminbi each month after the state took over his factory. Th-that was a sky-high salary back then. But he wasn't satisfied. He-he wanted more."

Wang's tone had shifted. Anger seeped into his voice. His stutter was back. Throughout his childhood, students and teachers had openly bullied him in class for being the son of a capitalist. His sisters were denied promotions at their factory. One sister had to be given up for adoption. The rest of his family nearly starved to death.

The Chinese had evolved into a people who had learned to detect the slightest ideological shifts in the ruling hierarchy so that they could quickly recalibrate their positions, protecting themselves and their families. Adjustment to ever-changing surroundings was a rule of life in China. Why hadn't his father adjusted?

Wang continued. "It was a very big burden for my mother to take care of so many children. M-my father isn't a kind-hearted person, either. He did something in the past. H-he did something that betrayed my mother," Wang said, exhaling a sigh.

This kind of phrasing made it sound like his father had a mistress or possibly a second wife, which wasn't uncommon for men of wealth at that time. I waited for Wang to continue, but he put the issue to rest. *"Bu-buyong duo shuo."*

The phrase meant "No need to talk about this further," and we didn't.

"My father spent his last years in a nursing home," Wang said. "I'm not sure what the specific diagnosis was. When he died, he was eighty-six or eighty-seven. I don't remember, exactly."

In a country with a tradition of worshipping family patriarchs, it was almost unheard of for a father with seven children to have to spend his final years in a nursing home. But if there was anything that was clear from reading Wang Ming's letters, it was that he had become used to solitude. By the end of his life, he had adjusted.

Wang Ming's ashes were buried in a family plot at a cemetery in his ancestral hometown in the countryside outside Shanghai. Neither his son nor his wife returned home for his funeral.

WANG XUESONG ARRIVED at JFK Airport on a China Eastern flight on May 12, 2008. It was his mother's eighty-second birthday. Mother Liu and her son were underwhelmed. "It didn't look much different from China," Wang said. "Shanghai's a big, modern city, and when we drove away from JFK, I looked around and thought it didn't look as nice as where we had come from. When we got to Flushing, it was full of Chinese stores and everything was written in Chinese."

After driving through blocks of Chinese storefronts, Mother Liu finally spoke. "Where in Shanghai are we?" she asked her son.

It was a serious question. Liu was suffering from the effects of Alzheimer's disease. "Her memory is gone," Wang said.

It had taken Wang and his mother twenty years to obtain residency visas for the United States. Sister Five had moved to the United States long ago with her husband, a Chinese-born American citizen. Big Sister and Sister Two had followed. The three sisters were scattered throughout the borough of Queens.

Wang's sisters helped him find a room in a duplex fifteen minutes away from the subway station. It was a two-story house crammed with five other Chinese families. Wang paid their Fujianese landlord $780 a month for a room on the first floor.

Prior to leaving for the U.S., Wang had worked as an engineer in a refrigerator factory in Shanghai. In New York City, neither this experience nor Wang's engineering degree from a Chinese university would be worth much without the ability to speak English. Within a few weeks of arriving in the U.S., a friend of his sister's helped him find a job that didn't require language skills: a Korean-run cellphone-repair plant in Long Island City. For eight hours a day, Wang worked on an assembly line scanning labels of hundreds of broken cellphones. It was a mindless, robotic job typical of China, not New York. In the mornings, when Wang walked past Cantonese groceries and Beijing dumpling shops on his way to an assembly plant full of Chinese factory workers, he began to feel the traces of senility that were plaguing his mother—here he was, back home again. There was no escaping China.

Wang made seven dollars an hour, more than he had made at his factory back in Shanghai. Still, it was less than minimum wage in New York at the time. I asked him how he was able to make ends meet. "I'm Chinese. I can make it work," Wang said over the phone. "We're not like Americans. We never spend more than we make."

He had never married. His six sisters had all wedded early and he had several nieces and nephews, but Wang was always too busy with other tasks—his studies, his work, taking care of his mother—to give marriage much thought. His mother had spent much of her life taking care of him and his sisters, and as the only son in a family without a father, he felt that once he became an adult, it would be his duty to look after her.

Wang Xuesong's favorite place in Flushing was the neighborhood's public library. He walked by the gleaming glass and steel structure each day on his way to catch the 7 train, and he soon came to learn that its role in the community was nothing like that of a library in China. In China, public libraries are scarce. For a population of 1.4 billion people, there are just 3,000 public libraries limited to the country's largest cities. By comparison, 350 million Americans are served by 17,000 public libraries located in nearly every town in the country. In China, the public library's role in the community is restricted to loaning government-approved books to residents. In America, Wang discovered, public libraries did much more. They were civic centers, learning centers, and in an immigrant community like Flushing, the library became far and away the single most important place in the residents' lives, offering free English classes, free computer classes, free high school–level classes, and a variety of workshops that helped new transplants adjust to their new home.

Wang spent all of his free time at the library. The fifty-seven-year-old took English classes there twice a week. On Tuesday nights and for seven hours each Saturday he took high school courses. By the time he turned sixty, he told me, he would earn his GED, the equivalent of a high school diploma. After that, he'd move on to college coursework. Wang's classmates at the library were some of his best friends. Many of them were from China, but he also had friends from India, Russia, and the Dominican Republic. Before he'd stepped foot inside the library, Wang told me, he didn't have a clear sense of how America was different from China. But here among the stacks of books and halls of classrooms was a place built for the betterment of the community; a place where people could, free of charge, learn new skills that would help them find better work and improve their lives. China didn't have places like this, Wang said. Each time he entered the bright and warm environs of the Flushing public library, he felt hopeful. He felt free.

I MET WANG on the steps of the Flushing library one rainy morning in May of 2014. It was the first day of the month—the Labor Day holiday in China—but in the U.S., it was just another workday. I was passing through New York on business, and I had called Wang the night before.

"I'm white, I'm tall, and I'll wear a black jacket," I told him over the phone.

"There are lots of tall white men at that library," Wang replied. "There are a lot of black and yellow people there, too. How about I wear a bright green jacket? I'm really short, and I'll wear a hat that says 'New York City,' okay?"

I arrived early. Despite the rain, the library was flooded with light. Downstairs, I peered inside the Adult Learning Center classrooms. Three classes of English were being taught. The rooms were full of Chinese immigrants. When I returned to the ground floor and walked outside, I saw a bright green jacket. Wang stood a foot shorter than me. He wore glasses and his small eyes often darted to the corners, as if scanning the area for any danger. On his black baseball cap, the Statue of Liberty stood in front of a Stars-and-Stripes-filled "NEW YORK CITY."

We sat in front of tall shelves of books on a bench facing an angled window that was being doused with driving rain. Two women sat across from us, speaking Fujianese. When we began to speak in Mandarin, the women halted their conversation.

"*Wah!* The foreigner's Chinese is good," one of them told Wang. "Is he American?"

"Yes, but he lives in Shanghai," Wang explained, turning back to me.

The woman looked confused. "How can a foreigner speak such good Chinese and here I am in America, and I can't speak a word of English?"

Her friend laughed at the misfortune of it all.

"He studied Chinese," Wang said. "You should study English. There are free classes downstairs."

"But we can't speak a word! We just got here from Fujian!" said the woman.

"It doesn't matter. They start at A-B-C. Go downstairs and register," urged Wang.

The women thought about it for a moment. "Nah, we're too old," one of them said.

Wang looked at them in utter confusion, a look that seemed to say: What kind of Chinese immigrant doesn't want to learn English?

I broke the awkward silence. "Auntie, have you found work yet?"

"No, we've only been here a week. We don't know where to look," the woman said.

Wang took out a piece of paper and a pen and wrote an address for them in English with some directions in Chinese. "Go to this agency," he said, handing over the paper to them. "You don't need to speak English at all, and they're always looking for workers. The pay's not bad, either. They take care of old people."

The women inspected the paper, looking skeptical.

"Don't worry," said Wang. "The old people you'll take care of are all Chinese. They don't speak English, either. Some of them even speak Fujianese."

The women thanked him and walked away.

Wang had adjusted to life in America. After six years on the assembly line, he had quit and was now collecting unemployment benefits. Each month, the government sent him a check for seven hundred dollars, around the same amount he had been making at the factory. He told me it was more than enough. Surviving the worst famine in recorded history alongside his siblings and an unemployed mother had taught him frugality. Plus, now that he wasn't working, he could spend more time taking classes at the library to improve his English and earn his GED.

When I asked him what his goal was, he removed an envelope from his bag. "This," he said, withdrawing a neatly folded pink sheet of paper. It was a carbon copy of a multiple-choice exam he had taken a couple of days ago. On top of the paper was the logo for the New York City Transit Authority. Under that was written "Revenue Equipment Maintenance Exam." Forty blanks were filled with letters written in Wang's careful penmanship.

"You want to work for the MTA?" I asked.

"It's an exam for a mechanical engineering job. Similar to what I did back in Shanghai," he said. "If I pass, I'll fix subway card machines. There are usually openings for this job. Just think about how many card machines are always broken. There's a lot of work out there. And they pay you sixty thousand dollars a year!"

This was something Wang could relate to: taking an examination in the hopes of landing a stable government job. It was familiar to anyone from China, where people competed for civil service positions the same way. Rainwater from his jacket dripped onto the pink answer sheet as he held it out for me. He carefully wiped the sheet dry and returned it to the envelope.

Wang told me he was also taking classes in Manhattan to become an office assistant, "but my English has to improve before I have any hope of finding a job," he said.

Wang wasn't in a rush to find work. He had spent his childhood learning about the evils of capitalist America from his school textbooks, but when he arrived in New York, he discovered its capitalists treated their poor much better than the Communists did back home. The U.S. government gave Wang's mother two hundred dollars' worth of food stamps each month. Its Medicare program paid for a nurse to arrive each day at their home to take care of his mother while Wang attended his free GED classes at the public library. Wang told me that between his mother's welfare payments and his unemployment benefits, they could afford rent while putting some money away each month. The way he saw it, you had to be pretty stupid to mess up an arrangement like this. "I was also eligible for thousands of dollars' worth of food stamps each year," he told me, "but I said no. I thought it would look bad."

Wang's favorite part of the day was the range of classes he took at the library. He smiled when he told me about studying world history from an American perspective and reading Shakespeare in the Bard's native tongue. He spoke about his prospects with the excitement of a teenager. His parents had lived long lives, Wang told me, and he had learned there would be plenty of time left to start over in his adopted country. "In America, you're never too old to begin again," he said.

Wang's mother was eighty-eight years old and in the late stages of Alzheimer's. Mother Liu was confused more or less all the time now. Wang removed his wallet from his jacket pocket and showed me a black-and-white photo of her. After reading dozens of her letters, I had formed an image of Liu in my mind's eye, and I was surprised to discover it was nearly identical to the woman I was looking at now. She was pretty—a long, thin face graced with high cheekbones. Like Wang, she had small, kind eyes. There was an anxiety in her gaze, like someone who was lost. "This picture is from last year," Wang told me, "around the time she escaped from home."

Wang was making breakfast for her one morning when he noticed she had left the house. He ran up and down the street shouting her name, but he couldn't find her. He called the police. Officers brought dogs to sniff her pillow for a scent and then they followed them through the neighborhood, but they couldn't locate her. That night, police dispatched a helicopter with a spotlight to search the surrounding neighborhood, but still there was no sign of her.

The police finally found Mother Liu at a local hospital where she was being treated for bruises on her face. She had likely fallen down a stairway somewhere. "The police in America are very good," Wang said, impressed. "That search must have cost a lot of money. They would never go to those lengths in China."

Wang took one last look at the photo of his mother in his hands, and then carefully slid it back into his wallet. "After she passes away, I'll have more freedom," he said with a sigh.

In six years of living in the United States, Wang had never left New York City. He told me that after he got his diploma, he planned to travel across the country in search of a better place to live. "Somewhere easy to find a job where the living costs aren't so high," he said. "I'd prefer somewhere quiet. I don't know. Where do you think I should live?"

I thought for a moment.

"Well, I'm from Minnesota, in the Midwest. It's a bit cold there, but life is good. It's quiet, it's safe, and it's affordable. My wife is from Texas. The land is affordable there, compared to New York. And the climate there is much better—it's more like Shanghai."

Wang listened to me intently, repeating the names of the states in Chinese. *"Ming Ni Su Da. De Ke Sa Si,"* he said slowly. "I'd like to live in different cities for short periods of time while I travel around. In China, you can't do that comfortably because of the *hukou* system, but the United States doesn't have *hukou*. You're free to move around wherever you want. It's more convenient here."

I nodded. I thought about Wang, free from the responsibility of caring for his mother, driving an affordable yet dependable car west out of New York City into the sunset. "It sounds like you're pursuing the American dream," I said.

Wang thought for a moment. "I don't see it that way," he said. "Life in Shanghai wasn't bad, either. Before I left, we lived in a nice neighborhood and the food was cheap and good. A lot of people ask me why I came to the U.S. when China has so much opportunity now. I tell them the main reason is the water and the air are so much better in America. Plus, I had waited thirteen years for a visa, and my chance finally came, so I took it. But I've learned that, for me at least, there isn't much of a difference between living in America or in Shanghai."

China had come a long way since the years of his youth. In a city like Shanghai, jobs were plentiful, schools were good, the streets were relatively safe, and people's lives had improved tremendously from a few decades ago. There was no reason for him to think life there wouldn't continue to improve for years to come. Yet for Wang, neither the American dream nor the Chinese Dream rang true. Wang's dreams were his own.

We had been talking for two hours. Outside, rain kept pelting the angled window in front of us, the din of millions of drops hitting the glass providing the perfect soundtrack for a library. I looked up at Wang. "I have copies of all those letters," I said. "Would you like them?"

Wang shook his head. "Nobody in my family cares about those letters. We already know what happened."

"But what about the younger generation—your nieces and nephews? Do they know?" I asked.

"They may not know, but they're not interested in this type of history. They have no memory of the Cultural Revolution or the famine or any of that stuff. They don't want to learn about it, either," Wang said. "There was a reason we threw those letters away. We Chinese like to think 'Let bygones be bygones.' People of my generation, we remember very clearly what happened and we don't want it to be repeated among the next generation in China."

I thought to myself: But isn't that precisely why they should have these letters? I had this conversation with other Chinese who had lived through trauma during the Mao years, and the answer was too often the same: *"Hide it and it will stay hidden."*

"My father has passed. Everything will pass. There's no reason to dwell on it," he said, uneasy with my silence. "My father was not a great man. He was just a *laobaixing*, a normal person," he told me.

In the distance, a cacophony of Mandarin dialects from a group of smiling Chinese seniors emerged from the stairway from their English classrooms below. Wang and I watched in silence. "Just talk to any Chinese who lived through that time," he said, motioning to them. "We all have the same stories."

11

Zero Risk

长乐路169号
Street of Eternal Happiness, No. 169

Behind a white-tiled kitchen thick with the pungent, oily vapor of fried scallion pancakes, is a room filled with boxes. They're stacked on both levels of a mattress-less bunk bed, heaped atop a hutch, and piled upon an armoire, puncturing a layer of cobwebs to the ceiling above. They're filled with Auntie Fu's work: Gatewang brochures, canisters of miracle tea, and packages of dried mushrooms, the clutter of products from various companies she's invested in. They loom over a dank room that also houses a queen bed, a small dining table, and a chest of drawers, and they trigger frequent heated arguments between Auntie Fu and Uncle Feng about a shortage of space.

But it wasn't the boxes I noticed when I first visited the couple's home. It was the televisions. Two of them. The hulking machines were the only signs of technology inside the room and the sole items of value. They faced the bed atop the chest of drawers, perched side by side. When I saw them, I turned to Fu with an expression that asked: *Why?* She looked at me as if I had learned nothing about them in the past year. "We can't agree on what to watch!"

I imagined the two of them in bed at night, exhausted from the day's quarrels, each watching their own program on side-by-side televisions, volume at peak levels, letting the machines continue their ongoing yelling match.

It was late February 2013, the eighth day of the Year of the Horse. My bike ride down the Street of Eternal Happiness was cold, wet, and quiet—four days of freezing rain had kept the neighborhood shuttered indoors. The last time I saw Auntie Fu, she'd promised Gatewang would list on the London Stock Exchange by Chinese New Year. When she answered my knock on her door, I was too scared to ask. Instead, I handed her a crate of oranges and wished her a happy new year, condensed breath streaming from my mouth.

Inside, Uncle Feng dozed under layers of covers. We stepped around the bed and sat at the table. "It's Spring Festival! Eat!" Auntie Fu said, scooping up raw walnuts and squeezing them together with both hands, crushing their shells, letting the fragments fall to the floor.

Auntie Fu had spent the holiday handing out copies of the story of the Ecuadorean girl who had toured heaven and hell with Jesus. She said most people took the pamphlet, looked at it, and then threw it in the garbage. "I told them throwing it away was sinful," she said. "Some people told me they were Buddhists and I said this story has nothing to do with the sutras, but they could bring it home and decide which one makes more sense."

Uncle Feng sat upright in bed and groaned in his wife's direction. The two had been stuck inside for four days thanks to the rain. The air in the room was thick with the tense remnants of bickering matches, and they usually started this way: Auntie boasting about her good deeds, then Uncle pouncing on her for sounding self-righteous.

He shook his head, picked up a remote control, and aimed it at the pair of televisions three feet in front of him. The one on the left turned on. Uncle Feng shuffled through the channels: Sino-Japanese War docudrama, Qing dynasty–era soap opera, a documentary on Venus flytraps. He finally settled on an episode of *Journey to the West,* a popular show from the 1980s based on a Chinese classic novel about the adventures of a monk, a pig, and a warrior monkey on their quest to retrieve sacred Buddhist texts from India. It was my favorite program when I first came to China in the '90s, because no language skills were required to appreciate it—all you had to do was sit back and enjoy the hyperviolent kung fu battles, cheesy special effects, and a story line that seemed to be riding an acid trip. When I finally understood the dialogue years later, I realized it didn't matter. The show still didn't make much sense, but it sure was fun to watch.

"The *CCTV Gala* was terrible this year," Auntie Fu complained, shouting over a kung fu fight onscreen. "The worst I've seen!"

Watching the gala while making dumplings is a New Year's Eve tradition for tens of millions of Chinese—the program attracts more viewers than the Super Bowl—but this year's gala had been mired in controversy. Chinese rock musician Cui Jian had been invited to perform, but authorities withdrew the invitation when they learned he was only interested in playing one song: "Nothing to My Name," an anthem of the 1989 Tian'anmen Square protests.

Auntie Fu offered me some dried apricots. "They're from my sister in Xinjiang! They're not like the sour ones here in Shanghai. Food in Xinjiang is so much better than the food here," she said.

"Then why don't you move back?" snapped Uncle Feng without diverting his gaze from the television.

Auntie rolled her eyes. Onscreen, the monkey had escaped from the clutches of a pair of bandits. The animal swung from a tree branch and landed on the back of one of the men, twisting his neck until blood spurted from his mouth. He then grabbed the first bandit's saber and swung it at the second one, lopping his head off.

Auntie stuffed a dried apricot in her mouth and continued to reminisce. "Chinese New Year was much more festive in my hometown in Sichuan than it's ever been here," she told me. "We'd visit relatives and sit along the streets. We'd make dumplings, too."

"She doesn't know how to make dumplings. She's as stupid as a pig," Uncle snarled, turning to his wife. "If you liked it so much better back home, then why don't you leave?"

"Because I'd rather stay here with you! You are so great!" Auntie Fu said sarcastically. "You're so handsome! Are you the emperor? Are you that great? Why don't you look at yourself in the mirror?"

Uncle slowly rocked back and forth on the edge of the bed, annoyed, bathed in the flickering blue light of the onscreen action. The monk and the pig were scrambling to heal the monkey, whose face was glowing red and changing shape. The monk laid his hands on the monkey's forehead while reciting a Buddhist sutra, and the monkey returned to normal.

Auntie glared at her husband in disgust. "God teaches us not to hate people, but how can you not hate someone like him?"

In the couple of years I had known them, the only visits free of yelling matches were the rare instances when one of them was at home alone. When I first met the two, I suspected my presence heightened the abuse. But after spending time with each of them separately, I came to understand this was simply the only way they knew how to pass the time with each other, stubbornly trading barbs in a never-ending struggle session that had raged since the days of Mao.

Each thought the other was crazy. Uncle Feng thought his wife too lazy to find a job and hopelessly naïve with her get-rich-quick investments. Whenever he and I were alone in his kitchen, he complained about the money she had lost in investment scams, wondering when she would figure out there was no substitute to earning it through hard work. In turn, Auntie Fu saw her husband as a simpleton. She believed he was blind to the opportunities in twenty-first-century China. She thought he was a lousy businessman, unaware of the most basic negotiating tactics.

Auntie once told me about an apartment they bought for their son's wedding. Their daughter-in-law wasn't happy with the neighborhood—"too many migrants," she complained—and the newlyweds promptly moved out. Uncle sold the apartment for the equivalent of around a hundred thousand U.S. dollars, half of what Auntie Fu thought it was worth.

After days of yelling at each other about the matter—with nightly intermissions of dueling televisions—Auntie told me there was only one way to get the money back. "I had to sue someone," she told me over tea one day when Uncle Fu was gone. "So I sued the agency that represented the buyer. But the court ruled the agency did nothing wrong. The judge said the real issue was our domestic problems."

That was one perceptive judge, I thought.

"So now I'm suing my husband," Auntie Fu said. "The judge accepted the lawsuit. We've got a court date coming up soon."

I wasn't sure I'd heard her right. "Wait. You're suing your own husband?" I asked.

"Yes! All of this was his fault. There's something wrong with his head!"

"But what happens if you win? He pays you?" I asked.

"No, no, no," she said. "I'm suing the property management company that helped him sell it, too. But his name needs to be on the lawsuit, because it was his decision to sell it. I'm suing both of them. If I win, he won't have to pay me any money. It'll just show he was wrong."

Auntie could tell I was confused. She stood up and rummaged through a plastic grocery bag full of files, looking for the court documents.

I took a sip of tea and shook my head. I should've known their squabbling would spill over into the courts. Auntie found a manila folder and placed it in front of me. "After I lost the first case, he wasted all the money he made off the apartment and he bought another one for some woman from Anhui!" she yelled.

Had I not just swallowed my tea, I would have spit it all over her papers in disbelief.

"Wait a second. Why'd he do that? Who's this woman?" I asked.

Auntie told me that when Uncle returned from Xinjiang

twenty-five years ago, he said a thief had tried to rob him in a train station on his way to Shanghai. A woman and her husband had helped him, he said, and after all these years, he had decided to return the favor by buying the woman a home.

"I told him he was right in returning the favor," Auntie told me, "but he didn't have to go and buy an apartment for her! Even the stupidest person in China wouldn't do that! I was so mad."

The story sounded implausible—a spectacularly bad lie. I let her finish.

"I finally called the police, and they interrogated her," she said.

Auntie fished out the police report from her folder, and we read it together. On May 5, 2011, police had interviewed a divorced woman from Anhui province named Bu. Bu confirmed that Uncle Feng had bought her an apartment in Shanghai and that her name was on the ownership certificate. According to the transcript, Bu was fifteen years younger than Uncle. She said she had known him for many years and that when she divorced her husband in Anhui and moved to Shanghai in 2010, Uncle felt sorry for her and proposed to buy a house where she and her two daughters could live comfortably. In return, Bu told police she had agreed to be Uncle and Auntie's caregiver when the couple grew too old to manage themselves.

I gently placed the report on the table, trying to make sense of it all.

"Do you think she's telling the truth?" I asked carefully.

"Of course not! She's from Anhui!" Fu said.

Urbanites often blamed outsiders for the problems that plagued city life—and not just outsiders in general, but specific ones. People in Beijing found their scapegoats among the migrants from Henan, one of China's poorest and most populous provinces. For residents of Shanghai, the people from Anhui, a poor, mountainous province within a day's drive of the city, were usually blamed for much of the lying, cheating, and stealing that happened within city limits.

"You're a foreigner. You don't understand. They're just bad people," my Mandarin tutor once told me when I questioned the stereotype.

But Auntie learned not everyone from Anhui was bad. She had

filed a lawsuit in a local court against Bu for tricking Uncle into buying her an apartment. The Anhui judge agreed and ruled in Auntie's favor. But Uncle refused to sign the verdict, and the house remained in Bu's possession.

"My husband isn't a bad person, but he's prone to being used and tempted by others," Auntie told me as I examined the court documents.

It was one of the nicest things I had ever heard her say about her husband.

"He really is a good person, but his mind is slow and he has a hard time figuring out whom he should trust," she said with a sigh.

Auntie put the court documents and police report back into the manila folder and walked across the room to place it into one of the dozens of boxes scattered around the tiny apartment.

"Perhaps I've sinned too much," she said, sitting back down again. "That must be why God is making me suffer so."

Auntie didn't know where else to look for an answer to why her life had descended into such chaos. There wasn't much to say other than a phrase in Chinese that seemed made for situations like this. "Luanqibazao," I said under my breath.

Auntie nodded quietly. It was a saying that described a circumstance where everything was in disorder, a hideous mess of a situation. And in a land of constant change, luanqibazao was often used to describe the indescribable clutter that had arisen from all this chaos.

Auntie didn't seem eager to seek order from the mess her husband was in. Maybe Uncle really was paying the woman from Anhui back for help two decades ago. The more likely conclusion, though, was that she was his mistress. Auntie wasn't interested in parsing out the details. The only thing that mattered to her was the money. Uncle had given away a valuable home meant for their son and their future grandchildren, and her friends and family had lent her tens of thousands of yuan so that she could afford the legal fees to try to get it back. "That's why I've been involved in all of these investments," she explained. "I've got to find a way to pay back all this debt."

THE CREDITS for *Journey to the West* rolled across Uncle's television. He turned it off, got up from the bed, said goodbye to me, and left with his bicycle.

"Always going out to play," Auntie muttered after he had shut the door.

It seemed like a good time to ask her about Gatewang. "Auntie, it's February already. Did Gatewang list on the London exchange?" I asked.

She stood up and began to tidy up the table, clearing it of walnut shells, distracting herself. "They originally told me January, but we're going to have to wait until March now," she said, pushing the fragments into her other hand. "They must want to wait until after the Chinese New Year," she guessed, keeping the tone upbeat.

"I'm not afraid, though," she said. "This is sure to bring money. The other company I invested in will get listed in March, too, so it'll be a good month for me."

Uh-oh. "What other company?"

Fu reached over to a manila folder and fished out a business card. The company's name was Liaoning Dingxu. Liaoning was a province in Northeastern China. *Dingxu* meant "Era of the Dawn." The two characters for *Dingxu* made up the first words of a poem scrawled atop a photo of a field of verdant green rice shoots on the business card. It read:

WEIGHTY CREDIBILITY IS GOLDEN,
THE SUNRISE SHINES OVER HEAVEN AND EARTH.

"What kind of company is this?" I asked.

"They grow mushrooms. The government gave them thousands of acres of land. They're going to get listed on NASDAQ in March."

I flipped the card over. Characters on the back of it promised "Investing in Dingxu's original shares will quickly multiply your wealth."

"The company organized a trip for eight of us investors from Shanghai so that we could inspect the operations," Fu told me with a touch of pride at being important enough to be invited on an inspection tour.

It was the first time Fu had ever flown on a plane. She was so impressed with Liaoning Dingxu's operations that before she boarded the flight back to Shanghai, she handed over the renminbi equivalent of fifteen thousand U.S. dollars in cash to company officials as an initial investment. She told me she had borrowed much of it from her son.

I began to voice a word of caution, but she was used to my warnings and she reassured me it was a safe bet before I could say anything.

"Don't worry. A lot of others invested, too. We all signed contracts with the company. There's zero risk!" she said with a smile, repeating the familiar phrase as if she needed to convince herself. "*Zero* risk."

RISK WAS THE ONE THING people of Uncle and Auntie's generation had learned to try to avoid, and yet most had not.

Many of their lives had been ruined serving as human guinea pigs for Mao's riskiest political and economic campaigns to reshape China. After those policies failed, they left their revolutionary roles in the countryside to rejoin civilian life in urban centers, where the rules suddenly changed. The revolution was over, capitalism was the new way of life, and risk—the thing they had come to fear most—crept back into their everyday lives.

The 156 million Chinese born in the ten-year period after the 1949 Communist Revolution were dubbed the Lost Generation. They didn't have much of a childhood, a family, or an education, and the experience had left them without the skills needed to succeed in this new China.

A prominent member of this generation summed the experience up in an interview on CCTV: "In the past when we talked about beliefs, it was very abstract . . . but it was emotional. It was a mood. And when the ideals of the Cultural Revolution could not be realized, it proved to be an illusion."

It was 2003, and the disillusioned interviewee was future president Xi Jinping. He was among a select group of his cohort who had flourished after the dust settled, thanks to having relatives within the Party leadership ranks.

But most weren't fortunate enough to ascend the Party's political ladder, and their lives had become a quest for order and stability. Their prime working years were spent serving the Party—sent off to the countryside like CK's parents, to a labor camp like Wang Ming, or to China's Western frontier like Auntie Fu and Uncle Feng—where one of the few lessons they'd learned was how to survive, while they had witnessed friends and family suffer and die. The trauma of the period's political turmoil was embedded in their psyche like the nightmares that haunt soldiers who have returned from war.

The Chinese I know between the ages of fifty-five and seventy appear to be normal retirees, but there's a thick layer of resentment just beneath that surface. All those years spent devoting themselves to the ideals of selflessness and egalitarianism have made them cynical about the rampant inequality plaguing China today. Their peers who have become rich and powerful are typically the most corrupt. They are those who had gotten to their positions of power through the same vicious and duplicitous tactics they had exercised as Red Guards in the 1960s: bullying their superiors and snitching on their friends. The generation's majority, though, have remained frustrated and poor, and they aren't afraid to speak out against the great injustice.

Those of the Lost Generation to whom I had become close all seemed to be going it alone, without much guidance. They had missed out on a formal education and the positive role models that come with that. This had forced them to become stubbornly independent in their actions, and it also meant they seemed perpetually at risk of making big mistakes. This was certainly true of Uncle and Auntie, and it was also a problem I saw with Mayor Chen and his wife, Xie, in Maggie Lane, who refused to compromise their quixotic mission to conquer the corruption of local officials, restore justice to their slice of China, and remain living in their home, happily ever after.

As their best-connected peer put it, their young lives had served an illusion. In their old age, many of them had pursued new illusions, ones that were less naïve. They might be out of reach in the system they lived under, but they were legally guarded rights elsewhere in the world. They were pursuits like investing in a trustworthy company, owning property, and realizing a national dream that strove to make everyone equal.

THE INFOMERCIAL BEGAN with a barrage of statistics: A quarter of all men have problems getting an erection. Half of all women suffer from low sex drive. Two out of every three men catch venereal diseases. The numbers flashed across the screen, superimposed on scenes of a middle-aged woman crying into a tissue and a forlorn man moping around his dimly lit home. The numbers didn't stop: More than half of all marriages end in divorce. Three out of every four divorces are caused by a lack of sexual harmony. Next, scenes of smokestacks and people shuffling down a smoggy street wearing air masks. China's worsening environment and the pressures of everyday life, announced a booming voice in Mandarin, are ruining your sex life. Auntie Fu's next investment opportunity promised to solve all these problems.

Over the phone, she insisted I attend. After watching her sink her pension into Gatewang and the mushroom company, I felt protective, so I tagged along. We met up at an abandoned, bankrupt shopping mall on Shanghai's outskirts. Inside, garbage piled up against empty storefronts. Escalators lining the empty three-story atrium were frozen in place. The elevators worked, so we took one to the top floor. As it lurched upward, I began to wonder what she had gotten herself into. Over the phone she said it was an investment meeting for a health product: "A big opportunity!" she gushed. But I felt nervous. What kind of company has its office in a dark, abandoned mall?

A loud *ding,* and the elevator doors opened to a dark hallway lined with construction scrap. We used the light from our cellphones to guide us to the only sign of electricity: a partially opened door to a lit office.

As my eyes adjusted, I made out a muscular middle-aged bald man extending his arm toward me. "Our esteemed visitor!" he boomed in Chinese, shaking my hand vigorously.

"See who I've brought?" said Fu, nudging him with her elbow. "A real American journalist!"

"A foreign guest! And he can speak Chinese! *Wah!*" exclaimed the man. "*Ayi,* your connections are far and wide!"

The bald man's name was Xue. He was a retired army helicopter pilot from Sichuan. He looked like a Chinese version of Mr. Clean: shaved head, bull neck, and a tight white T-shirt. He appeared calm at first, but after he began to speak, I noticed the left side of his face contorted every ten seconds or so, a facial tic that distracted from his pitch.

Behind him, seven seniors—all potential investors—lounged on black leather chairs around a long wooden table that faced a flat-screen television. On the opposite end hung a framed Chinese calligraphy painting penned by former president Hu Jintao. The characters read: "Be Honest."

"This is what we're selling," said Mr. Clean, shoving a box into my hands before turning to face the others. "It's a great product, for both men and women. It's now available in forty countries around the world."

He paused to pivot in my direction: "Including America."

Heads nodded around the table. I examined the box. "Personal Ecological Care" was written in English below a large photo of a buff white model with his shirt open a couple of buttons. He looked like an older, more mature version of tennis star Novak Djokovic, with salt-and-pepper-colored hair. Below him, an English description of the product:

CREATING POWERFUL DETOXIFYING, CONFIDENT LIFE
GET RIT OF TOXINS, BEAUTIFUL APPEARANCE

The Chinese description was less baffling: Each box contained thirty pads saturated with traditional Chinese medicine. You affixed them to the inside of your underwear. Within days, it promised to detoxify your body and restore a youthful sex life. The Chinese name of the product was *Lian Zhi Yang*, "Nurturing Lotus," and a company named Golden Days International made it.

Mr. Clean turned on the television.

The narrator of the Nurturing Lotus infomercial had a smooth, powerful voice packed with emotion. At the end of each sentence, he sounded as if he were on the brink of orgasm. In my fifteen years in radio, I hadn't heard a voice-over actor who commanded an audience quite like this. "Nurturing Lotus pads," he crooned, "are *infused* . . . with thirty . . . *different* . . . kinds . . . *of* . . . *HERBS!*"

"But *none* more important," announced the host, "than *Saussurea involucrate, a flower* . . . that *grows* . . . in the *remote mountains* . . . *of* . . . *XINJIANG!*"

Auntie elbowed me excitedly. Never had her Xinjiang sounded so mind-blowing. I looked around the room. The other seniors sat up straight, alert, smiling.

"It *warms* the uterus," the host said in a sultry voice, "*stimulating* menstrual flow . . . *con-tracting* the uterus!

"In *men* . . . it *stimulates* . . . *libido!* It cures *im-po-tence* . . . and *prevents* . . . *VENEREAL DISEASE!*"

Onscreen, an image of a hand stamping the Nurturing Lotus's patent with the words *United States of America* dissolved into a scene of Chinese technicians in lab coats jumping up and down, cheering, high-fiving one another.

The infomercial's final scene was of a woman, stretching her arms out, head tilted back, as rain poured down, soaking her, purifying her, ridding her of all her toxins. "Your . . . *sexual* . . . *health* . . . *is* . . . *RE* . . . *STORED!*" the host bellowed, gushing one last time.

"That's it," said Mr. Clean, turning the television off. "The company's global headquarters are in Singapore. That country's president and first lady are using the products," he claimed.

Auntie took a box and removed one of the individually wrapped pads. "Heavenly Happiness" was written across the wrapper. She opened it and removed a white pad that smelled like a cross between Tiger Balm and rotting fruit.

"You put this in your underwear!" she said, giggling. "You peel off the back and stick it to the bottom so that it's touching your little brother!"

The rest of the room erupted in laughter at Auntie's vernacular.

"I've used them for a few days now," Auntie announced. "They really work!"

I paused. I thought about Auntie and Uncle's deteriorating relationship. I thought about their separate televisions, and their separate lives. I began to wonder how, exactly, her sex life had improved. Then I shuddered a little and stopped thinking about that.

Mr. Clean handed me a folder. Inside were dozens of photos. Everyone in the room huddled around me as I examined them. The first one was labeled "Male's Heavenly Happiness Pad after First Use," and it showed a pad filled with a discharge that bore a resemblance to blackberry jelly.

"Wah!" Auntie shouted while we all stared at it together.

"What's that?" I asked, pointing at the black jelly.

"Toxic discharge!" shouted Mr. Clean from the other side of the room.

I winced. "You mean this came out of his . . ."

"Yes! His little brother!"

More laughter. People passed around the photo, impressed with Heavenly Happiness's results. It looked more like Hellish Misery.

The Chinese typically weren't squeamish about bodily discharges. The gory images of bodies mangled in traffic accidents were commonplace on local television news, and I had once been treated at a hospital that, in its waiting room, displayed a series of gruesome photos of a farmer who had managed to impale his skull with a steel pole. A poster described how the hospital's talented team of doctors had successfully treated the unfortunate man.

Mr. Clean passed the photo back to me and I glanced at it again.

"That's just awful," I said.

"It's not painful at all," said Fu. "It feels nice and cool. It begins to take effect after just ten minutes!"

I looked at the other photos spread across the table. Brown, black, and yellow discharge covered an array of Heavenly Happiness pads. One photo of a pad covered in dried blood claimed to have been from a woman who had gone through menopause. She was now menstruating again, thanks to the wonders of Nurturing Lotus.

Mr. Clean put his hand on my shoulder. "Here," he said, giving me a Heavenly Happiness package. "The restroom's down the hall. Go put one inside your underwear."

I reflexively crossed my legs. "Um . . . no, thanks," I said.

Mr. Clean's facial tic fired once more before turning into a frown. "I've used them for two months. They're very comfortable. You won't feel a thing."

I shook my head.

"It'll boost your sex drive!" Mr. Clean assured me, smiling. "You're a journalist, right? You should try it so that you can report on it from your own personal experience."

"I report on China's economy, not on sexual health pads," I said firmly.

"Then maybe you can report on my husband's other company," said Mr. Clean's wife. "He's the CEO of a helicopter business. In ten years, everyone will be riding around in helicopters! There's an eighty percent chance of it getting launched," she said confidently.

Mr. Clean nodded. I glanced over at him and imagined what his life must be like: one day recruiting people to sell underwear pads, the next day, selling shares of his commuter-helicopter scheme to poor people.

I looked around the table at the others—all of them were retirees like Fu. They spent their days in and out of investment meetings like this, trading secrets, championing their favorite merchandise, recruiting one another, receiving and delivering sales pitches for products that were too good to be true. One day they were predators, the next, prey; selling and buying from each other, spinning and spinning until hunter and the hunted had circled one another so many times they could no longer recognize which side they were on, only knowing they were all in this together, a human pyramid, bound by the force of *guanxi*.

I picked up a box of Heavenly Happiness and turned to Mr. Clean. "So how much do these cost?"

"Three hundred and ninety-eight renminbi for a box with twenty pads," he replied.

I did the math. It was equal to $75, nearly $4 a pad. Uncle Feng would have to sell 150 scallion pancakes to afford a box.

"That sounds expensive," I said.

"It's a very good deal," Mr. Clean said with a serious face. "And if you sell these, you'll make a lot of money. Once someone tries it, they keep buying them."

I looked at the photos spread across the table and tried to fathom why someone would keep buying a product that triggered uncontrollable discharge and made your underwear look like a soiled diaper.

Mr. Clean sensed my skepticism, and his face twitched. "Once you stop using these pads, you begin to feel very uncomfortable," he said with a facial tic wink. "Before you know it, you feel like you can't live without them, and you'll always come back for more."

He picked up a black dry erase marker. He began writing numbers on a whiteboard next to the television. It cost ¥4,000—around $700—for a membership that included fifteen boxes of pads. After I sold those, he said, I would get half off my second order. Once the discount kicked in, he said, I would have a ¥200 profit on each package of Heavenly Happiness I sold.

Auntie ran the numbers for me. "That's a forty-five-percent profit!"

Mr. Clean nodded. "It's that simple," he said.

"What if I recruit other people to sell boxes of this?" I asked, playing along.

Mr. Clean's face twitched with excitement. "And with your connections abroad, I'm sure you will!"

He turned to the board and scribbled more numbers. "If you find someone to help sell, you get a 'first generation income,' which is 25 percent of your friend's sales. And let's say he finds others to sell the pads, too. Then you'd get 'second generation income' of 15 percent, and it goes on to 10 percent of third generation, and then it's 9.5 percent extending to the tenth generation. Just follow me here, and I'll explain how it all works."

Mr. Clean feverishly covered the whiteboard with dots and then turned to us. "You see this?" he asked.

We nodded.

"Now watch," he said.

He turned around and drew lines connecting the dots, filling the board with small triangles, his face twitching more rapidly. He then connected all the triangles, and turned to us, out of breath. On the board, the shape was clear.

"This," said Mr. Clean, "is a pyramid."

I looked over at Auntie. She smiled at me, and motioned to the whiteboard.

Mr. Clean continued, pointing his marker at me. "Let me ask you something. Would you rather I give you one million renminbi after a month's time, or I give you one renminbi the first day of the month and then multiply it by two each day after? Which would you choose?"

I played dumb. "I think I'd take the one million," I said.

Auntie couldn't contain herself and let out a snort of laughter.

"Okay," laughed Mr. Clean. "You take that and I'll take the one-renminbi option. Let's see who made the right decision. The first day I get one yuan; the second day, two; the third day, four; the fourth day, sixteen . . ."

Mr. Clean scrawled the numbers furiously while the rest of the room chanted the calculations in unison. "Then 4,096! Then 8,192! Then 16,394! Then 32,768!"

By day 25, Auntie was slapping her knee excitedly as Mr. Clean again took over the chanting, his booming voice overpowering the room. "Then it's over two hundred million! And on day thirty it's over five hundred million! *Wah!* But you," he said, pausing to take a breath, "only get one million. You see? That's how our sales work!"

It was a neat multiplication game, but sales didn't work that way, particularly sales of overpriced Chinese medicinal sexual health pads.

"How many people have you recruited?" I asked Mr. Clean.

His face twitched a little as he considered an answer. "Five or six," he said.

"How long have you been selling these pads?" I asked.

"Three months," he answered.

Auntie put her hand on my knee. "A friend of his from Wenzhou recruited him to sell these here in Shanghai!" she said.

Of course, I thought: a Wenzhou connection. "How much have you made?" I asked Mr. Clean.

"I've just started!" said Mr. Clean, forcing a smile. "Plus, I'm also preparing to start my helicopter company, so I've been busy with that."

One of the women in the room stepped forward. She was in her eighties, and before the infomercial began, she told me she had made so much from investments like this that she could afford to send her granddaughter to a university in Australia. She put her hand on my shoulder, sensing the conversation had gotten off topic.

"*Aiya!* You journalists don't make much money, right? How much do you make? Not a lot. Only businesspeople make a lot of money. Selling these pads could help you earn some extra income."

Auntie nodded. "They'll give you a trial box that you can share with your friends. If they like it, then come back and ask for more."

"Bring this product back home to the United States," urged the old woman.

"But I thought you said you're already selling them in America," I said.

"She's just asking you to help promote the product there," assured Auntie.

Mr. Clean stepped in. "We'll help you connect with the company to discuss how to bring it to the American market."

The old woman touched my hand. "It's a good opportunity,"

she told me, patting my arm. "We're honest people. We would never cheat others."

"157 SENIORS IN NINGBO Have Their Investment Dreams Smashed, Over RMB 12 Million in Pensions Poured Down the Drain."

This headline was the first to appear on a Chinese search engine after I typed in "Liaoning Dingxu," the name of the mushroom company into which Auntie Fu had poured much of her pension. "More than 100 Ningbo seniors are suspected to be mired in a Ponzi scheme," began the article in the *Southeastern Business Report* of May 15, 2014.

The article claimed Liaoning Dingxu had drawn capital from all over China. Its target investors were Chinese in their seventies and eighties.

The city of Ningbo was just two hours south of Shanghai. I wondered if the perpetrators there were the same ones who had flown Auntie to the company's mushroom farm and taken her fifteen thousand yuan.

The company's CEO had been arrested along with two others at the Ningbo branch office. They were charged with stealing millions of dollars from 157 seniors, some who had invested their entire pensions into the company. The suspects had convinced the seniors they would earn an annual interest of 15 percent on their investments once the company was listed on NASDAQ.

Separate articles had reported the company was on the verge of bankruptcy. The *Liaoning Evening News* had discovered the greenhouses supposedly growing mushrooms—the same ones Fu had toured—were a façade, and had actually been rented out to local farmers who didn't work for the company.

According to the article from Ningbo, the seniors who lost their pensions refused to believe they had been tricked. "Despite the fact that the case was nearing the sentencing period," read the report, "several investors still wanted to discuss the U.S. listing with the defendants."

The judge in the case was astonished. Prior to sentencing the defendants to prison, he took one last look at the conned investors assembled in his courtroom and asked them, incredulously: "Do you still believe the company will get listed?"

He then uttered a traditional Chinese saying, called a *chengyu*, from the bench—*"Ku xiao bu de"*—*I don't know whether to laugh or cry.*

IT WAS IMPOSSIBLE to know how many people in China had fallen victim to investment scams. The government didn't keep track of these sorts of things. Both companies Auntie Fu had bought shares in—Gatewang and Liaoning Dingxu—had promised listings on reputable stock exchanges in the West. At the time, several Chinese companies were listing on NASDAQ and the New York and London Stock Exchanges to great media fanfare.

When it came to pyramid schemes like Nurturing Lotus, China's government had a little more experience. In 2014, China's State Administration for Industry and Commerce allowed forty-nine companies to legally participate in direct sales, the selling and marketing of a company's products between individuals instead of through fixed retail locations, as long as those companies and their army of *laobaixing* salespeople agreed to follow Chinese laws. The forty-nine included foreign ones like Amway, Avon, and Herbalife. Unsurprisingly, Nurturing Lotus didn't make the official list and was therefore an illegal operation. But even for the companies on the list, there were problems. More than a few had been venturing into the recruitment and brainwashing techniques typical of pyramid schemes.

As one scholar who studied pyramid schemes in China put it, China's Communist Party has always kept a close watch on these direct sales networks for good reason. "The growth of [these] grassroots networks is very similar in some ways to the Party's own early organization and its early fervor. They harken back to the sects and cults that have traditionally thrived in the Chinese countryside, where the Party once found its most zealous supporters."

That's why I worried about Auntie Fu. She had grown up an

uneducated peasant in the mountains of Sichuan. She was recruited by the Party to farm a desert in Xinjiang. Then she followed her husband across the country to the wilds of Shanghai, a place where money seemed to be everywhere besides her own pocketbook.

Like so many people of her generation, she didn't know how to make money in this new China, so she gravitated toward what was familiar to her from the Mao years: a smiling recruiter promising a path to happiness and prosperity. And, just as a wide-eyed village girl was an ideal convert for Party recruiters in the 1960s, a poor elderly woman with little education and no access to the Internet was even easier prey for scam artists in twenty-first-century Shanghai.

THERE WERE NO DECORATIONS in Auntie Fu and Uncle Feng's spartan room, save a poster of a Renaissance painting above their bed. The winged man in the painting appeared to be the Roman god Saturn. In one hand, he carried a nude woman and was poised to fly off with her. In the other, he gripped a sickle, using it to jab a man who was languishing on the ground.

"Why do you have that painting on the wall?" I asked the two.

I'd stopped by to have a heart-to-heart with Auntie about her investments after what I had found out about Liaoning Dingxu, but Uncle had been at home alone. When Auntie finally showed up, they started bickering. I needed a diversion.

"It's from Germany," Uncle said. "It's an ancient painting. It's depicting history. It's about the feudal society."

I wasn't sure how he had come to this conclusion. Maybe it was the sickle the winged man was holding. Maybe it was the pastoral background. Auntie didn't believe him, either.

"History? What do you know?" she said. "They're not even dressed properly. How can you call that history? You're talking like Chairman Mao! Feudal society! Class struggle! Aiya."

"You don't understand anything," Uncle shot back. "You're talking nonsense."

"Mao was evil and cruel," Auntie said to her husband.

"You can't say he's evil," he said, glancing in my direction. "He was just following a different path."

"He killed my father. He killed my uncle too, just because he graduated from a Kuomintang school. They were both innocent," Auntie said. "Now all I've got left is one uncle who is barely surviving."

"Then why don't you go and visit him and share all that money you must be making from all those investments of yours!" shouted Uncle.

"I will when I'm through with this lawsuit," she said.

"You and your stupid lawsuit!" Uncle shouted. "What the hell is the matter with you, filing a lawsuit! If it weren't for me, you'd still be poor, toiling away in Xinjiang."

"The air in Xinjiang is good!" Auntie screamed. "The food is safe. Everything's cheaper! The climate is cool in the summer and warm in the winter. Where else can you find such a place where life is like heaven?" she asked.

"Then go back!" shouted Feng.

You just watch, old man, I thought to myself, *she will.* For Auntie Fu, Xinjiang represented a time in her life when she was happy, when life was simple. She didn't live in a cold, dark hovel in Xinjiang, and she wasn't in debt. There wasn't a mistress in Xinjiang, and Auntie wasn't driven by greed or revenge.

Auntie Fu pointed to Uncle's back. "You want me gone so that you can do bad things while I'm away!"

She turned to me. "The only reason we're in Shanghai is because of our children. The education system is better here, but everything else is better in Xinjiang."

"Oh! It was for the children!" mocked Uncle. "How much money did you give the children? Did you buy a house for them? No! I'm the only one who helps them. All your money has been cheated away! You buy health products and other garbage and now you're spending money on a lawsuit? What bullshit!"

I stood up to leave in the most polite way I knew.

"I've really got to go," I stammered, looking at my phone. Auntie's face was red with anger, her ears deaf to my departure notice.

She grabbed my arm, stopping me. "Remember when I told you about how he forced me to come home to give birth in Shanghai? Remember that?"

I remembered. She had told me the story the day we met. We were in the middle of the underground church service; the rest of the congregation was singing a hymn. I had been struck by how her story—departing Xinjiang to give birth in her husband's ancestral home—was similar to the story of Mary and Joseph, leaving for Bethlehem to comply with the Roman census. Instead of giving birth in a manger, Auntie Fu had gone into labor on a bus in the middle of the desert and disembarked to give birth to her son at a run-down clinic. Afterward, she had suffered from complications of the birth and a doctor had introduced her to the teachings of Christ.

"Yes, I remember," I said.

Auntie Fu wiped her eyes and took a breath. "That son died," she said.

Uncle looked up from his television and glared at his wife.

She pointed to her husband. "*His* mother took our son to Anhui with her. One day he drowned in the river. He was studying to be a doctor at the Shanghai Medicine University. It was 1990. He had just turned eighteen. His mother brought him to Anhui, and he died in the river, just like that."

I sat back down and braced for another fight, but the two fell silent, leaving the voices of the doctors on Uncle's health program to fill the cold, dark room.

Three long minutes later, Auntie grabbed a bag of dried fruit from her cupboard, opened it, and offered me some. "Have an apricot," she said with a soft smile.

I took one and looked at Uncle Feng. He stared into his television, listless. He didn't say another word.

12

Country Wedding

长乐路109号

Street of Eternal Happiness, No. 109

For much of Zhao Shiling's adult life, the trip from her flower shop on the Street of Eternal Happiness to her hometown in Shandong province took 13 hours. Then, on the afternoon of July 1, 2011, a high-speed rail line appeared. What used to be a slow, bumpy overnight journey on a rickety sleeper bus suddenly became a 3-hour, 200-mile-per-hour jaunt on a bullet train gliding so smoothly above the rice paddies of the Yangtze Delta that you could stroll from the dining car back to your plush window seat without spilling a drop of your latte.

I took a sip and looked out the window at the Chinese countryside. It soared past so quickly it was difficult to focus on anything for more than a second or two. Before China built high-speed rail, a train ride was ideal for contemplation. I would often stare out an open window watching people work, and sometimes they would notice the foreigner and wave with a smile as the train crawled past. I would stick my head out, take a deep breath of country air, and wave back. I would think about the work they would have to do before the sun went down. I would think about their children who were studying at the village school, and I would imagine the life they led out here in the spaces in between. The sealed vestibule of a speeding bullet train offered no such opportunity for contemplation. You no longer breathed the same air as the villagers; there was no longer time to inspect a river gorge from the bridge above. These days, a train ride in China was spent engrossed in a movie on a tablet or checking email on your phone. If you were bored enough to have a look outside, the instant your eyes managed to focus on a farmer hoeing his field, he was gone.

It was as if he and the countryside he tilled had never existed.

IT WAS MAY DAY, a five-day holiday, and when I stepped off the train at Zaozhuang Station, I climbed a broken escalator to the ground level where Zhao and her youngest son were waiting. It would be the last time I would be allowed to touch my suitcase. "Give it to me! Hand it over!" shouted Little Sun, wresting the bag from my hands and hoisting it into a cab.

I barely recognized Zhao. The return-to-the-village uniform of two decades ago—a blue factory jumpsuit—was now a stylish formal dress decorated with flowers, hair styled with curls that graced her bare shoulders, topped off with mascara, lipstick, jewelry, and a sun hat.

Zhao was dressed for a wedding, but not the one we were there to attend. Her nephew was to be married the following day in the countryside, yet she had come with a mission to arrange her eldest son's marriage with a local girl. In a land of floating lives and families scattered to the cities to work, a hometown wedding was no longer about the bride and groom. It had become an event where family business was conducted, marriages arranged, and futures planned.

"I can't believe you're here!" Zhao shouted, touching my arm.

"When I told my nephew you were coming to his wedding, he was thrilled. Out here, we only see foreigners on television!"

Zaozhuang looked smoggy and flat, and construction cranes towered over the skyline. Some cities in China are celebrated for local cuisine. Others are known for their ancient cultural sites. Zaozhuang draws its fame from fighting. This part of China is flat and green—fish and rice country, the Chinese call it—but its fertile plains are prone to devastating droughts. Weishan Lake, the local source of water, forms the midsection to China's ancient Grand Canal, a waterway constructed fifteen hundred years ago. It makes up the border between Shandong, Anhui, and Jiangsu provinces, and tens of millions of people depend on it for their livelihoods. During dry spells, Zaozhuang's men often wage water wars against their neighbors. In the last sixty years, there have been more than four hundred recorded cases of cross-border conflicts over Weishan Lake. Hundreds of local men have been killed or injured.

The lake wasn't the only thing the men of Zaozhuang shed blood for. During the Japanese invasion in the late 1930s, a local team of guerrilla fighters—farmers and workers from the surrounding coal mines—became national heroes after they launched a series of raids on the invaders, killing enemy soldiers and taking control of their trains to steal guns and explosives.

The city had a bloodstained history, and the more I learned about it, the more I realized that Zhao's stories about the lawlessness back in her hometown weren't exaggerations. Zaozhuang's men had never been ones to turn down a good fight.

Zhao hoped Big Sun would make a life here. For his future family, she had bought an apartment on the twenty-first floor of a building named People's Harmony Park. It was one of the tallest high-rises in the city, and it was next to Zaozhuang's biggest tourist attraction: the Railway Guerrilla Memorial Museum. "There it is!" said Zhao, pointing out her open cab window at a building that looked like a castle. "I'm renting it out now, but someday Big Sun will move there."

The only thing missing was a wife. Zhao pulled her arm back inside the car, slunk into her seat, placed her hat in her lap, and closed her eyes, exhaling hard, letting the warm spring air blow through her hair. She had prepared for this weekend for more than a year. Ever since Big Sun had dropped out of high school and returned to her flower shop, Zhao had felt responsible for his path in life. Now it was time to help him find a wife, and this was the closest she had ever come. Big Sun and the girl had even struck up a friendship over WeChat, texting each other each day leading up to this weekend.

"They met for lunch today," Zhao said, her eyes still closed. "She's very pretty."

Until today, all she had to go on was the girl's profile photo on WeChat—the one where half her face was covered with a Hello Kitty air mask.

"He's meeting with her parents and relatives now," she said, sounding a little worried. "They don't seem to be very happy that Big Sun is a hairdresser. That's not a popular job in my hometown. They don't think his income will be very high."

They were right, of course, but their daughter's income wasn't high either. She made the equivalent of $150 a month managing the warehouse of a grocery store, and she had no desire to leave her hometown for better pay. After they married, Big Sun would be forced to return here to find work, and his options would be limited. He was naturally smart, but he had dropped out of high school and his work experience was limited to a golf course and a hair salon. Most jobs in Zaozhuang were at the coal mine, in the wheat fields, or in construction, but Big Sun shunned manual labor. Zhao worried what the girl's parents would think about that, and she hoped the apartment at People's Harmony Park would sweeten the deal. "In our village, there's a saying," Zhao said from the front seat: " 'You can only catch a bird after you buy a cage.' "

Zhao had another cage. It was a spacious flat on the seventeenth floor of a blue-and-white-tiled building rising from a lush green grid of wheat and corn on the outskirts of town. When we arrived there, the bird—Zhao's daughter-in-law Zhang Min, the wife of Little Sun—had flown off to accompany her hapless brother-in-law in his meeting with the Hello Kitty girl. Big Sun had gotten himself lost trying to find the girl's home and had made an emergency call. "*Aiya!* He doesn't even know how to chase a girl!" lamented Zhao when she heard the story.

The apartment was an empty concrete shell. After Zhao bought it for Little Sun and Zhang Min, the couple had married, left for Shanghai to work, and had a son in such quick succession that they had never gotten around to decorating it. Someday when they had made all they could in Shanghai, they would return to settle down here with their little boy, Shuo Shuo. When Zhao retired, the third bedroom would be hers.

Little Sun picked up the two-year-old Shuo Shuo and gave me a tour. It was around a thousand square feet—large by Chinese standards—and had three bedrooms. The living room window overlooked a large courtyard with a basketball court and a man-made creek filled with boulders. Below, teenagers were shooting hoops, and young boys were molding their own mini-river, corralling a trickle of water from a leaky fire hydrant. "I can picture Shuo Shuo playing down there," said Little Sun, smiling in the sunlight.

Whenever I saw him at his mother's flower shop on the Street of Eternal Happiness, Little Sun was in between work shifts and he usually looked depressed and stressed out. But in Zaozhuang holding his young son, he was relaxed, optimistic, and happy. He was home.

His big brother, on the other hand, had needed a tour guide for his own hometown. When Big Sun and Zhang Min arrived fresh from his meeting with his future in-laws, he still looked lost. He saw me and murmured a "*Ni Hao,*" briefly glancing my way before fixing his defeated gaze onto the floor. He had dressed in a paisley shirt and carefully ripped black jeans for the occasion.

"How'd it go?" I asked.

"I don't know," he moaned. "We were supposed to have lunch, but that didn't happen. Having lunch is a sign her parents have accepted me into the family. Instead we just sat there and talked nonsense. Now I have to wait for them to let me know."

Big Sun had brought a get-well gift—a basket of fruit—for Hello Kitty's father, who was recuperating from surgery. It was a gesture Zhao saw as courteous and filial but that the girl's family had interpreted as too forward a step in the delicate dance of countryside courtship. Her parents had acted as if accepting the gift from this slick urbanite meant they approved of him as their daughter's future husband. Zhao and Big Sun simply thought it was customary. It was a cultural misunderstanding between city and country. For rural folks, a gift was never just a gift. It was a debt that needed to be repaid. As Zhao thought to herself about what to do next, I thought about how she and her son seemed out of touch with their hometown's customs.

Zhao looked up. "Where is she now?" she asked Big Sun.

"She's at work at the grocery store," he said with a sigh.

Zhao stood still and stared sideways in deep concentration. There was only a day left to finish this. Where her son saw a dark pit of hopelessness, Zhao saw opportunity.

Ten minutes later, the entire family was outside the grocery store, demanding to talk to the girl. Big Sun and his mother stepped up to the warehouse door at the back of the store. The rest of us retreated half a block away, trying to look inconspicuous. But the presence of a foreigner this far afield from the big city began attracting a throng of onlookers. "*Laowai!*" someone yelled: *Foreigner!* and then there were more yells.

Zhao nodded her head, and Big Sun knocked. Zhao walked away to join us down the street. She had done all she could. Her son would have to take it from here.

More people stared at me. On the street, rubberneckers in their cars stopped; one of them honked his horn. Big Sun glanced back at us with a look of horror. His courtship was turning into an event.

The door opened, and the girl stepped into the doorway.

Hello Kitty looked more Shanghai than Zaozhuang—she was petite and very pretty—but she had the temper of a local girl, and she looked to be on the verge of losing it when she saw Big Sun. "Why are you bothering me at work?" she screamed at him, flailing her arms.

We stepped around the gawkers to get a clear look. Zhao stood in front, holding the hand of little Shuo Shuo, who sucked on a lollipop.

Hello Kitty turned her head and finally saw us. "Eh? Who are all these people?" she shouted, stretching an arm toward us.

The gathering mob now had something else to stare at: a live soap opera unfolding on the streets of Zaozhuang. For a moment, all was quiet as the point of distraction shifted. The only sound was the loud slurping from Shuo Shuo, who was busy with his lollipop. Big Sun looked dumbstruck by the scene, unable to answer. Hello Kitty flew into a rage. "What the hell's going on here?" she yelled in exasperation. "What is this? You're going to get me in trouble!"

Big Sun suddenly found his voice. He stammered that he only wanted to invite her to his cousin's wedding. This prompted more frantic screaming.

Zhao watched the scene she had created, shaking her head. "Big Sun is useless," she said under her breath. "It's not difficult to find a wife here, but it's so difficult for him. He's just useless."

More screams. The mob slowly surrounded the two, eager to watch a fight. This seemed to energize Hello Kitty, and she yelled even louder at Big Sun. He nervously glanced at the people surrounding him, hands in his pockets, mortified.

"Girls here are more interested in scoundrels who waste their money on booze, gambling, and prostitutes," Zhao said out of the side of her mouth to me while watching her son. "Big Sun's too much of a nice guy," his mother said sympathetically. "He's too innocent, too honest. He's useless."

The girl slammed the door in Big Sun's face. He stared at it for a few seconds, pondering whether to knock again, but persistence wasn't in his nature. The crowd dispersed, disappointed with the abrupt ending. Big Sun turned and walked toward us, his head sunken into his chest. "She's not coming," he grumbled, stating the obvious.

Before we got into a waiting cab, Big Sun glanced one last time at the warehouse door. Goodbye, Kitty.

He slouched next to me in the backseat, and we set off for Tanghu, the village where the wedding would take place. Zhao sat in the front seat, staring out the window.

Her phone rang. It was Hello Kitty. "*Wei?* Ah. I understand.

That's fine. Please don't be angry . . . relax. He told me your father was sick, and I told him he should come and visit him, regardless of whether you two will be married or not . . ."

There was a long pause. Zhao shifted the phone to the other ear. Hello Kitty's voice sounded angrier.

"Right, right. That's fine. Don't feel embarrassed," Zhao said into her phone, reassuring the girl. "We were waiting outside because we had a friend who came from America to meet you . . . yes . . . I understand your boss was there . . . I know . . . Big Sun really likes you, I can tell."

I looked over at Big Sun. He stared out the window, limp. Outside, city had turned into country. We passed a cart pulled by a donkey.

Zhao glanced at her son as she spoke. "Perhaps you don't like him, perhaps it's because he grew up in the South; he's not familiar with how northern girls expect to be treated. But I know he likes you. It's my fault. I was never good at educating him . . ."

Big Sun's face turned from mopey to annoyed. He barely knew Hello Kitty; apart from the texting, he had only seen her twice. This was his mother's deal. But he was still angry about what had just transpired. When Zhao hung up, he sat upright. "What did she say?"

"She said her bosses were all there and she couldn't leave work. She acted like you were going to drag her out of there like a caveman!" Zhao shouted. "*Aiya*, people here! The way they think—they're so *fengjian*!"

The word meant "feudal," and I had heard urban transplants like Zhao use it when describing the habits of people in their rural hometowns.

"How could I drag her out of there?" asked Big Sun defensively. "I've never even touched her!"

Zhao looked back from the front seat. "She felt that since you were outside the door asking her to come with you, she was losing face in front of her boss."

"Too *fengjian*!" shouted the driver with a burst of laughter.

The cabbie was a burly man with a crew cut and aviator sunglasses. He looked eager to participate in the conversation.

Big Sun looked at the driver's eyes in the rearview mirror. "In Shanghai, if someone likes you, isn't that something you feel happy about? Isn't it normal for me to pursue a girl?" he asked. "But here in our hometown, it has to be this protracted and painful process. I can never figure this place out!"

"It's Confucian!" shouted the driver, turning around to explain it to the foreigner in the cab. "His hometown is down the road!"

The great sage had hailed from Qufu, an hour away, and people here—the same people city-dwellers often considered *fengjian*—still lived by many of his traditions.

Zhao and the driver talked about her son's predicament in the front seat.

Big Sun slumped in the back, growing angrier. "She's as stubborn as a bull!" he shouted. "I go and meet her mother, and she doesn't give me any sign whether they approve of me or not. So they bring me to her father, and I bought a little gift for him! That's just being polite! But after I go and buy it, she gets angry with me."

"You were in the right," the driver said decisively.

"I mean, who am I marrying? Her or her father?" Big Sun asked, exasperated.

"Ha ha ha! You hit the nail on the head!" roared the driver, slamming his hand on the dashboard.

This was about as close to a therapy session as you could get in China. Shanghai cabbies usually ignored the banter in their backseats, but not their rural counterparts. They owned the car and any conversation that occurred inside. It was natural for them to insert themselves into discussions of the most intimate personal matters as if they had a stake in it, too, acting as a sounding board while troubleshooting perplexing Confucian duties.

"Listen," the driver said, looking at Big Sun in his rearview mirror. "Your mom mentioned you work in Hangzhou, right? You've seen the world. You've got a foreign friend. This bumpkin girl makes a thousand yuan a month at the supermarket! What's the big deal?"

Big Sun considered this point for a moment. "Property prices are going up across the country, and the price of a wife is, too," he said.

"Yeah, but you've already got a place in town, right? After hearing about your situation, I think it'll be easy for you to find a girl. If I were that girl, I'd be flattered you came to see me at work."

The driver stopped his car along a dusty main street lined with run-down shops. Fields of bright green wheat lay beyond. He twisted around. "I was going to turn in for the day, but I saw you had a foreigner with you! I'm almost fifty and I've never seen one before! And you, young man," he said, pointing to Big Sun. "Don't worry about a thing. You'll find a better girl than her."

Zhao took out a fifty-yuan note and handed it to the driver, paying him for the ride. The therapy session was free.

HAD BIG SUN grown up in Zaozhuang, he might have already found a better girl. His cousin did. "They met in graduate school," Big Sun said as we watched romantic photos of the bride and groom dissolve into each other on a flat-screen television.

We were in the courtyard of a two-story concrete farmhouse. Workers stepped around us to construct the stage for the next day's wedding ceremony. Behind us came the machine-gun-fire sound of women chopping meat and vegetables for the banquet dinner. Buckets of live fish and soft-shelled turtles covered the courtyard. Canvas tents lined the alleyway outside the house, extending to the wheat fields beyond. Neighbors were unfolding dozens of tables underneath them. Nearly all the village's residents had come to help marry off Big Sun's cousin.

A photo of the couple staring into each other's eyes appeared onscreen. The groom looked up at his tall bride. He had a pudgy face, narrow eyes, and what the Chinese call a "garlic nose," nostrils flaring out like a bulb of garlic. The bride was thin and had an angular, freckled face. They stood on a rocky beach, the ocean behind them.

"Where's that?" I asked Big Sun.

"Qingdao. That's where the bride is from."

It was a scenic port city on the opposite side of Shandong province, where the couple had met.

As photo after photo of the couple floated by, I thought about the different paths Big Sun and his little cousin had taken in life. His cousin had grown up in this tiny village, studied hard, and had tested into a reputable university in a desirable city. He attended a good graduate school where he met a city girl. He found a job as an engineer at a pharmaceutical company; she worked as a manager at IKEA, and now here they were, poised to live happily ever after. Had Zhao not left to work in Shanghai, Big Sun would likely have forged a similar path. He certainly had the smarts and drive to do so. Instead, here he was, a migrant hairdresser striking out with an inscrutable hometown girl.

By the time we had arrived at the village, the entire family had already heard about Big Sun's debacle. Out here among the corn and wheat fields of rural Shandong, news traveled fast.

"Which girl was this?" asked an older cousin with a smirk. "The pretty one whose photo you sent me? The one wearing the mask?"

Big Sun nodded.

"I think the key here is you haven't done anything to show you like her," he lectured. "You're just not romantic enough."

Big Sun sighed. "Sometimes I joke that love between a man and a woman is only useful to make babies. True love is between men."

It was a comment that—in the West—might raise questions about his sexuality. But here in a land where courtship rituals were the source of endless frustration that strengthened the bonds between fellow men, it seemed to fit.

A squat, rough-looking fellow stood to the side of the scrum of cousins: Big Sun's father. This was the mountain man who had emerged as the only local bachelor willing to marry Zhao after her leukemia went into remission. He was a coal miner who routinely beat her until she finally left for the big city, only to return for holidays, weddings, and funerals. He was a quiet man with big hands, bushy eyebrows, and a garlic nose. He stood several inches shorter than his wife, and when he looked up at others, he had a habit of squinting, making him look perpetually confused. Zhao had gussied him up for the weekend festivities with a navy blue blazer, blue-checkered shirt, and khakis. The old coal miner awkwardly picked at his new duds like a boy who can't wait to change out of his church clothes.

I shook his hand. "See?" Zhao shouted. "I told you he was ugly!"

Zhao belted out a hearty laugh. Her husband ignored her, shaking my hand, looking perplexed at how his wife had come to know a foreigner in that faraway city on the sea.

We were in a shaded part of the courtyard. Zhao's husband was here with a dozen old men huddled around a table watching a bespectacled man in a Mao suit carefully inscribing characters into a small red booklet. They were connected to the groom's family by blood or soil, and each of them held red envelopes stuffed with money in their callused hands.

The first man handed his envelope to a man in a suit sitting beside the scribe. He was the village accountant, and he was the only one whose hands were clean. The accountant opened the envelope, slowly counting the money out loud: "ONE hundred, TWO hundred, THREE hundred . . ." The others pressed forward to watch. When he was finished, the scribe took a red booklet from the top of a large stack and wrote the name of the donor into a formal invitation for the next day's wedding.

Everyone here was accustomed to the ritual. They knew precisely how much to give based on a variety of factors: how you were related to the family, whether you someday *wanted* to be related to the family, if you did business with the family, how much the family had given at your son's wedding, whether you owed the family any favors. It was like the opening scene of *The Godfather* cast with Chinese farmers. But here in the village, there was no secrecy—everyone was free to look at the accounting book to see what their neighbors had given—and many did just that prior to handing over their red envelopes.

It seemed like a nerve-racking role, going through the motions of being a guest at a country wedding. But if you had a problem with it—as the driver reminded us in the cab—you could take it up with the godfather of all Chinese traditions. His hometown was just down the road.

I WOKE UP the next morning to the piercing blast of a trombone. In an instant, my body jolted itself up in bed. My mind felt its way through a pounding headache to work out where I was, what time it was, and why a trombone was blaring "Jingle Bells" outside my window.

I stumbled out of bed and opened the curtains. Directly below the window, a six-piece marching band of elderly men in bright red suits hunched over their instruments: a man on trombone, another pounding a big bass drum, one on snare, and the rest of them smashing cymbals together at intervals detached from any sense of rhythm. It was clear and sunny. I sat down on the edge of my bed trying to recall what had happened the night before, while the cacophony outside streamed into my room . . . *Prancing through the snow, in a one-horse open sleigh* . . . I had obviously gotten drunk, and my clothes smelled like smoke. . . . *O'er the fields we go, laughing all the way* . . . I noticed a crumpled cigarette atop my notebook on the nightstand. "Suyan" was scrawled just above the filter in traditional Chinese characters. Ah, yes. I had accepted the countryside greeting between men—a cigarette—and that had eventually snowballed into Suyan after Suyan. I had written the cigarette's English name in my notebook—"Sequoia"—and below that, I had taken note of the eloquent English motto written on each pack:

FOLLOWING THE TRACK OF THE GALE,
I AM CHASING THE SUN.

I coughed up some phlegm and winced. My throat felt like I had chased the sun, caught it, and swallowed it whole. Foggy snapshots of the evening began to surface. I recalled sitting at a table with women and children only to be lured by Sequoias to the men's table, seated between two drunken fishermen who were sharing swigs from a bottle of grain alcohol. After we polished the bottle off, we moved on to local beer. I had a memory of looking over to the women and children's table and noticing little Shuo Shuo on his mother's lap, sipping on cup after cup of red wine until he passed out in his mother's strong arms. My drinking partners laughed and said the two-year-old could put away more than me.

I remembered frequent visits to an outhouse where the walls seemed to be moving. Then I took a drag from a Sequoia and the orange embers lit up the grimy stall, revealing a wall crawling with maggots. When it came time to return to the motel, I remember quietly walking upstairs in the groom's country home to retrieve my bag in one of the bedrooms and startling a pregnant woman who was inside. I stammered an apology, explaining who I was, but before I could finish speaking, she had vanished through the door.

The next morning when Zhao picked me up at the motel, I asked about the woman. We were seated in a tiny covered vestibule on the back of a three-wheeled motorcycle cab on our way to her cousin's home. Thin red-velvet curtains blocked the windows, making everything inside appear rose-colored. "That was the wife of the groom's younger brother," Zhao said. "She's in hiding."

"Whom is she hiding from?" I asked.

She looked at me, disappointed by my stupidity. It was obvious why a pregnant woman in the countryside would be in hiding.

"The family planning bureau!" Zhao said.

The agency was in charge of enforcing China's planned-birth policy. Zhao told me the woman and her husband already had a little girl, and they had tried again for a boy. In China, doctors aren't allowed to reveal the sex of the child, so Zhao's relatives visited an illegal clinic to find out. An ultrasound revealed another girl. The couple made an appointment for an abortion. "But when she got to the doctor's office," Zhao said, "she didn't have the heart to go through with it. So she's hidden upstairs in that bedroom ever since. She's usually locked inside. If she's discovered, she'll have to pay a sixty-thousand-yuan fine. That's a lot of money out here."

It was a tragic situation, but Zhao spoke about the girl's dilemma without a hint of emotion.

"What's going to happen to the baby after it's born?" I asked.

"The family's already decided," Zhao said. "Her sister and brother-in-law have tried to have children, but they keep having miscarriages. She'll give the baby to them and they'll register the child as their own."

Out here, there were all sorts of ways to get around the rules of the system, and when a relative had a problem like this, family members worked together to solve it internally rather than let the state intervene. There was nothing that shouldn't be kept in the family, especially its newest member.

The motorcycle cab jolted to a stop outside another relative's home. Zhao stepped out and embraced a woman who looked to be her age. She had shoulder-length hair and was thin and pretty. She smiled with the bottom half of her face. Her eyes looked sunken and sad; her droopy eyelids made her look sedated. "I told you about this cousin!" Zhao yelled to me. "She's the one who doesn't need to work. Her husband is quite capable! Whereas me, bah! I work too hard."

It dawned on me that I had heard stories about this cousin back at the flower shop in Shanghai. This was the wife of the infamous tax official, the cousin who was routinely beaten by both her husband and his young mistress, the one who had attempted to kill herself by swallowing pesticide. We had come to discuss Big Sun's courtship disaster. It was this cousin who had helped Zhao arrange the pairing.

Inside her cousin's fifth-floor penthouse, Zhao didn't bother sitting down. "She didn't give us face at all!" Zhao said, skipping any small talk.

"This isn't your fault," Zhao's cousin told her. "It's Big Sun's problem."

Zhao shook her head. "He's so unreasonable! *Gao bu cheng, Di bu jiu!*" she yelled.

It was a Chinese saying describing someone who can neither

accomplish something big nor settle for something small. It seemed appropriate for a young man whose dreams had been lost somewhere between the big city and the countryside.

"*Aiya!* He's nearly thirty years old!" said the cousin, slapping her white leather sofa. "There's something wrong with the girl, too. She kept giving him excuses not to meet. 'I'm too tired,' 'I'm sick,' she just didn't want to meet him."

"That just shows she's not interested. Still: suppose you worked in the supermarket and a group of people came to see you. Wouldn't you go out to say hello?" Zhao asked her cousin.

"You have to! It's common courtesy! You must give face!" her cousin yelled.

"Of course you must! She lacks any culture! How impolite!"

Their cackles bounced off the walls of the bright, airy apartment. A fountain with an angel as its centerpiece jutted from an interior wall. There were framed photos throughout the apartment of Zhao's cousin and her children. There was no trace of her husband—he paid the rent and sometimes showed up to beat her, but for the most part, he lived across town with his mistress.

Zhao and her cousin went on howling about Big Sun, the girl, and the indignity of it all. The two were a curious pair of matchmakers: both of their marriages were train wrecks, and Zhao told me neither of them had been in love before. Yet here they were, beside themselves as to why Big Sun wasn't interested in any of the girls they had arranged for him.

After they settled down, Zhao's cousin turned to me. "You're from America, eh? Is your house in America bigger than this one?"

"Um . . . yes, but houses in America tend to be bigger, generally speaking. Your house is very nice," I said.

Zhao's cousin flashed another dead-eyed smile. Her expression remained completely sullen.

"I have four others," she said.

"HER HUSBAND IS SO capable," Zhao said.

We were back in a cab on our way to the countryside wedding.

The banquet the night before was just a warm-up for today's festivities. Zhao's voice carried a tone of envy. The man may have abused her cousin and taken a mistress, but he was rich and powerful—more than could be said for most men in her hometown, especially her own husband.

"He's very well connected and he works all the time," Zhao continued. "He and my cousin are actually second cousins."

"They're related?" I asked, a little confused. "Wait. You're related to him, too?"

"We're all related," Zhao answered. "They've got three kids—their son has a genetic disorder—something's wrong with his eyes—but their two girls are fine."

The windows of the taxi were open and a warm wind blew through Zhao's hair. Outside, the apartment blocks of the city made way for fields of newly planted wheat and corn. I thought about the life of Zhao's cousin and how messy and chaotic it had become.

"The women here aren't like Shanghai girls," said Zhao, her arm out the window, grasping the door. "They're not feminine and soft at all. Women here—when they've had enough of life, they drink pesticide."

The driver, a man with cropped gray hair, nodded. "I know a lot of women like that," he said.

The meter had dropped. Another taxicab therapist was in.

"So do I," said Zhao. "It's common out here."

The driver grinned and shook his head. "Their husbands beat them, and they feel like there's no other way out," he said.

I wondered if he beat his wife, too.

"My cousin drank half a kilogram of pesticide. It wasn't enough. They pumped her stomach and she was in the intensive care ward for days," Zhao said.

"*Wah,*" said the driver, impressed.

"Another cousin of mine was able to do it right—she drank a whole bucket of pesticide and died, just like that," Zhao said.

"A lot of women here jump off the suspension bridge into the river," offered the driver.

Zhao nodded. "After my cousin survived drinking pesticide,

she jumped into a well. That didn't work, either," she said with a chuckle.

It was a hell of a conversation for a sunny springtime drive to a wedding. Zhao and the driver chatted and chuckled as if these things were funny. Both claimed to have firsthand experience.

"I don't have the courage to drink pesticide or jump into a well," said Zhao. "I admire them for that. Sometimes I want to die, but I can't bring myself to do it."

"Why would you say such a thing?" I asked.

Both Zhao and the driver laughed at my show of concern. "If it were easier to kill myself, I would've done it a long time ago!" Zhao said. "All I do is work, eat, and sleep. It's meaningless."

A gust of wind blew through the car. The driver smiled and nodded his head in agreement.

"TODAY IS MAY FOURTH, 2014 A.D. Today, the sun shines and the wind is gentle. The sweet fragrance of the osmanthus tree is in the air. It is an auspicious and festive day. We gather together in the most happy mood to witness the ceremony of this beautiful young couple!"

A responding chorus of Hao—Good!—erupted from the audience. A tall young man with a microphone stood between the bride and the groom. The couple had forgone the red traditional outfits for a Western look: a black tux and a poufy white dress. To honor tradition, the groom sported a red tie, and the bride, red-framed sunglasses.

The pair had arrived in a rented white BMW. As they stepped out of it, family members lit a thirty-foot-long roll of firecrackers that unraveled into the shape of a heart. They exploded like machine-gun fire for nearly a minute, triggering alarms in cars parked along the village's main street. Next, a row of red cannons released one exploding rocket after another. Little Shuo Shuo, hungover from his red wine binge the night before, wailed in panic through the racket.

Inside, more than a hundred family, friends, and neighbors

crammed into the courtyard. They quietly watched the bride and groom ascend the family wheat-threshing platform. It had been converted into a stage framed by a pink curtain bearing the single red Chinese character 福: "happiness."

"Groom! Please take one step forward and face the people!" shouted the man with the microphone. "Today's groom is handsome with an imposing appearance. Let me ask everyone here: Is the groom handsome?"

The man pointed the microphone at the audience, but they missed the cue. Most of them had never attended a Western-style wedding ceremony and they couldn't fathom why a man with a microphone would be talking to them when they weren't the ones getting married. For a moment, the only sound was the background music, a sappy violin piece seeping from the speakers onstage. A machine propped up atop one of the speakers spit out hundreds of bubbles that hovered just above the heads of the mute audience.

The host cleared his throat. He was a handsome man with glasses dressed in a black suit resembling a Catholic priest's frock, but he was no man of the cloth. He was a professional wedding host the family had rented for the afternoon.

"Ahem. There are tens of thousands of brides in the world, but today's bride is the most beautiful!" he continued. "As the bride stands here, the sun is stunned, the cosmos is shattered, and the earth is paralyzed. Why? Because she's a fairy of the earth! Let's prove that with our applause!"

The stunned, shattered, and paralyzed audience broke from their trance and responded with a loud ovation.

The ceremony went on like this for an hour. The host seemed to be working from a memorized script that was often interrupted by a videographer and a cameraman who walked on and off the stage whenever they felt like getting shots of the couple and their families. They would interrupt the wedding by shouting, "Three, two, one: Eggplant!" as family members smiled and shouted it in return. The word in Chinese, *qiezi*, pushes your mouth into a smile when you say it, much like "cheese" does in English.

Children from the village dressed in school track uniforms

with red handkerchiefs around their necks filtered in and out of the courtyard. They sat on the edge of the stage, giggling at the spectacle. At one point, a cameraman hurled a curse word at a child who was in the way of his shot. The child's father, a cousin of the bride, shoved the cameraman into the audience, shouting obscenities at him. The host turned off the microphone, and the audience was entertained with a brief intermission as the two men swung their fists at each other wildly, neither of them landing a punch. Face lost, the guest gathered his wife and son and stormed off, disappointing those who were hoping to watch a good fight with their Western wedding.

I stood next to Zhao's two brothers. They were large men with thick necks, broad bellies, and fat cheeks. Both reeked of grain alcohol. Zhao had warned me about them. "When those two get together, they drink too much," she had told me, "and they'll expect you to drink, too."

The older brother was a truck driver. He boasted of dropping out of local school at the age of fifteen after repeating the second grade for eight straight years. The younger brother had done slightly better in his studies, but had ultimately dropped out after primary school and had followed his sister to Shanghai, where he worked in construction.

Keeping up with what seemed to be local tradition, each brother juggled a wife and a mistress, and from the looks of it, the younger brother continued to be on the prowl, eyeing a young woman in front of us who was a friend of the bride. He whispered, "You're beautiful" into her ear, slurring his speech.

The woman jerked her head away as if a bee had been hovering over her. The older brother laughed. "He's a wild beast when he drinks! My dad used to chain him to the dinner table at home because he was so wild!"

As the ceremony wound down, I watched Zhao from afar as she greeted long-lost family and friends. She smiled as easily as ever, gliding across the courtyard with the grace and poise of a sophisticated urbanite.

In this hometown of hers, filled with wild men, abused women,

and forgotten children, her quiet civility stood out. Family spoke to
her with deference, friends sought her advice. Inside a courtyard of
her closest relations, she was the first person who had *chuqu*, "to
go out," yearning to see the world outside the narrow realm of her
hometown. She had worked hard to earn money to buy a home for
each of her boys, something her family and friends expected of a
man, but not a local woman. Among the women here, Zhao was a
pioneer. Among the men, she inspired both fear and attraction: she
was a woman with power.

"Now is the moment we've all been waiting for," shouted the
host into the microphone. "It is time for the bride and groom to face
each other!"

This was the cue for the groom to kiss the bride, but the couple
demurred and hugged each other awkwardly instead, prompting
catcalls from the audience and shouts demanding a genuine kiss.

"You should be more impulsive and your head should be on this
side," instructed the host into the microphone, moving the groom's
head, "and the bride's head should be like this," he said, positioning
her face with both his hands as if she were a mannequin.

The couple hesitated again, before giving each other henpecks
on the cheek, triggering more howls from the courtyard. Finally,
Big Sun climbed atop the threshing platform. With both hands,
he pushed their faces together, forcing a real kiss. The courtyard
erupted in laughter. Whether the young couple liked it or not, their
family had decided: they were now husband and wife. With her sons
at her side, Zhao stood next to her brothers and sisters who had
gathered together on the platform with the bride and groom. They
posed for the photographer and smiled. "Three, two, one: Eggplant!"

"THAT PLACE IS no longer my home," Zhao told me inside her flower
shop on the Street of Eternal Happiness. "I'm merely visiting family and friends when I go back there. This is where I'm most comfortable now. This is my home."

It had been two weeks since the wedding, a rush of business
from Mother's Day had subsided, and Zhao was now alone in her

shop on a cool, misty day in mid-May, hunched over her phone, exchanging text messages with friends who had heard about Big Sun's disastrous performance in Zaozhuang. The search for a mate had resumed, and this time around, Zhao was leaving friends from her hometown out of the matter. "Yesterday, my neighbor here in Shanghai found a new girl for him, but Big Sun refused to see her," she complained. "He said she was too young. He's simply hopeless!"

Back in Zhao's hometown, talk of Big Sun's fiasco had reached mythical heights. Zhao told me there were rumors circulating among her relatives that the girl was a *Tongzi*: a human who, under Taoist belief, had spent the previous life as a fairy and was reincarnated to carry out a special mission. According to legend, once the mission was fulfilled, a *Tongzi* would be called back to the spirit world. *Tongzi* were said to be attractive humans who had terrible luck in relationships and life in general. "The gods gave her a beautiful face," Zhao explained to me, "but not a beautiful fate."

Maybe Big Sun is a Tongzi, too, I thought. I could tell from Zhao's furrowed brow that she may have been thinking the same thing. By her estimate, she had set Big Sun up with at least three girls a year for the past eight years. None of them had panned out. I was no expert on Taoist deities, but the odds of Big Sun meeting more than two dozen reincarnated fairies seemed to go against the laws of numerology.

"My brothers liked you," Zhao said, changing the subject. "They enjoyed drinking with you."

"I enjoyed drinking with them, too," I replied, not entirely truthfully.

After the wedding ceremony, her brothers had filled me with as much grain alcohol, beer, and Sequoias as they could before I excused myself to stagger onto a train back to Shanghai. *Following the track of the gale,* I thought as the high-speed train picked up speed and barreled southbound under the night sky, *I am chasing the sun.*

"Each of my brothers has two wives," Zhao told me matter-of-factly. "My younger brother was finally able to divorce his first wife, but my elder brother is too nice of a guy to let go of the first one."

I wondered if there was a man in all of Zaozhuang who managed to survive with just one wife.

"Your husband doesn't have another wife, does he?" I asked her.

The question triggered uncontrollable laughter. "You saw him! He's not good-looking at all!" shouted Zhao between bursts of laughter. "If he had two wives, I'd love him a lot more! The more wives you have, the more capable you are!

"If I had to live back in my hometown with my husband, I would have drunk pesticide a long time ago," Zhao told me, turning serious. "I've tried for years to divorce him, but he just won't let go."

Zhao had told me a number of times that one of her biggest fears was that her husband would come to live with her in Shanghai after he retired from the mine. "After the wedding, my sister cried and blamed my mother for not taking better care of our marriages. I have four sisters, and the men she found for us are all hopeless. Each one of us women is the pillar of our families."

Zhao took out her phone to check and see if her friends had made any progress in their search for a suitable match for Big Sun.

Outside, a mix of smog and rain had reduced visibility to just the cars steadily driving by in front of us, each one of them sounding like a duck landing on a lake. Zhao turned off her phone and sighed. It appeared her firstborn son would remain single for the foreseeable future. She shook her head, exasperated, and said, "All men are useless."

13

CK's Pilgrimage

长乐路810号

Street of Eternal Happiness, No. 810

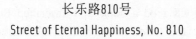

CK began to feel the *qi* one day three years ago. He was hanging out with a couple of friends playing videogames when he decided to lie down and rest. "That's when I felt something," CK told me. "There was somebody talking with me. It was another me."

"It sounds like you were high on something," I said.

CK smirked. "Actually, in that moment my mind was very clear."

It was a sunny and warm Sunday afternoon in May of 2014. Outside, the plane trees were bursting with bright green foliage, people were enjoying walks along the Street of Eternal Happiness, and, for a change, *2nd Floor Your Sandwich* was busy.

CK's waitstaff handled the traffic while their boss sat in the corner, talking to me about how he found the *qi*.

"The *qi*—the energy—it traveled through my body," CK said.

"The other me guided the real me in how to breathe and relax my body. Suddenly I couldn't feel anything. I was just lying on my bed in another space. All colors disappeared and everything turned to black and white. And then I saw them. Lotuses. Lots of lotuses. And then there was someone else with me."

"Someone else apart from you and the other you?" I asked.

"Yes," said CK with a serious face.

CK didn't know it at the time, but he now thinks it was Buddha.

"All I knew for sure was that it wasn't a man or a woman. There was suddenly no difference between the two, just like there was no difference between right and wrong. Because in that space, all there existed was peace. There weren't even any colors."

Afterward, CK read a book that described Buddha as being gender-neutral, and it reminded him of his vision. He began to study Buddhist scriptures, and soon after, CK met his master.

"He's a monk at a small temple outside the city. He told me I was born to be a monk, too. The first time I met him, he asked me to cut my hair and stay in the temple."

"Do you think you have the discipline to be a Buddhist monk?" I asked.

"Not at the moment. It'd be too hard to quit sex," CK said, pausing to take a sip of coffee. "I told my master I'm not ready for a commitment like that yet. I'm still too accustomed to life in the city."

CK's sandwich shop had turned a corner and was finally making a profit, and his accordion business was thriving. There were few other cities in China—or in the world, for that matter—where you could make a decent living selling sandwiches and accordions.

But life in Shanghai had its disadvantages. When I'd arrived, I noticed a bandage on CK's left ear. He was also sporting a three-inch gash on his chin. "I blacked out at a club," he explained. "I fainted and fell down the stairs. When I woke up I had blood all over my face and my ear was ringing."

Doctors had stitched up his chin and had performed surgery on his ear. "Were you drunk?" I asked.

"No, just two glasses of wine. I'm just not getting much sleep these days. And business—I mean, it's stressful, you know?"

The sandwich shop was busier now, and CK hadn't had a day off in months. He had grown accustomed to working twelve-hour shifts at his café while handling orders over the phone for his accordion business. When I asked him about sleep, he replied, "Not much." He was getting by on four or five hours a night. Going out with friends after he closed up shop was usually too tempting.

The pressure of life in the city had made CK feel out of sorts. He sought balance and quietude, anything that could calm his anxiety and his desires. When a friend introduced him to a Buddhist monk, CK felt he had found what he was looking for.

The temple was a four-hour drive from Shanghai. He went there once a month with a few friends who also worshipped and studied there; "brothers," he called them. Their master was the same age as them. Like CK, he was born in the countryside and when he was eighteen years old, he had told his parents he was leaving for a temple in Shanghai to become a monk. Years later, he saw a vision of Tibet while he was meditating. In the vision, CK said, the master met an elder monk in the mountains who had instructed him to establish his own countryside temple.

"It's a small temple without any visitors," CK said. "It's just him and four other monks."

And maybe someday, CK hinted, he would become the fifth.

THE PEOPLE I KNEW along the Street of Eternal Happiness were no strangers to religion. At the corner flower shop, Zhao had learned about Christianity from her devout mother. A block away, Auntie Fu had been converted after she gave birth to her firstborn son in a remote desert in Xinjiang and was now a regular underground churchgoer. And just a couple blocks south of CK's restaurant in Maggie Lane, Mayor Chen and Xie, like many Chinese who grew up in Shanghai, were lifelong Christians.

For the under-forty set, however, religion was something few had time to consider. Weiqi, who grew up on the land where I now lived and had earned his PhD in the United States, didn't seem interested. For Henry, the adman who worked in the skyscraper across the street from CK's restaurant, practicing yoga was as spiritual as he got. CK, on the other hand, seemed hungrier than the others for some guidance.

Buddhism was a natural choice. CK disdained the materialism surrounding him in Shanghai. Capitalism was undergoing a renaissance in China, but it had just started. Those who were rich in twenty-first-century China were *nouveau* riche, and they usually acted the part. They drove neon-colored Ferraris, wore Prada, and spent weekends clubbing. Buddhism's rejection of desire and materialism—beliefs shared by Chinese Communists before they came to power—appealed to young Chinese who felt uneasy with this new era of greed.

Yet China's sudden wealth was also funding Buddhism's rise. By 2005, there were just as many Buddhists in the country as there were people in the United States, a number that had tripled from 1980. One of every five Chinese was Buddhist, outnumbering Christians in China two to one, and their money flowed to temples throughout the country. Tours of historic Buddhist sites across China were popular among the new consumer class. Local officials, eager to profit off religious tourism, helped fund the repair of Buddhist temples destroyed during the Mao years. Though the Party was officially atheist and it discouraged members from practicing religion, local officials understood the value of the renminbi, and for them capitalism was more important than atheism.

Money wasn't the only reason the Party looked favorably on Buddhism's revival. The country was in the grips of a moral crisis. Just a few decades ago, China was an agricultural society where people relied on the help of their community. The economic boom spurred 250 million of them to migrate to the cities. Suddenly, few people knew their neighbors, and trust was in short supply. Videos of incidents capturing pedestrians ignoring others who were having medical emergencies routinely went viral on China's Internet, and a national discussion about morality and social responsibility followed. Tens of millions of Chinese were turning to Christianity to rediscover these values. But Buddhism had two millennia of history in China, and Party leaders were more comfortable promoting it as a safe way—when not mixed with ethnic or political concerns as in Tibet—to restore an ethical value system. Doing so would help fulfill one of the Party's top priorities to keep itself in power: greater social stability.

I occasionally had coffee with Henry, the philosophy major I had met in the ad agency high above the Street of Eternal Happiness in the skyscraper across the street from CK's café. When I told him about CK's conversion to Buddhism, he was hardly surprised. He was a post-eighties generation member, too, and he faced many of the same hurdles in life. "Theoretically, you're supposed to move up in life," he reasoned. "Otherwise, what's the point? You've already fed yourself; you've got a comfortable life. What else is there? You fill a black hole."

Many Chinese CK's age were embarking on spiritual quests, and they reminded Henry of the Beat Generation writers of the 1940s and '50s in the United States who grew up during a similar stretch of economic growth and social change. Like the Beats, today's young Chinese were exploring paths to enlightenment through religion and philosophy indigenous to China. Taoism was undergoing a rebirth rivaling that of Buddhism. The number of Taoist temples in rural China had multiplied sixfold from the 1990s. And in urban China, more and more study centers were devoted to the scholarship of Confucian classics.

One of these centers was in an alley off the Street of Eternal Happiness, behind CK's restaurant. Many of its members worked across the street in the assortment of multinational companies piled atop one another in Henry's office building. The name of the center was Guoxue Xinzhi, "new knowledge of sinology," and it occupied a renovated first-floor apartment.

Xu Yuan had established the center. He didn't have a background in the Chinese classics; he had studied electrical engineering at Fudan. The idea for a Confucian center came to him when he read about how universities in the United States required students to take a smattering of humanities and literature courses before they moved on to their majors. China's schools had no such liberal arts requirements, and classical studies courses offered by even its best colleges were typically weak.

"Chinese society has been through a lot of revolution and trauma that has destroyed our traditional culture," Xu said between sips of tea at his center. "Many of us have completely forgotten about the essential characteristics of being Chinese, but they're reflected in our everyday habits and in our daily lives. When we discover the origins of these characteristics, we can better understand ourselves."

Xu was a tall and lanky man in his thirties with puffy lips and eyeglasses that framed a calm and serious gaze. In just two years, more than fifty thousand young people had attended his weekly events. It may not seem like a lot in a city as populated as Shanghai, but given the center's mission, it was impressive.

Xu noticed that—as his new members reacquainted themselves with Confucianism—many struggled to incorporate the philosophy's core tenets into modern life. "One consequence of China's urbanization is the loss of filial responsibility," he said.

Xu hoped to channel the deep-seated responsibilities young Chinese felt for their parents toward helping the elderly in their adopted neighborhoods in Shanghai. It was a goal that seemed to fit neatly under the umbrella of leader Xi Jinping's Chinese Dream and government efforts to restore Confucian traditions in China. In my reporting trips across the country, I had begun to notice propaganda posters extolling traditional Confucian virtues and tenets, often topped with the characters 中国梦, 我的梦: "China's dream, my dream."

Xi Jinping may have grown up on a healthy diet of Marxist ideology in Yan'an, the birthplace of the Communist Revolution, but China's new leader was also steeped in the Chinese classics, and from the moment the Party elected him to rule, he had vowed to return the nation to its traditional values and glory.

If you drew a timeline of China's rulers across a piece of paper, the Communists would represent a tiny red sliver less than an inch long at the end of a five-foot-long line filled with emperors, but that minuscule red segment had a lot more in common with the rest of the line than outsiders thought.

It was refreshing to chat with Xu. From my work as a teacher and later as a journalist, I had always felt more comfortable with Chinese who were in touch with their own cultural traditions than those who had shed those traditions for Western beliefs, including Communism.

"I'd say most Chinese traditions are being revived by *laobaixing*," Xu said, referring to China's masses from the countryside; "they're not being revived by intellectuals at the top. China's intelligentsia and the upper echelon of society are more Westernized and have been heavily influenced by the Soviet Union. But the needs of the *laobaixing* will someday awaken their memories."

This grassroots revival would take time. But in China, old traditions and beliefs had a way of reappearing after periods of neglect, like a seed patiently sitting out a drought, waiting for rain. It reminded me of something Henry had said about Confucius's core philosophy; something I applied to people like CK and Zhao, who, in order to achieve their goals, had learned to be patient for the right moment to head into the storm of the system.

"The Chinese value the lotus flower. Why? Because it grows from the mud but it is pure and beautiful itself," Henry told me. "Confucius tells us that even though you are not living in an ideal world, you can still search for ways to find meaning in your life, whether from political pursuits or individual pursuits or spiritual pursuits. There is always a way."

THE PILGRIMAGE BEGAN when I arrived outside CK's apartment at six in the morning. CK waited for me on the sidewalk beside two boxes and a backpack. On any other early Saturday morning, he could be found lurching home along the winding streets of the French Concession to sleep off a night of clubbing. But on this sunny, sweltering May morning, a temple was waiting.

We heaved the boxes into the trunk of a cab and slumped into the backseat. I handed him a coffee and asked what was in the boxes. "Fruit and grain alcohol," CK said. "Offerings for the temple."

He yawned and rubbed his eyes underneath a pair of aviators, wooden Buddha beads around his wrists swaying with each twist. He wore a tan shirt left unbuttoned to his stomach, revealing a red beaded necklace that rested atop his hairless concave chest. He looked like an Asian Jim Morrison. The bright green leaves of the plane trees rushed by for a few minutes and then disappeared underneath us as we climbed onto an empty elevated highway toward the edge of the city.

A few dozen people waited for us outside the bus. A group of men helped us with our bags and boxes and loaded them in the bus's cargo hold. CK thanked them, addressing them as *"Shixiong,"* "brother-in-learning." I had wrongly assumed the bus would be full of people CK's age—there were just a handful of them. The rest was a smattering of everyday Chinese society: families with children, single middle-aged professionals, the elderly; there were engineers, white-collar office employees, retired factory workers, construction laborers, teachers, and a Buddhist nun. It was about as accurate a microcosm of urban China as you could find, all on their way to explore the mysteries of life together.

CK waited outside as a *shixiong* performed roll call. He leaned against the bus and lit a cigarette, completing his look. A girl in a black muscle shirt and ripped jeans disembarked and came to rest her elbow on CK's shoulder. Without looking at her, he removed a pack of Marlboro Reds from his pocket, flipped it open, and held it up in the air. She removed one, he closed the pack, and with his other hand he opened a lighter, holding its flame to her cigarette. She took a drag and exhaled before nuzzling his neck.

"This is Jackie," he announced.

Jackie had long, jet-black hair, a thin oval face with a slender nose and high-set eyes, giving her the look of a northern Chinese from the border of Mongolia. She wore beads, too, but her black fingernails and mascara added a goth element. If CK was Jim

Morrison, she was Avril Lavigne—a pair of rock 'n' roll lovers on a pilgrimage to find Buddha. CK mentioned in the cab he had been dating her for a month, "but I'm not sure it's going to work out," he admitted. "I'm just having fun."

Jackie looked to be a sixteen-year-old schoolgirl, but was actually a twenty-five-year-old secretary. She had met CK at his sandwich shop. She wasn't religious, but CK had turned her on to Buddhism and she had come along to learn more. Her parents, shop owners in a northern district of Shanghai, had assigned her older brother and his best friend to go along and keep watch over her.

The trip hadn't even started yet and the two chaperones already had their hands full. Jackie's brother nervously watched his sister slip her arm around CK's waist. Her brother was tall, lanky, and had a long face that was devoid of any symmetry: one eye was bigger than the other, his nose bent slightly to the left, even his smile was crooked. His friend was big and round with eyes that seemed to disappear into his fleshy face. He wore an extra-large Baltimore Ravens T-shirt that failed to contain his expansive belly. Wherever CK and Jackie would roam that weekend, the bumbling pair of men trailed them, like Laurel and Hardy chasing a crook, wondering how they had gotten themselves into this mess.

The bus soared out of the city thanks to an absence of early-morning traffic on the elevated expressway, the height of the high-rises crowding Shanghai's suburbs gradually shrinking with each kilometer. We were headed five hours west, following the muddy Yangtze River and crossing its many tributaries into the fertile delta countryside the Chinese call yu mi zhi xiang, the "homeland of fish and rice." I sat next to a friend of CK's named Sun. He had moved to Shanghai from the northern Chinese city of Xi'an. "Have you been?" he asked me.

I had, and I responded the way many Chinese were expected to respond, by praising his hometown's food and tourist sites. Xi'an was home to one of China's most important cultural treasures: the Terracotta Warriors, an army of statues found in an underground catacomb thought to be guarding the still-unexcavated tomb of

China's first emperor, Qin Shihuang. *"Jiade,"* Sun spat, using the Chinese term for "fake." "He's not buried there. They haven't discovered a thing there."

I thought it better to ask Sun about his attraction to Buddhism. "I was looking for something to believe in," he said. "I started by reading books and anthologies, and then I visited the temple for the first time this past Winter Solstice. I asked the master many questions, and he told me I should study the Buddhist scriptures. He seemed smart, so I've done that for months now."

Sun was thirty years old. He had studied industrial design in Xi'an and accepted a position with a Shanghai firm after attending a local job fair in his hometown. But after he arrived, the job was not what it seemed. *"Wo bei pian le,"* he told me—*I was cheated.*

The firm had lied to him about the position and the salary in order to lure him to Shanghai to help sell foreign-looking villas in Jiading, a sparsely populated district on the outskirts of the city. "Business is terrible," he complained.

This was hardly surprising. China's property market was over-saturated, a bubble waiting to pop, and places like Jiading had become ghost towns filled with vacant neighborhoods of luxury villas. Sun admitted occasional pilgrimages to his temple were the only bright spots in his life at the moment.

I turned to CK and asked him about the temple. He told me his *shifu,* or master, helped manage it with funding from dozens of worshippers in Shanghai. "Only Shanghai?" I asked.

"Yeah, all of the worshippers are from Shanghai," he said.

It seemed odd that a temple so far away from Shanghai would exclusively serve the city's population. I said so and asked CK why. "The government is strict with religion," he said, choosing his words carefully. "My master teaches us a lot of different Buddhist practices, and he wants to do that somewhere quiet where he won't receive any government interference."

"What kind of practices?" I asked.

"Secret ones," CK said softly, making sure the others didn't hear us.

I rolled my eyes and CK grinned. "Okay," he whispered,

surrendering. "He teaches us about Tibetan Buddhist practices and religion."

There was nothing illegal about teaching Tibetan Buddhism in China. It's a state-sanctioned religion and Tibetan Buddhists are, by law, free to worship. However, Chinese authorities keep a close eye on the religion and its practices. Many Tibetans have long sought independence from China, and their sect of Buddhism follows the teachings of their spiritual and political leader, the Dalai Lama, whom the Chinese leadership considers a separatist and a threat to national sovereignty.

CK told me his master was interested in Tibetan Buddhism for religious reasons, not political ones. "The purpose of our studies is to find a way out of *Lunhui*—the reincarnation cycle," explained CK. "Our master believes the best way to do this is through Tibetan Buddhism."

CK said his master had neglected to inform local officials about the Tibetan Buddhist practices at the temple, and they didn't seem interested because it paid its taxes and few locals worshipped there. The "secret" method of instruction helped explain why CK's master exclusively catered to worshippers from a faraway city rather than to locals—if locals were involved, nearby authorities would inevitably hear about the goings-on at the temple. This way, CK's master could freely teach his students a path to enlightenment in peace.

THE BUS CAME TO A STOP along the main street of a village lined with farming supply shops. We disembarked and carried boxes of supplies and offerings down a long alleyway to the entrance of the temple. Everyone pitched in except for Jackie, whose black-tipped fingers were too busy texting her friends back in Shanghai. She wandered down the middle of the alley as if in a trance.

"Isn't the sky here so blue?" asked CK. "You can actually see the clouds!"

I looked up. The sun was directly above us, heating up the countryside through a pale blue sky dappled with clouds whose outlines were blurred by a veil of brownish smog. It was still polluted out here, but less so than Shanghai, where a sharp azure hue was unusual. Jackie took a break from her phone to point her head up, smiling. I looked behind me and noticed Laurel and Hardy squinting their eyes and pointing their phones toward the sky, immortalizing nature's rare appearance.

There was more of the natural world inside the temple. A pair of red tubs filled with two dozen soft-shelled turtles lay in the shade next to the kitchen. The animals scrambled on top of one another, clawing those underneath them to escape. The last time I had seen this many turtles in one place, they were ready to be boiled alive for a wedding dinner in Zhao Shiling's hometown. Laurel and Hardy poked at them, picking them up by their tails, grinning at their helplessness.

"We're going to set them free later," CK told them, motioning to the river behind the temple.

This was common practice among Chinese Buddhists—buying live animals at the market to set them free later—but the ancient ritual in compassion sometimes backfired. "800 Carp Ceremoniously Set Free in China Netted by Fishermen Moments Later" was one of dozens of headlines from years' worth of local stories capturing the rising tension between spirituality and self-interest in China. "We're quiet about where we release them," CK assured me when I mentioned this modern contradiction. "We usually do it at night so that the locals won't snatch them downstream."

The temple was a work in progress. The master had overseen the construction of five interconnected red-tile-roofed buildings. There were meeting rooms, living quarters, a canteen, and two large worship halls that rose high above the rest of the surrounding village. The project had proceeded in fits and starts—contingent on a seasonal cycle of donations—over the span of ten years, and it would probably take another ten before it was completed. Atop the roof of the main temple hall—named "The Brightest Hall" in Chinese—sat a pair of golden deer facing a dharma wheel, a symbol of Tibetan Buddhism, with flowing golden Tibetan script written underneath them. In the middle of a square in front of the temple stood a two-story-tall golden statue of a monk dressed in robes holding a staff in his right hand. "That's Dizang *pusa*," CK told me as we backed up to get a better look. "He's the only *pusa* who chose to remain in hell."

A *pusa*, or bodhisattva, is an enlightened being who has dedicated his or her life to helping others attain enlightenment. The most popular bodhisattva in China is Guanyin, a female *pusa* associated with mercy and compassion who is typically worshipped as a deity. Dizang, known as Ksitigarbha in Sanskrit, is a lesser-known bodhisattva who, according to Buddhist tradition, chose to go to hell to help save those who suffered there.

I shielded my face from the sun and squinted upward at Dizang. He was bald with long earlobes that nearly grazed his shoulders. His half-shut eyes gazing past the rice paddies in the distance looked detached and confident. Dizang seemed like a good fit for CK. As a hell dweller, he was easily the most rock 'n' roll of the bodhisattvas.

We spent most of the day waiting for the master to appear. He hadn't met the bus when it arrived—he was inside his living quarters meditating, CK explained—and worshippers slowed down as they walked past his two-story home to catch a glimpse of him through a window. After it was clear it would take some time for him to finish meditating, CK and a few others laid yoga mats in front of Dizang *pusa* and began to prostrate. They held their hands together in prayer, lifted their arms above their heads, squatted to their knees, and dropped their bodies to the ground, pushing forward to stretch out, briefly lying on their stomachs before reversing the motion and standing back up again. They were supposed to do this 108 times while contemplating their sins. In the sweltering, sweaty forty-five minutes it took CK to complete this, Jackie, Laurel, and Hardy sat in the shade of a temple eave, contemplating their smartphones.

At three in the afternoon, we filed into a conference room filled with dozens of chairs surrounding a long wooden table. A wall of windows looked out onto a bend in a river flowing through lush green rice paddies. After we sat down, the master appeared, seating himself at the head of the table in a black leather chair. He looked around the hushed room with a frown, slowly taking inventory of who had come, unconsciously pulling a string of gray beads through the bloated fingers of his left hand, holding each bead between his middle finger and thumb before moving on to the next. Though only in his thirties, the master commanded a room like a seasoned military leader, narrow eyes darting from one person to the next. This aura was aided by his burly physique, like that of an offensive lineman draped in a bright yellow robe. His large head was shaved, accentuating an asymmetrical face dominated by fat, protruding lips stuck in a permanent pout, revealing a pair of buckteeth whenever they parted.

After a minute of silence, he spoke. "What did you call me in here for? I forgot what you wanted to know," he said, slightly irritated.

A young girl sitting on her mother's lap ignored the master, asking another child to hand her a toy. Her mother shushed her. The master reserved a smug smile for the children, the only ones here who weren't under his influence. CK, who sat beside him, spoke: "Master, can I put a thangka near a fireplace?" he asked.

"That wasn't the question I was told you would ask," the master snapped. "What was your original question?"

CK shifted his weight to the edge of his seat, nervous. He turned to Jackie, slouched into her chair. "Ask the master to interpret your dream," he stammered.

"What dream?" the master barked.

"She dreamed of a *pusa*," said CK.

"Ah? Which *pusa*?" the master asked, looking mildly interested, fingering his beads.

CK turned to Jackie, who looked too scared to speak. "Just tell him!" he shouted nervously.

"Ah, I don't remember exactly," Jackie murmured. "I dreamed I was in a small town, and I saw a very large statue of a *pusa* with beautiful lights in the background. I thought the *pusa* said something to me, but I couldn't remember."

"Do you know which *pusa* it was?" asked the master.

Jackie shook her head.

"Fine. I'll go find a *pusa* brochure and you can page through it," he said sarcastically, eliciting snorts of laughter from CK and the others.

"Master, how about my previous question?" interrupted CK. "I live in an apartment with an old fireplace that we don't use anymore. Can I hang a thangka over it?"

The master pursed his lips at what seemed like another silly question. A thangka was a Buddhist painting on fabric. What did it matter where you hung it? "So you're using a thangka as a decoration inside your home?" asked the master, his eyebrows curved, his fingers stroking his chin.

"Not really," answered CK. "We're supposed to worship Buddha at home, and my thangka is part of my shrine. I was just wondering if the fireplace was a respectful place for it."

The master forced a perplexed look from his face. "As long as you don't hang it in the bathroom," he said to more laughter.

The master took a sip of his tea and grimaced. "Who made this tea for me?" he shouted.

The room fell quiet; the only sounds were the hushed voices of children who continued to play, oblivious to the master. "I did," a young man in glasses answered, raising his hand.

"What a prodigal son! Why fill my cup with so many tea leaves?" the master yelled. "What a waste of money! I could drink for two days with this many leaves. Is this tea or soy sauce?"

Isolated giggles rippled through the room. It had been half an hour, and the Buddhist master had yet to speak to someone in a compassionate tone. I began to fear the master would call on me, too, but he had ignored me since we had entered the room. Before we arrived, CK had warned the master a foreign journalist would be present—maybe he was avoiding me.

A woman at the opposite end of the table spoke up. "Master, I've brought my daughter back," she said, motioning to a girl who looked to be around ten years old.

I had noticed her when I boarded the bus in Shanghai. The girl was tall, skinny, and had striking, wild eyes that focused to the side of whoever spoke to her. She had trouble sitting still and would break the silence with bursts of nonsensical words as she danced up and down the aisle to a soundtrack inside her head. She didn't smile. The other children kept their distance from her.

The master turned his gaze to the girl, who was quietly talking to herself, staring out the window. "There is still hope for her," he said. "Don't make her take random medicine. There will be bad side effects. You just need to stay calm."

The woman nodded her head. "Whenever she goes through a bad spell, I don't say anything. I just quietly say a prayer to the *pusa*."

"Good," nodded the master. "The more of a fuss you make over her, the worse she'll get. After a while, she'll get better."

The woman nodded. She was tall and she sat up straight. Her long hair was pulled back. She had the same eyes as her daughter. "Once when I was shopping along the street, we passed a temple with a statue of Guanyin *pusa*," she said. "She kept hitting me, trying to force her way in. I eventually let her go inside."

"Not bad, not bad," said the master.

"Last year, I brought her to see a local witch doctor," she continued. "She told me my girl was crazy and that when she reaches sixteen years, she'll be normal."

The master sat up straight. "What?" he asked.

"I thought this woman might be talking nonsense," said the woman. "She prescribed some tea for her to drink. She said she was a nun, too. I didn't believe her. She said my girl is being followed by Guanyin."

The master's face turned serious. "No," he said curtly. "That's not it. It's that your girl *follows* Guanyin. She was a disciple of Guanyin in a past life. She was known as the daughter of the dragon. Do you understand?"

"Yes," answered the woman; the master had told her this before.

I glanced at CK with raised eyebrows. CK lifted his head a little with a motion that said: We'll discuss this later. Keep paying attention. I turned my attention back to the girl and her mother.

The mother glanced at her daughter. "I feel terrible when she has her fits," she told the master. "She cries so hard. Sometimes she even throws bowls and plates at me. I don't know what to do."

"As long as she's not putting herself in danger, you should let her be when she's like that."

"This morning she woke up early," she said. "I asked her, 'Where are you going?' She said, 'I'm going to see the master!' She was so excited."

This seemed to please the master, who smiled warmly at the girl. The girl could feel the master's gaze. She knew the room's attention was focused on her. She glanced at the master briefly and then looked at the ceiling and screamed, "Bye-bye! Bye-bye! Bye-bye!"

"Bye-bye?" asked the master, amused. "You just got here. Where are you going?"

The girl ignored him, turned her head to resume staring out the window. The sun had sunk closer to the horizon, its rays lighting up the conference room. The girl watched the silhouette of a shirtless farmer in the distance struggling to pull a long bamboo pole four times his size out of the water, the parachute-shaped fishnet slowly rising from the murky river. The woman put her hand on her daughter's leg. "The doctors say she has *zibizheng*," she said quietly.

When strung together, the words meant "self-obstruction illness." I quietly withdrew my phone from my pocket and checked my Chinese dictionary: "autism."

"Autism doesn't work this way," the master said. "Tell me: which hospitals told you she was autistic?"

"The Children's Hospital in Beijing and Xinhua Hospital. They both told me that," she replied nervously.

These were the best hospitals in China and it was a costly decision for a woman of her means to go to the expense of traveling from Shanghai to Beijing to consult the country's best doctors.

The master wasn't impressed. "Go tell the doctors in Beijing to check their *own* heads," he said. "It sounds like *they're* the ones with the problem. You can keep analyzing her brain, but I'm telling you she isn't autistic!"

The woman suddenly looked sad. "She used to be normal . . ." she began to say.

"That's because you kept feeding her Western medicine!" the master snapped. "Those drugs made her dumb."

"I didn't give her many drugs," the woman protested quietly. "I stopped after a month because her energy level was low."

"Okay, then. Here's what you need to do," interrupted the master, pointing at the woman. "Go to Mount Putuo. Pray to the Guanyin *pusa* at the temple there. Do you understand? Bring your daughter. That'll work. Pray to Guanyin multiple times."

"How often should we go there?" asked the woman.

"The more you go, the better your girl will be. Just go to Mount Putuo and we'll observe the results later. But don't feed her any more medicine."

Chinese Buddhists consider Mount Putuo to be one of the country's four sacred mountains. Its hundred-foot-tall golden statue of Guanyin is a site of pilgrimage for millions of worshippers each year. It wasn't unusual for a Buddhist monk to suggest their pupils make a pilgrimage to the mountain. The manner in which CK's master had done so, though, made me feel uncomfortable. It was likely the girl was autistic; pediatricians at two of China's best hospitals had diagnosed her as such. The master's condescending refusal of the diagnosis made it seem like he was testing the woman's loyalty—not to her faith, but to him. He had given the woman what she wanted to hear: the reason for her daughter's behavior wasn't a mental disorder, rather a miraculous twist of fate concerning who she had been in a previous life. Her daughter was a special being, assured the master, and the woman would only have to look as far as him to confirm this. I kept quiet and scanned the faces of others around the room to gauge their reactions, but nobody seemed to share my discomfort.

"How about you?" the monk said, motioning his head to a middle-aged man in glasses sitting near the window. "You seem like you've got something to say."

The man nodded and sat on the edge of his seat. "My baby

daughter has a high fever every two weeks or so. It usually comes with a rash. We have no idea what's wrong with her."

The master thought for a moment. "How do you feed her? Breast milk?"

"We feed her formula and everything else she's supposed to be eating," the man replied.

"Did you breast-feed her?" the master asked.

"Yes, until she was seven months old."

"Then why is this?" asked the master, pausing to think some more, his fingers pulling the beads of his bracelet one by one. "Was she born naturally or by cesarean?"

"My wife wasn't able to give birth naturally, so we were forced to do a cesarean birth."

The master shook his head impatiently. "Just say 'Cesarean'!" he said, turning to the others with a smirk. "He always answers questions in a winding manner!"

Several others in the room snickered along, and the man began to laugh nervously. The master sat up and spoke. "You need to release captive animals. Any animal will do."

Before the master could turn to another pupil, the man interrupted. "Forgive me, master, but we've already released some animals in Shanghai," he said.

The master looked surprised. "What kind of animal was it?"

"Snakehead fish," he said.

"You misunderstand the scriptures!" the master said. "Next time release turtles! But remember—you can't let turtles go in those rivers in Shanghai, because there aren't any natural banks and they won't have a place to get out of the water and they'll drown. Do you understand?"

"Yes," said the man.

"And be careful about where you release them. Last time we let go of some turtles here, the neighbors caught them and ate them. Find a place away from people with soft mud nearby," said the master. "Of course, if someone catches the turtles later on, I am not responsible for that."

"Thank you," the man replied with a smile and a nod.

The master slouched back in his chair and slowly looked around the room. The girl diagnosed with autism was quietly humming to herself, and now that the room fell silent, she sang louder. When she finished, she asked the master, "Did I sing well? Did I sing well? Okay, bye-bye! Bye-bye!"

The master nodded. *"Emeituofo!"* he shouted—*May Buddha preserve you.*

"You, then," he said, pointing to a woman in her thirties sitting next to the girl. "You came last time with a problem. What was it again?"

The woman's long hair was pulled back, revealing a youthful, pretty face. She wore glasses and spoke too softly for anyone to hear, including the master. "Speak up!" he said. "Don't be shy."

The woman cleared her throat. "I'm not ovulating," she said loudly.

The master nodded. "Have you visited the doctor? Did he tell you why?"

The woman nodded silently.

"It's too embarrassing to say," guessed the master. "Did you see a Chinese doctor? How could a Chinese doctor fail to tell you the cause?"

A friend of the woman spoke up. "She went to see a Western doctor," she said.

"Go see a Chinese doctor!" said the master. "How old are you? Don't keep it secret! There is no secret with your master!"

"Thirty-five," said the woman.

"Okay, fine," said the master. "If you haven't cured this by the time you reach forty, we'll need to find another way. Let's think about why this happened to you. Think hard and think in relation to the past," he said, staring at the woman.

The woman averted her glance toward the floor. The master continued. "At a critical moment, I tried to help you, but you didn't listen. I told you that you and your husband weren't a good match. Now look. Do you want it this way, or does he want it? You must figure it out together. I'm telling you seriously now. Once you took a wrong step, everything else went wrong. I don't know what to tell you now."

The woman continued to stare at the floor, dejected.

The master moved on. There were a few people who sought advice on business matters—he responded with a promise that they would speak later in private—but for the most part, people had come here needing medical consultation. There were two other women who had problems conceiving children, a woman with an enlarged thyroid, and a man with a bad case of psoriasis that had spread to cover his neck and face. Doctors had diagnosed them and they'd undergone treatment, but for one reason or another their conditions had persisted, medical bills were piling up, and many of them were running out of money. China called its state health insurance program "universal," but in practice, it covered only the most basic of health problems. Appointments with a specialist were barely covered, and if you didn't have a Shanghai *hukou*—the situation that most people in this room found themselves—you'd have to pay even more out-of-pocket costs at city hospitals.

Even if you had saved enough to see a specialist, you'd be fortunate to receive thorough care. Chinese hospitals were typically overcrowded and underfunded. Doctors were considered government employees and were paid an average salary of less than a thousand U.S. dollars a month. It wasn't unusual for doctors to expect patients to hand over red envelopes stuffed with cash to perform any type of specialized procedure so that they could supplement their meager incomes. Doctors also routinely received kickbacks from pharmaceutical companies in return for prescribing their drugs. The practice was so entrenched in the system that it had coined the popular Chinese phrase *Yi Yao Yang Yi*: "feeding hospitals by selling drugs."

This muddled healthcare landscape had left people confused, desperate for solutions. The types of treatment their master had prescribed—a pilgrimage to Mount Putuo to make the signs of autism disappear, releasing turtles in the river to ease a child's persistent fever, and reevaluating a marriage so that a woman could start ovulating again—seemed just as reasonable to them as the medications their doctors had prescribed and were at price points they could afford.

"People don't know where to turn for some of their problems," CK told me later. "They've been to so many doctors and they eventually end up coming here to find answers."

AT DINNER THAT EVENING, the mother of the autistic girl sat next to me. Over a meal of stir-fried eggplant, stewed carrots, and pressed tofu, we talked about her daughter's behavior. She had come here because she was trying anything to help the girl. "I *know* she's autistic," she whispered with a frown about her master's afternoon diagnosis. "She was only three years old when we figured it out. She began talking and acting strangely. It's lucky we live in Shanghai. At least there they have special schools for kids like her."

I asked her if it cost extra money for her to attend a school like that. "No, it's free, but I pay a little extra to the teacher on the side so that they'll pay special attention to her," she said. Doctors weren't the only professionals who relied on red envelopes.

She told me most of the children at her daughter's school suffered from cerebral palsy, and she considered her daughter to be the most functional student in class. She asked me how American schools handled children with autism. "My mother's a primary school teacher," I said, "and in her school, autistic children go to class with all the other students."

"They'd never do that in China," she said. "They'd see that as too much of a distraction to the other children, and parents would definitely complain."

I told her the autistic children in my mom's school were typically assigned aides who escorted them from class to class to help them through their days. "*Wah!*" she shouted, elbowing her friend. "Did you hear that? In America, my daughter would get her own personal teacher!"

"*Meiguo hao,*" said her friend—*America's good*—and she stuck her thumb up. "*Pingdeng.*" *Equal.*

"Not China!" complained the mom. "China would never do

that for a disabled child. Hey—I heard the U.S. government gives all children free milk. Is that true?"

I told her there were some federal assistance programs that did that, but if the U.S. government gave free milk to all American children, it'd likely go bankrupt. America may seem like a nice place, I said, but it had a lot of problems, just like China. The woman shook her head, correcting me. *"Meiguo hao,"* she said again. *"Meiguo hao."*

THE CEREMONY BEGAN at nine o'clock the next morning. Overnight, the winds had shifted, and a cold, steady rain began, soaking the countryside. The temperature had plummeted, and worshippers in sweaters and jackets silently ate breakfast huddled around the coal briquette fire inside the temple's kitchen. A few of them cracked smiles when they heard the shouts of the autistic girl next door in the canteen going through a school morning exercise routine: "One-two-three-four! Two-two-three-four!" she yelled, waving her hands wildly and pacing in circles around the table where Jackie, Laurel, and Hardy sat, too busy staring into their phones to notice.

CK told me the master had held a special prayer ceremony for the girl the previous evening in the presence of a *pusa* statue. It ended when the girl began screaming loudly, kicked her mother, and ran out of the temple, sobbing. CK said the ceremony was meant to give the girl positive energy.

Before the morning's ceremony commenced, the congregation was split into two groups: those who believed, and those who didn't. We nonbelievers filed into the temple's main hall first, seating ourselves on leather cushions lined up against the sliding doors to each side of the entrance.

There were ten of us. As we waited for the believers to enter, we gazed up at a twelve-foot-tall bronze statue of Buddha. He sat in the lotus position, his hands resting on his lap in prayer, with two forefingers rising up to touch each other. His eyes were barely open and he was smiling. To his right, a stoic-looking guardian stood atop a white elephant holding a lotus stem. On Buddha's left, another guardian stood upon a blue tiger, raising a sword up in the air with his left hand. I took out my phone to snap a picture, but a young woman sitting next to me whispered that phones were forbidden inside the temple. On my other side, Jackie, Laurel, and Hardy sat on their cushions looking miserable. It would be an hour before they were allowed to look at their phones again.

While we waited, I asked the woman what she thought of the place. "It's my first time here," she whispered. "My friend brought me. It's nice. But I don't think I'll come back."

"Why not?"

"I don't believe in these kinds of things," she answered.

The master's four apprentice monks filed into the hall and took their positions to the side of the altar. They wore yellow robes and slippers and their heads were shaved. The ceremony began when one of them softly hit a bell with a mallet, letting the tone reverberate through the cold, empty hall. Another monk smashed a pair of cymbals together, while the third monk swung a curved stick and hit a large drum hanging by a rope tied to a beam above. The fourth monk led the others into a chant while the master stood inside the doorway, prostrating toward the statue of Buddha three times. CK was directly behind him, following his motions along with seven others. The rest of the believers stood behind this elite group, outside in the rain.

One by one, they entered the hallway, taking incense sticks and raising them above their heads with both hands before sticking them into a pot full of sand in front of the Buddha. The fragrant smoke swirled to the ceiling of the temple. Below, worshippers chanted, bowing in unison before filing out of the temple. The rest of us followed, walking single file under the eaves of the temple to protect ourselves from the rain, circumambulating the temple grounds before heading back to the main hall. I looked behind me and noticed Jackie using Hardy's massive body as a barrier from the cold, wet wind.

On our slow march back to the hall, the autistic girl began to scream, *"Wo zhiyao haochide! Wo zhiyao haochide!"* over and over. *I only want something good to eat! I only want something good to eat!* she cried, growing more frantic with each outburst.

It was a chant whose shrieking volume had managed to rise above the others'. Her mother grabbed the child's arm and shook it, urging her to stop, only making matters worse. I thought about the master's diagnosis, *"She's a disciple of Guanyin,"* as the rest of us watched the mother remove her distraught daughter from the ceremonial line, heading back toward the canteen in the pouring rain.

We returned to the main hall and chanted and prostrated before the Buddha for half an hour. The rhythm of the chanting picked up speed, cymbals and drums banged with a quicker tempo, *boom-crash, boom-crash, boom-crash!* I watched CK. His eyes were firmly set on the statue of Buddha as he walked toward the shrine. He closed his eyes and offered incense to the master. The master accepted it and stuck it into a pot atop the shrine. CK then pivoted with military precision and slowly marched away, his hands clasped together, deep in prayer as the tempo of the percussion quickened.

Through the incense smoke, CK's face looked sincere, earnest. He really wants to be a better person, I thought. Many people I knew didn't. They were too burdened by making enough money, helping their children, and among many here, finding sound medical help before they could begin thinking about improving themselves. And while the master of this temple was no medical doctor, he was a spiritual one. Just as Fu had learned to do at her illegal church, CK was carefully bypassing the master's dodgier traits to glean what he could from him, like a lotus flower twisting through the mud, as this was the best opportunity he had found in his search for the light.

CK and the others returned to their cushions. The monks to the side were now crashing the cymbals and pounding the drum in a frenzy, and the worshippers responded by prostrating in one wave after another, faster and faster, alongside the furious pace of the deafening metallic collisions, thumping, and chanting. Finally, the master stood, seized a mallet, and struck a bronze bell.

In an instant, the noise ceased, the temple fell silent, and the vibrations of the bell resounded through the temple, blending with the rhythms of nature outside. Suddenly, the sound of rain pounding on the concrete was all we heard. I peered through the temple's latticed window and noticed an elderly couple walking along the swollen river with hoes over their shoulders, on their way to their rice paddies to resume work.

LATER, BACK IN THE CANTEEN, we waited for a final meal before the bus took us back home to Shanghai. CK sat with me and asked me what I thought of the weekend. "It was interesting," I said. "It seems like you've found something special here."

CK nodded. "I've come here many times, but this time was different," he said. "I'm surprised the master chose me to worship directly behind him."

The master had given CK homework: prayers, chants, and a meditation schedule. I had requested an interview with the master, but he had instructed CK to tell me that he was too busy for questions from a foreign journalist. "You can write whatever you want about the weekend," CK told me, "but my master has only one request: please don't write where the temple is located. We'd like to keep that quiet."

I nodded. I asked CK how his new faith was improving him. He thought for a moment. "Before I came here, I drank a lot, smoked pot sometimes, you know, if a friend wanted to get a drink, I'd stay up all night and drink with him. But after coming to temple, I don't feel the need to do that anymore. It feels unhealthy—both for me and for my energy.

"Everything was out of control," he continued. "I feel like I'm taking back control of my life now."

The door opened and people shook their umbrellas in the entryway, walking to the kitchen to help set the tables for lunch. CK and I watched them. "I like going somewhere I can worship with others who feel the same way as me," he added. "We're doing it together, no matter who we are."

All his life, CK had yearned to find a place where he truly belonged. He stood up to go help the others. Outside, the raindrops continued their steady beat, filling the river with ripples.

As we waited for lunch, I wandered into a storage area behind the canteen. Half-finished carved doors were stacked to the ceiling next to a wheelbarrow and an old circular saw. Light from the temple hall above shined through the cracks and onto discarded drums and broken incense pots strewn about the dirt floor. I could hear the faint voices of people upstairs mixed with the sound of raindrops outside.

Tucked away in a corner of the storage room behind a broken cabinet was a glass box as tall as me. Inside it, a statue of Mao, wearing his trademark gray suit, stared straight at me. I froze when I saw him. The Chairman was the last person I expected to meet in the basement of a Buddhist temple. But here he was, smiling, his face made to look like Buddha's, with only his haircut and trademark mole above his chin giving him away.

I guessed the master had kept this display handy in case of a visit from local Party officials. But there was no such visit today. The people upstairs were merely *laobaixing,* commoners, who had learned everything they needed to know about this figure in the temple's basement. Now they were searching for something more. On each side of the old leader hung red ribbons with black characters. They read:

ALWAYS REMEMBER CHAIRMAN MAO
NEVER FORGET THE COMMUNIST PARTY

Home

家

A month after the demolition of Maggie Lane, Mayor Chen and his wife, Xie Guozhen, wrote a letter to the mayor of Shanghai:

> *We are now homeless. The weather is getting colder. Our property rights and our rights to live in peace have been ignored. We hope our leaders can look into this matter and restore a sense of fairness and dignity to our lives in this beautiful city of Shanghai.*

The couple had lost their home, but they had found shelter. After boarding in run-down hotels for a couple of months, they rented an apartment down a quiet lane in another part of the former French Concession. "This place is better than the Summit," joked Mayor Chen when I visited.

Their new place was a two-room apartment with high ceilings that had been the upstairs of a European-style villa a century ago. We sat at a table in front of a pair of French doors that opened onto a balcony overlooking a garden. The couple rented the apartment for the equivalent of four hundred dollars a month, a little more than half their monthly pension.

Mayor Chen seemed unusually upbeat, given the circumstances. Shanghai's mayor hadn't responded to his letter, he hadn't been able to retrieve his belongings, and local journalists wouldn't talk to him. "There are simply too many forced demolition cases in China," Mayor Chen recalled a reporter from Xinhua News Agency telling him over the phone. "We've run out of good angles to pursue."

He told me that I was the sole journalist who remained interested in Maggie Lane, and he wondered if it made sense for us to visit the district housing bureau together. The last time I had done that was two years ago when I had accompanied Old Kang, who had been homeless ever since his house was torn apart by an excavator.

"After you visited their office, the officials were scared, so they agreed to give Old Kang a thousand yuan a month in compensation," he told me.

Mayor Chen said it was enough money for Old Kang to afford rent in an apartment on the outskirts of Shanghai. I paused, unsure of what to think of that.

"Actually, I'm not sure if that's a good idea," he said, responding to my hesitancy. "They'd probably make me sign something promising I'll stop bothering them."

Mayor Chen had no intention of doing that. On his bedside table was a book he had checked out from the Shanghai Library, *Regulations on State-Owned Land: Demolition and Compensation,* a volume he had filled with bright yellow bookmarkers. He opened the book to a well-worn page, following the tiny Chinese characters with his forefinger: "Look at this passage—it couldn't be more obvious," he told me. "Regarding forced relocation: 'The notary bureau must inform the property owner to be on site. If not, the notary bureau must make records of seized property. Then the property must be recorded and checked, one by one.'"

On the day their home was demolished, Mayor Chen and Xie returned to Maggie Lane and discovered the notary bureau officials didn't have time to make a list of their belongings. Instead, officials had thrown their possessions into large plastic bags and hastily tossed them into trucks so that excavators and bulldozers could flatten the house as quickly as possible.

Mayor Chen flipped through the book to another marked page. "See here: even if they were to demolish our home, they have to notify us in advance," he said, raising his voice. "Beijing must dispatch an investigative team down here! They've severely violated the people's interest."

Xie had been sitting quietly on the edge of the bed, but hearing this made her giggle, almost making her spill her tea. "Xi Jinping would never send 'an investigative team' down here!" she said, scolding her husband. "There are endless cases like this in China. What happened to us is just a drop in the ocean! Why would he bother?"

Mayor Chen shut the book with an angry snap. Xie ignored him. "He believes in a China that appears on television and looks perfect and nice," she said, pointing to her husband. "But what's happening right here, right now? This is the real China."

Mayor Chen turned to his wife. "I honestly believed they wouldn't demolish our house like that," he said. "They kept on saying they would protect the people's interest. I still have a hard time believing what happened to us that day."

Xie shook her head and looked at her husband like a master looks at a puppy that won't stop chasing its tail.

"I wanted to ask you," Mayor Chen said, turning to me: "My brother lives in New York. Do you think we could appeal to the United Nations?"

Xie bit her lip and looked to the ceiling in exasperation.

"I'm not sure that would work," I said.

He nodded, studying the cover of his book. His brother owned a house in Brooklyn and had urged him to move to the United States, too. Mayor Chen had never considered the possibility. Plus, he told me, he could no longer leave the country. He had left his passport behind inside his house—now a pile of rubble. In the months following the demolition of their home, Mayor Chen's outlook had developed an icy stubbornness. Before, he'd felt it was his right to remain in his home inside an abandoned demolished neighborhood. Now, with his home and neighborhood wiped off the map, those feelings had only hardened. He was still holding out for the Xuhui District government to compensate him and his wife with a home near their demolished neighborhood, an unlikely outcome.

"At what point do you just give up?" I asked him. "When do you stop fighting and move on?"

He bristled at the question. "Impossible," he blurted. "We've agreed among us neighbors that we'll keep fighting. We just have to keep finding new ways to fight."

"What does your brother in the United States think of all of this? He grew up in the house, too," I said.

"We talk every day on the phone. He's also asked me whether I'd just take one step back and compromise, maybe ask for homes in the countryside as compensation," Mayor Chen said.

"Wouldn't that be a better solution?" I asked.

"Why would we do that?" he asked. "We're not slaves. We're the masters of our house. It belonged to my father, and now it belongs to my family. It's ours. The government has no legal right to it."

"But these laws you're talking about," I said, "they may be written down somewhere, but the Party is above the law. If you've got a legal dispute with the government, these laws are as good as *jiade*."

The word meant "fake," and Mayor Chen shook his head vigorously at the sound of it. "No!" he shouted. "These laws are real. The government in this case just refuses to follow them. How about the Chinese constitution? I suppose that's not real, either? You can't just say these things are all fake. Even the Party insists they're real."

They were real—for the Party. The Party had created these laws and the Party's leadership—not China's 1.4 billion citizens—had the final say on how they should be interpreted. If any legal disputes arose between the citizenry and the state, it didn't take a genius to figure out who would win.

A WEEK AFTER my visit to Chen and Xie's new apartment, a court in Beijing heard the case of a local legislator who called on the Party to enforce its own constitution on behalf of its citizens. It was January of 2014. The man's name was Xu Zhiyong, a forty-year-old who carried the physique of a marine and a mind that had made him one of China's brightest lawyers. In 2002, state television had named him one of the "Top Ten Figures in the Rule of Law." In his work as a legal activist, Xu had called on the government to give children of migrant workers better access to educational opportunity, the sort of thing that had dimmed the hopes of Zhao Shiling's sons Big Sun and Little Sun back on the Street of Eternal Happiness. Xu had also made a public plea for China's leaders to disclose their assets, a sensitive topic for leader Xi Jinping, whose family members were discovered by *Bloomberg* to have amassed hundreds of millions of dollars in assets.

Xu had formed a group called the New Citizens Movement. It sought to push for reform from within China's system to ensure the rule of law. At the time, his demands weren't that different from those of China's leadership. Key figures in the government were also pushing for educational reform, and Chinese president Xi Jinping had overseen an anti-corruption campaign that had removed thousands of corrupt officials from office and brought them to justice. Yet when Xu called for an end to corruption, he was arrested and removed from his second term in office as a representative to the National People's Congress. And on that cold day in January, he was sentenced to four years in prison. As Xu was led away by guards, he told those present, "The court today has completely destroyed what remained of respect for rule of law in China."

When I saw the headlines of Xu's imprisonment on foreign news sites the next day, I thought of Mayor Chen. He fought with the same zeal and sense of righteousness as Xu did. Would he end up in prison, too?

LATER THAT YEAR, I woke up to the rumbling sound of an excavator clearing the rubble of Chen and Xie's house. The bright orange mechanical dinosaur lurched forward, scooping red bricks, crushed concrete, and pieces of splintered wood. It jerked and swiveled, lifting all of it high up into the air before dropping the debris into a green dump truck with a terrific crash. It took just a day to remove all traces of a neighborhood that had lasted eighty years. Later, a work crew in orange jumpsuits appeared. They poured concrete and built a red-roofed dormitory for workers. The rumor among residents at the Summit was that the land had been leased to a developer and work on a series of new high-rises would soon begin.

"*Bu dui,*" Mayor Chen told me when I called him. "That's incorrect. The district hasn't sold the land. They're not going to do anything until they settle our complaint. The city's got a bunch of public works projects this summer. That's just temporary housing for the workers."

Each morning that summer I ate breakfast and watched the workers—migrants from the countryside—mill outside their dorm rooms, squatting in the sun, sipping gruel from their bowls. They would leave together to repair a street or install a new gas line, and they would reappear in the early evening, exhausted and sweaty, a day's wage earned, a little more money for their families back home.

As night fell, so did the lights from their windows. They would fall asleep and dream where Chen had slept and dreamed as a child, and where countless others had slept and dreamed before him. And like everyone else, one day they disappeared. In the autumn, the workers in orange jumpsuits reemerged to dismantle the structure, and by the end of the year, Maggie Lane had reverted to a walled-in abandoned lot where stray cats roamed through a wilderness of chest-high weeds. For now, it was a quiet jungle in the middle of China's biggest concentration of humanity, indifferent to anyone who bought it or sold it or called it home. It sat still, awaiting its next reincarnation.

◆◆◆

WHEN I MOVED TO SHANGHAI in 2010, the wall surrounding Maggie Lane read "Better City, Better Life." Five years later, the message read:

FULFILL OUR CHINESE DREAM
AND VITALITY WILL FILL CHINA

The first sign was nailed to the other side of the wall from where Mayor Chen and Xie had lost their home, facing the street. Every twenty feet after that, another one appeared. Each carried a different saying or poem, all with the same message: Embrace the Chinese Dream and love your motherland. The framed propaganda posters followed the wall as it snaked around Maggie Lane and wrapped around two corners, the last sign facing the spot where Weiqi's father had burned to death trying to protect his home from a demolition crew.

In Hong Kong, a storm was brewing when Weiqi answered the phone. "The weather's been terrible—every afternoon around this time, a storm comes that looks like the end of the world," he told me. "It reminds me of home—kind of like *huangmei tian* in Shanghai."

They were known as the plum rains in English, and they arrived each June, coinciding with the appearance of yellow plums in the countryside. The few weeks of stormy weather ushered in the oppressively humid summer to the Yangtze Delta.

But on this day in late May, the skies over Shanghai were blue, the air crisp, and a warm breeze blew through the window of my eleventh-floor office. I stood at my window, watching old men fly kites in the sculpture park below. On the other end of the phone line, Weiqi was in a vacant conference room overlooking central Hong Kong, opting to watch the approaching storm instead of the markets. We were both playing hooky.

Weiqi talked about wedding preparations. His fiancée was from Yunnan, in China's rural southwest. She had met Weiqi while completing her master's at Cornell. They would marry in the fall, and Weiqi's mother had taken a hiatus from her petitioning to help out.

The ceremony was planned for the Xijiao Guesthouse, a luxurious state-owned hotel where China's leaders stayed whenever they visited Shanghai. It seemed an odd choice for the son of a woman who was in and out of prison for protesting China's leaders, but Weiqi didn't think this way. Contradictions like this were everywhere in China, and he was too busy planning his wedding to notice.

He was also trying to hold on to his job. China's economic growth had cooled, a bear market had emerged, and there were layoffs throughout Hong Kong's investment banking sector.

Outside my window, students in white jumpsuits and red handkerchiefs tied around their necks burst from the doors of the school below my building. Groups of them walked toward the park to steal some playtime before another night of homework. High above them, a flock of homing pigeons flew in the afternoon sun, flying this way and that, all changing course whenever the ones in the lead felt the instinct to do so. They stuck close together, none of them straying from what appeared to be a random flight pattern.

"You report on China's economy. What do you think will happen?" Weiqi asked.

I got this question wherever I traveled in China. This was one of the most perplexing economies in the world to figure out, yet the inquiry was a logical one: I was a foreign journalist and I was free to travel around China to investigate the matter, unlike most local journalists. The question always made me feel like I had performed terribly at my job. It was unanswerable. "The more I learn about China's economy, the less I feel I really know," I told him. "A big part of the economy is off the books, so it's impossible to know what's really going on. All I can go on is the anecdotal evidence I see from my reporting trips."

"And what has that shown you?" asked Weiqi.

"There's more money in China than ever, but much of that money has gone to build wasteful projects that probably won't ever serve anybody," I said.

"That's what I'm seeing, too," Weiqi told me.

He had noticed a surge of investors moving their wealth out of China. "People say that if your money is in Mainland China, then it's not real money," he told me. "If you're living inside a system that doesn't respect personal property, then it's never certain your money is actually yours."

Weiqi had spent a lot of time thinking about property. His father had died for it, his mother devoted her life to fighting for it, and he had spent years in one of America's finest universities studying its impact on the flow of capital. After all this time, he concluded that the Party's respect for personal property would ultimately determine whether it succeeds or fails. "Once a government shows respect for personal property, then it gives itself a chance to build wealthy, powerful groups of people who won't fear for their safety," Weiqi explained. "After a period of time, these groups will become relatively reasonable and they'll learn to compromise with each other in terms of setting up the new rules for a better country."

If that were to happen, Weiqi predicted, then people might someday have the right to *truly* own their own land in China, instead of leasing it from what had become the biggest landlord in the world.

And while he had learned not to place too much faith in any one leader of his country, Weiqi was more encouraged by President Xi Jinping than of anyone else who had come before him. "When you grow up in a senior official's family, you're educated well and the chances are higher that you've become a reasonable person," he said. "His 'Chinese Dream' is an ambition to bring China to a better place, and that's great, but I don't think the power of a single person can change China's path at this stage. It really takes time, because, to be honest, it's not just his country."

Weiqi had plans to someday return to Shanghai. "I hate Hong Kong," he confessed; "it's a messed-up city.

"Most people here are miserable; they can't even afford to own property. Shanghai has a lot of problems, too, but I'm still willing to live there, despite all that's happened to my family. I've already been through a lot. I'm no longer scared."

A warm breeze blew through my window. Outside, children ran after one another through the park below. I could hear their distant giggles from the eleventh floor. Above the trees, the sky was clear, and the pigeons' afternoon flight was over. They had instinctually followed one another back to their cages down one of the lanes behind the park. While they were away, their master had cleaned their pens and filled their cups with seed. I imagined them hungrily pecking at their dinner, filling their stomachs, content to be back home.

♦♦♦

FOR FIVE YEARS, Wang Xuesong's American existence was neatly contained within a three-mile radius of the Flushing library. His world would soon expand. He would celebrate his fifty-eighth birthday by earning the equivalent of a high school diploma. Then, maybe a job that would pull him away from Queens. "I'm already going all the way to Manhattan for job training," Wang told me with a confident smile.

Wang seemed more interested than ever in the world beyond Flushing. It was autumn of 2014, and I was visiting New York again. I was staying with my brother's family in New Jersey, and I took the train into the city. Wang asked me how long it had taken, and whether I had run into any trouble on my journey. He asked a lot of questions about New Jersey. What was it like? Were the houses big? Did you see wild animals out there? Did any Chinese live there? He had only heard of the place. To a man who had never strayed beyond New York City, the Garden State sounded wild and exotic.

Wang's unemployment benefits package included government-subsidized job training. For the next two years, he would venture into Manhattan once a week for classes in office management. "I suppose it'll help me qualify to work at a front desk in a clinic or a hospital," he surmised. "Or maybe at a law firm downtown or something like that."

He sounded like a high school senior who had just begun to ponder the mysteries of the labor market. The last time I had seen him, half a year ago, he had taken an exam with his heart set on becoming a repair technician for the MTA. "I failed," he told me without a hint of sadness in his voice. "My English wasn't good enough."

In the meantime, he had applied for part-time sales jobs at the Gap and at a duty-free shop at JFK Airport, but he hadn't heard back from either.

Though Wang was beginning to venture out a little, he still insisted on meeting at the same bench we sat at last time, inside the window of the Flushing library. It was a late-autumn morning, and the leaves on the trees had begun to change colors. The street across from us was lined with shop fronts in Chinese characters: "Cuijiang City Supermarket," "Bright Star Number One Beauty Salon," "Peaceful Good Health Pharmacy," and so on. Its foreignness reminded me of what the Street of Eternal Happiness was beginning to look like back in Shanghai, as more Western restaurants and cafés were opting to advertise themselves in English. Wang wore a cream-colored button-down shirt with a paisley pattern tucked into black dress pants. "These are your letters," I said, handing him a plastic bag full of papers that sagged with the weight of a bowling ball.

Over the summer he had given the matter of the letters some thought, and when I called him from Shanghai to let him know I'd be in town again, he had mustered up the courage to ask, "W-w-would you mind making copies of them for me?"

"*Wah!*" he said, lifting the bag. "I didn't know there were so many of them! This must have been very troublesome for you, carrying these all the way from Shanghai and then on your train trip from New Jersey!"

"*Meiyou,*" I replied, using the catchall Chinese word for "no."

Wang reached into the bag and pulled out the stack, flipping through them. He stopped when he saw a letter written by his mother. She had etched "1960" at the top of the page. She was thirty-four years old. Wang was just two. "I remember my sisters telling me about this," he said, pausing to read the rest of the letter. "The government had t-t-taken our home and we had to pay rent on it. They charged us 8.5 yuan a month. That was only a dollar, but my mother couldn't even afford to pay that. Sh-she was raising six children—we were all so young."

He placed the letter on his lap. "After a few months, o-o-officials from the housing department showed up. They told us if we didn't pay, they'd send us to Gansu province. They promised there'd be jobs and houses there. Of course they were lying. My m-m-mother knew of people in the neighborhood who had g-g-gone to Gansu and ended up b-begging to survive before they escaped and made it back to Shanghai. My mother cried. She t-t-told the man she couldn't do that to her children. They finally left us alone. Otherwise, we all would have ended up in G-g-gansu," said Wang, his gaze lost in his mother's handwriting. "The famine was t-t-terrible in Gansu—people were eating grass and tree bark and worse. So many people starved to death there. We p-p-probably would've died there, too."

The province was among the mountains and high desert of China's northwest. In a three-year period, more than a million people had starved there. Reports of cannibalism weren't unusual among those who had survived.

I imagined Liu, crying in the doorway of her quiet lane in Shanghai, her children wondering about the strange man who had made their mother so sad. I pictured the official, deciding whether to go through with sending this woman and her children off to die in the countryside for being late on their rent. What had made him change his mind? Was it pity? Was it late in the afternoon of a long day and had he been too tired to complete the paperwork? Whatever it was, his split-second decision was the reason Wang and I were sitting here talking fifty-five years later, in a library on the other side of the world.

The fates of others had been decided that day, too. I asked Wang about his sisters. Big Sister, Sister Two, and Sister Four lived with their families in New York; their children were in college. Baby Sister—Wang's sister who had been given away—had divorced and remarried. She had retired early and moved to Vancouver with her husband and daughter. "She was very good at business and made a lot of money. My older sisters are all doing well, too. They all own their own homes. In comparison, I'm the worst!" he said with a chuckle. "Here I am, nearly sixty years old, and still learning English!"

Wang felt he should have tried to study English when he had been young, but he admitted it would have been difficult, since school had often been canceled for political rallies when he was a teenager and English had been considered a language of the capitalist class. "English should become a universal language for the world," Wang told me. "Much of the world already speaks it, and just imagine if everyone in the world all spoke the same language? So many international problems boil down to poor communication. There must be a solution."

When he had arrived at his new home, all of his friends were Chinese. Five years later, he had befriended classmates from Russia, India, and Cuba. They often shared stories of their home countries, and had chatted about the world's problems. "I have a business idea that probably seems a bit immature," Wang admitted. "I'd like to start a dating company. My goal would be to introduce people from different countries to each other. I think it'd be better if someday everyone belongs to the same race and speaks the same language. There wouldn't be any differences. Everyone would be equal."

Wang sounded energized by the spirit of New York City. "However long that takes, what kind of government do you think people will have?" I asked him.

"Some of my friends here think the Chinese political system is more efficient," Wang told me. "Nothing needs to be dragged on. One person can make a decision instead of a good idea being stalled by bickering from opposing parties."

Wang paused to give the question more thought. "But if that one decision-maker isn't good, or he doesn't have enough knowledge about running a country and he makes bad decisions, then we're all done," he said. "I think a political system like the one in the United States is superior."

Wang hadn't voted yet. Becoming an American citizen would mean giving up his Chinese citizenship. Once he did that, he'd lose the property rights to his family's home on the Street of Eternal Happiness.

Wang wrinkled his forehead in thought. "But I need to deal with this problem," he said. "After all, one can only live in one place at a time. Once I've made the decision to call America my home, I suppose I'll sell the old one."

Home was calling. Wang had news for me, and he let it slip toward the end of our conversation on that autumn morning: "I just got married," he told me softly. "My wife is in Guangdong. She hopes to come here next year for good."

Wang looked embarrassed. He had always taken his filial duties seriously, and in a household without a father, he understood his role as his family's only son. He had spent his life looking after his mother, taking on the duties of the husband she had lost. But his mother's blank stares these past few years had taught him he was slowly losing his companion.

It was an arranged marriage. A friend of Wang's had introduced the woman to him, and after months of chatting online, he had flown to the southern province of Guangdong to meet her. A few days later, the two had married in her hometown. She was a thirty-eight-year-old divorcée from the countryside. "She's nineteen years younger than me!" he said, laughing. "She's applying for a U.S. visa now."

"Does she speak English?"

"Not really," Wang said. "She can start out here working as a nurse. She speaks Mandarin and Cantonese, so that will help her get a job."

In Flushing, speaking two Chinese languages was more useful than a command of English, and Wang's unemployment and welfare benefits were more than enough for them to get by. "Do you have a picture of her?" I asked.

Wang couldn't afford a smartphone, so he kept a few photos inside his wallet. He looked inside and realized he'd forgotten her photo. "I don't have it here. Anyhow, she's not very good-looking," he said happily.

He seemed particularly pleased by this last point. Like many Chinese pairings, it was a marriage of convenience. The woman was from a poor region in northern Guangdong, and Wang knew his U.S. residency was the primary reason she would agree to marry someone nearly two decades her senior—if she were too pretty,

Wang reasoned, he would constantly worry about her leaving him for someone else once she made it to New York.

"Do you want to have children?" I asked him.

Wang smiled. "That's our wish," he said, looking outside at the clear blue sky over New York City.

Wang carefully returned the copies of his parents' letters to the plastic bag, unzipped his black duffel bag, and packed it neatly alongside his high school textbooks. Class was about to start. His friends were trickling into the library; they waved to us before descending the stairs to the classrooms below. On the other side of the planet, his wife was preparing for the journey of her life. Wang stood up and smiled. "Everyone needs a family," he said, shaking my hand to say goodbye. "You can't always be alone."

15

Chinese Dreams

中国梦们

In the ten years CK had been away from Hunan, his family had never asked him to come home. Then one morning in the winter of 2014, he got a phone call. "Grandma had a stroke," his father told him. "Half her body's paralyzed. We need you back home."

CK's father was feeding Grandma three times a day, pushing her wheelchair outside for air in the afternoons, and stumbling out of bed twice a night to carry her to the bathroom. He could leave her side only for an hour or so each time. Meanwhile, his own health problems were mounting. He had suffered a minor heart attack and he was scheduled for surgery. CK was summoned home for a month to take care of Grandma.

CK could manage the accordion business by phone. *2nd Floor Your Sandwich* was another story. His partner, Max, had gotten his girlfriend pregnant and was headed back to his hometown to marry. "You're on your own," he had told CK.

The father-to-be would become a minority shareholder, and CK would take over day-to-day operations. With months of hard work ahead, CK knew this might be the last time he would see his grandmother. He packed his suitcase full of books about esoteric Tibetan Buddhism, tossed in a few changes of clothing, boarded a high-speed train, and rode 750 miles to Hunan.

It was a respite from the temptations of the city. Since we'd journeyed to see his master together, he'd made several more pilgrimages to the temple, and CK seemed healthier and much happier. After closing his shop for the day, he'd been accustomed to heading out for drinks with friends, but lately he preferred to go home to meditate before bedtime.

"Born for faith, Fight for faith, Die for faith," proclaimed his WeChat profile. Posts that once chronicled night after night of partying now displayed photos of him and his brothers-in-learning building extensions to his master's temple. "We're installing 1080 Sakayami statues inside the upper roof," read one post. "If anyone wants to leave a virtuous gift for us, it's RMB500 per statue. Your honorable name will be carved on the lotus seat of each statue. May Buddha preserve you!"

GRANDMA WAS NINETY years old. CK had heard her tell stories about her privileged childhood. She was the daughter of a banker and the family chauffeur would escort her to a private girls' school each day. After she graduated, she married a literature professor. She was twenty-five years old when the Communists took China, seized her family's assets, and slapped the label of "landlord class" onto her family. The Red Guards assigned her family a new label several years later: "counterrevolutionary." As a young man, CK's grandfather had been recruited as a soldier for the Kuomintang, who had seized control of his hometown, and fought the Communists.

At the height of the Cultural Revolution, Red Guards knocked on Grandpa and Grandma's door at three o'clock each morning to question and threaten him. This happened every night for months. Grandpa lost sleep and the stress drove him mad.

"There was no way to fight against the system," CK told me. "Either you killed yourself, which a lot of people chose to do at the time, or you just suffered. There was no other way. Everyone was brainwashed, and everyone was afraid."

By the time CK was born, Grandpa had moved out, choosing to suffer alone in a tiny, smelly room downstairs from his family's apartment. Grandma would go to his room every day to cook for him. "He couldn't think straight," CK told me. "His body was always shaking, and he was always scared of people knocking on his door at night to come and take him away." Human interaction had made him sick.

This reminded me of something Wang Xuesong had told me when I visited him at the Flushing library. Occasionally while in the throes of Alzheimer's, his mother would suddenly sit up in the middle of the night, terrorized by what she was certain were Red Guards pounding on the door of their New York apartment. They're waiting to question me, she'd tell her son.

CK knew never to ask his grandmother about what had happened to his grandfather. It was this same understanding that led him to suffer alone at such a young age, struggling to cut his wrists while his grandmother dozed inches away, oblivious to her grandson's misery.

But these events were in the past. Opportunities had grown immeasurably for CK's generation. His parents and grandparents may have been completely tied to the system, simply trying to survive, but he had grown up with options. He had chosen his own career, his own religion, his own home, and his own dreams.

Yet CK hadn't chosen where he was born. Among the requirements of those who grew up in China were filial duties. And so, for three weeks, CK woke at four o'clock each morning, carried Grandma to the bathroom, and then to the kitchen where he made breakfast for her. He'd go to the market for groceries, then stop by the hospital to see his father before heading home to cook lunch and dinner for Grandma. He would roll her wheelchair outside each day for fresh air. During the night, he would wake twice to carry her to the bathroom. When his father had recuperated enough to return home, CK took care of him, too.

"It wasn't easy to live with my father again," CK told me after he returned. Grandma could no longer speak, so his father had become accustomed to living in silence. He filled the void by talking to himself, and had stopped responding to CK when he spoke to him.

This silent treatment was a departure from CK's childhood, when his father would spend hours patiently listening to his father's rants about *the system*. Now his father had become a mumbling, empty shell. CK admitted he didn't know which was worse.

There was one time CK's father had become coherent enough to order him to liquidate the sandwich shop. It was losing too much money, he told his son.

"Someday I might take his advice," CK said with a frown. "But I've still got savings. I honestly don't know how much I've got in my bank account, really."

I took this as a good sign. He lived frugally, and had enough padding from his Polverini work to fatten up a retirement fund. And for years, he'd been able to send two thousand yuan home to each parent to cover their monthly expenses.

ONE AFTERNOON while CK was alone in the apartment with Grandma, she asked him to carry her to bed.

"The way she asked me, something in her face, I felt strange," CK told me. "I said, 'Okay Grandma,' and put her in bed."

Two minutes later, CK still had a bad feeling about the request. He pushed open the bedroom door.

"She had tied one end of a scarf around the pole of the headboard," he told me.

The other end of the scarf was tied around her neck. She was trying to roll herself off the bed. CK frantically stepped toward her and lifted her frail body back onto the center of the mattress. He unfurled the scarf from her neck and the two collapsed upon the bed, grandson embracing grandmother, in the quiet bedroom they'd shared long ago.

+++

"BUSY MEANS you're making money. Once you turn idle? That's when you start to lose it," Auntie Fu said, motioning to her husband.

Uncle Feng was tucked under the covers, flat on his back, snoozing through a health program that blared on his television. Auntie had switched hers off when I arrived.

It was the dead of winter. On my bike ride over, the brittle, naked plane trees lining the street allowed a clear view of the buildings above: low, ornate villas built by Europeans a century ago set against a towering backdrop of glass and steel built by the Chinese. Amid the past decade's flurry of construction, it seemed no one was ever idle in Shanghai.

Especially Auntie Fu. At the end of the Year of the Horse, I tallied her tangle of investment schemes: the sexual-health-pad pyramid scheme, a Wenzhou firm dealing in gold bars, a company that dubbed itself "China's largest antique trading platform," an Inner Mongolia business that sold medicinal tea squeezed from a shrub called sea buckthorn, the mushroom company that had flown Fu to their headquarters, and of course, Gatewang, the e-commerce terminal company.

None appeared to have a real future. The mushroom company had been labeled a scam by a local judge, and the company employees promptly sentenced to prison. Gatewang was the subject of several online forums concluding it was fraudulent, too. And those were the only two I'd looked into.

All told, Fu had dumped the equivalent of fifty thousand dollars into get-rich-quick schemes. It was nearly her entire life's savings.

The pair's property investments seemed just as dismally chaotic. Since returning from Xinjiang in 1993 after the birth of their first son, the couple had acquired five properties. I took stock of their real estate portfolio: Two were eventually demolished to make way for Shanghai's development, one was discovered to be illegally converted, Uncle Feng sold another to buy his mistress a new home, and the last was the run-down ground-level unit the couple shared on the Street of Eternal Happiness. Among these, two were at the center of lawsuits Fu had filed years ago, one of them against her own husband. Neither had been resolved.

How did a life's work come to this? Auntie Fu and I reviewed the details with cups of sea buckthorn tea, over which she'd occasionally lapse into a sales pitch. "It's good for your heart! Buy a box and sell them to your friends!"

I glanced over at Uncle Feng under the covers, and yearned to curl up in a fetal position beside him. On the surface, these two appeared to live a life of simplicity—a tiny apartment, modest pensions, children and grandchildren to visit each weekend—yet underneath were chaotic lives filled with deception, heartbreak, and greed.

Uncle Feng snored while we finished our tea. Auntie quietly picked up the remote control beside him and turned his television's volume down. She walked over to the corner of the room and reached into a box with both hands. She gently pulled out a photo album. She stood, illuminated against the light of the TV for a moment, wiping the album carefully with a single square of toilet paper. She put on her eyeglasses and sat beside me at the table.

"Last time you were here, you said you wanted to see our old photos from Xinjiang," she said, handing me the album.

It was covered in white silk and displayed a picture of a mother panda eating bamboo with its cub. The photos inside spanned decades. I paged through it slowly, pausing to take a look at the earliest photo of the couple. It was a black-and-white portrait from 1971. Auntie and Uncle were newlyweds in their twenties. Uncle Feng sported a newsboy cap tilted to the side, and a tattered collared shirt with horizontal stripes. The shirt opened to reveal a broad chest and skin darkened from days spent outside in the desert sun. His teeth were white and perfectly straight. He looked confident and handsome and he smiled with his whole face, without a trace of the cynicism that had come to define his personality.

Auntie Fu sat in front of him, leaning backward, nestled into his shoulder. Her dark cheeks framed a broad, joyous smile. The two looked like a happy young couple in love.

The studio backdrop was a painted landscape of a pine forest along the shores of a still lake reflecting snowcapped mountains above. "That's an actual place in Xinjiang," Fu said, gently placing her index finger on the backdrop, ignoring her and her husband's smiling faces. "It's not far from where we lived."

Fu smiled, tapping the photo. "Once Gatewang is listed and I make my fortune, I'm going to buy a house there and move back."

This was her dream: to return to the untamed frontier, where rivers ran freely and mountains were reflected in crystal-clear alpine lakes, a place of beauty and simplicity.

It would be a long wait for her ticket home. Her shares in Gatewang remained worthless; the company would likely never be listed. Each time I visited, I asked about Gatewang's progress.

"Not yet," she would say with a trace of disappointment. But then her face usually lit up again. "Just wait till next month!"

I had heard her repeat this eleven times in the past year.

That spring, the month finally arrived. "Gatewang's on the London exchange!" Auntie announced. "I should be collecting my money any day now."

I hurried back to my office to confirm the news, only to shake my head with disappointment. Zhu Jun, Gatewang's executive director, had acquired an interest in a similar-sounding company based in London named GATE Ventures. It was a shell company that had just listed on the Alternative Investment Market, a submarket of the London Stock Exchange that had fewer regulatory requirements.

Conveniently, the stock code for the company was GATE, and Mr. Zhu announced at Gatewang's annual meeting, in March 2015: "We've listed!" Investors asked for the ticker. "GATE," he told them, referencing the code for a completely different shell company with a similar name.

"This sort of fraud is remarkable," exclaimed one investor blog about Gatewang's maneuver.

Fortunately, Gatewang wasn't Auntie Fu's only ticket back to Xinjiang. Her sister lived there, and Auntie could stay with her while she searched for a retirement home. Still grasping her photo album in their dark apartment, I glanced back at Uncle Feng. He was sound asleep. "Would you both move there?" I whispered.

"No," she said without bothering to lower her voice. "I'll go alone. And I don't intend to come back."

We flipped through the photo album some more. The last picture I saw was from the early 1980s, after they'd had three children. Their youngest son, who looked to be about four years old, sat on Auntie Fu's lap. Their daughter and their eldest son—about eight years before he was to drown in a river—stood behind their parents.

I looked closely at the older boy. He was tall, he had Uncle's good looks, and his hand rested on his father's shoulder. Uncle Feng wore an army uniform and a dark green cap with a red star on it. The three children stared into the camera, stone-faced. Uncle looked angry, as if he had just yelled at his wayward offspring. The backdrop was another beautiful Xinjiang alpine setting, this time a meadow of wildflowers with snowcapped mountains beyond.

The only one smiling was Auntie Fu.

JULY IS LOW SEASON for flower sales. Official functions are on hold, weddings are usually pushed off to the drier, milder spring and autumn months, and there is not a single Chinese holiday.

One Sunday afternoon in July of 2014, I pedaled down the Street of Eternal Happiness toward Zhao's flower shop. The pavement was wet from a midday thunderstorm, and the sun had just emerged from behind the clouds. I slowed as I passed *2nd Floor Your Sandwich* and caught a glimpse of CK serving up pasta to lunch patrons. Farther down, Fu and Feng's kitchen window was pulled down and padlocked; Feng had given up the *congyoubing* business for the summer. When I arrived at Zhao's, I found her lounging with her daughter-in-law Zhang Min on tiny wicker chairs in the shade of the plane trees in the shop's doorway. They fanned themselves as two-year-old Shuo Shuo raced miniature sports cars inside.

"You're here! Eat!" shouted Zhao, dropping her fan. She slid a butcher knife into a fat watermelon. I grabbed a chair and sat down between the two women. Zhao handed me a slice. The sun was high in the sky, pushing the temperature past 90 degrees. In the green canopy above, the first cicadas of the year had hatched. The pitch of their loud, mechanical drone wavered in a natural harmony with the breeze blowing down the street. Below, we quietly ate and watched traffic on the street surge then stop, surge and stop—Shanghai's slow and steady heartbeat.

This was my favorite month in the city. Schools were out and most of the French Concession's foreign residents had returned home to the United States, Europe, Australia, and other countries for the summer; the absence of locals gave the neighborhood a feeling of tranquillity.

Typhoon season would soon begin in earnest; the winds that normally blew from the polluted north and west would gradually begin shifting, carrying clean air from the East China Sea.

July was Zhao's month of rest and contemplation. From her perch underneath the lush foliage of the plane trees, her thoughts naturally hovered over matters unsettled.

"Big Sun's turning twenty-nine after the next New Year. He's too old!" she groused, tossing her watermelon rind on the sidewalk. "I've already got two girls lined up in our hometown. One is twenty-four, born in the Year of the Horse. The other is an older woman—thirty! But she's educated. She majored in engineering in college."

Zhao took her phone from her pocket and showed me a photo of the younger girl puckering her lips toward the camera. "He already told me he's not interested in this one," she said with a sigh.

Zhao had good news. Big Sun had quit his job as a hairdresser to accept another as a futures trader in Shanghai. He had landed a job with a company that helped Chinese investors buy shares on the New York Stock Exchange. It was commission-based, and he would have to live with his mother, but Zhao was pleased. It presented an opportunity to submit him to an intensified barrage of blind dates. It was also fitting relief for the guilt she had felt since he was forced back to Zaozhuang for school.

Although Big Sun had always been driven to learn, the poor results in school meant he had wandered from one dead-end job to another without fulfilling his intellectual needs. Yet the menial work gave him the free time to teach himself. He had shown a passion for investment strategies, and he spent many hours over the last couple of years sitting in an empty barber chair poring through books on the subject. This was a career path that would bring out the best in him, Zhao believed. Most important, her boy would be back home with her in Shanghai.

Where one son would return, the other would leave. Little Sun and his wife faced the decision Zhao had more than twenty years ago when she arrived in Shanghai: a son's education. Little Shuo Shuo's fate was connected to his hometown. Would Shuo Shuo attend kindergarten in Shanghai, an outsider among Shanghainese, or would he go back home to Zaozhuang, where his *hukou*, or household registration, allowed him to eventually attend middle and high school?

"It's not just about his studies," his mother said, fanning herself. "It's about his socialization."

Zhang sighed loudly. "If you don't have enough money, nothing is easy."

She continued. "Other kids' fathers are engineers or managers. Yesterday someone in the park asked him what his father did for a living. He said he didn't know, and he asked me. I said, 'He works in a kitchen.' He said, 'Oh, my daddy works in a kitchen.'"

Zhao nodded her head. "When Big Sun studied here, the other kids called him 'farmer.' I don't want my grandson to have to deal with that."

"If you're not from Shanghai," said Zhang, "no matter how good of a student you are, it's useless. Teachers won't cultivate you."

There were many reasons for this. Migrant children didn't have parents inside their teachers' social network like Shanghainese children did, they didn't speak the same native dialect, and their parents generally weren't as involved as Shanghainese parents in their educational progress.

Back in Zaozhuang, Zhao believed, teachers would help him along. It was simply a matter of pride. "Teachers will say, 'There's talent from Shandong.' But in Shanghai, teachers wouldn't bother. They just see us as *waidi ren*—outsiders."

Zhao had dealt with this discrimination for years. She was a good neighbor, always buying fruit and snacks for the shop owners on her block. She took care of her neighbors' children when parents had errands to run, and her neighbors—nearly all of them migrants, too—took care of her in return. When she had broken her ankle, the entire block came to her aid. But her Shanghainese neighbors seemed to lack this community spirit.

"Local Shanghainese don't like us," Zhao said. "They're jealous of us if we make more money than them, and if we don't, they see us as impoverished thieves. The truth is, the Shanghainese are generally lazy. They don't want to eat bitter."

"At least back in our hometown, nobody's going to call him 'farmer,'" said Zhang.

Both of them giggled. "Stop being so polite! Eat more watermelon!" Zhao urged me.

I took a piece, and so did Zhao's daughter in-law.

We ate together, three outsiders sharing thoughts on the insiders.

Little Sun and his wife would likely send Shuo Shuo back home, that much was clear. But would they go, too? Little Sun worked as a chef at a Greek restaurant, earning at least twice as much as he would make back home. His wife, Zhang, was now a manager of a small French restaurant, earning more than her husband. They had considered asking Zhang's mother to take care of the boy, but the woman was barely literate, and she couldn't help with homework. One of them would have to give up his or her job and head home with their son.

"It'll probably be me," Zhang said with resignation. "I can adapt anywhere. I'm like a cockroach." I reflected again on how much she reminded me of Zhao: plainspoken, strong, and she learned quickly. She wasn't as approachable, but she was only twenty-six years old. She had plenty of time to practice the art of customer relations. I imagined her starting her own flower shop or café seven hundred miles away in her hometown of Zaozhuang.

Her husband, on the other hand, was probably best left to what he knew: making Greek food in Shanghai.

"In our hometown, men either have skills or strength," Zhang explained. "My husband has neither."

Zhao spit out a few watermelon seeds in laughter. The two had spent many days like this, complaining about their worthless spouses, and Zhao was well past the point of defending Little Sun. Zhang continued. "He could work as a construction worker if he was strong, but he's not," she complained. "He could make more than he's making now if he could lay tile, but he doesn't have any skills."

"That's not true!" Zhao smirked. "My son knows how to make Greek food!"

The two roared with laughter. China was changing fast, sure, but spanakopita would probably remain underappreciated in a place like Zaozhuang.

"We still haven't decided," Zhang said. "Maybe he'll live with my mother for a year and we'll see how it goes."

Zhao smiled sadly. "I never expected our Shuo Shuo would be a left-behind child," she said, looking at the sidewalk. "He'll be just like his father. Two generations of left-behind children! *Aiya!*"

But even as she said this, something in her look revealed she knew this wasn't true. Shuo Shuo wouldn't be stuck in a coal-mining town like his father was. He'd live in a middle-class suburb in a spacious seventeenth-floor condominium with hardwood floors that his grandmother had bought for the family. He wouldn't be misdiagnosed and left in a school for autistic children. He'd be escorted to and from a good kindergarten just a block away from home. What used to be a twelve-hour sleeper bus journey from Shanghai was now a three-hour high-speed train ride. Mom and Dad could visit him every other weekend. In just twenty years, China had begun to transform into a modern, developed country. *What would it look like in another twenty years?* Zhao wondered aloud. Maybe the country would do away with *hukou* laws altogether.

A refreshing breeze from the east blew down the Street of Eternal Happiness. It rustled layers of green leaves from the plane trees above, and speckles of sunlight danced across the street, glinting off the watermelon rinds that littered the sidewalk. Little Shuo Shuo emerged from the shop with his arms outstretched, vibrating his lips, making motor sounds. "B-b-b-b-r-r-r-r," he babbled, running down the sidewalk, veering onto the edge of the curb, jumping into the street to avoid pedestrians. The boy did this a lot, and it always made me nervous. But neither his mother nor his grandmother paid attention to his antics. Shuo Shuo had lived nearly every day of his short life here, on this patch of the street, and he had learned what he could get away with. Whenever a car or a scooter raced by, he reflexively jumped back onto the sidewalk in the nick of time.

I stopped watching him and noticed both Zhao and Zhang had closed their eyes. They had tilted their heads back to let the breeze caress their faces as they listened to the steady rustle of leaves. The strong wind made the plane trees sound like rapids on a river: always rolling, its flow eternal. The gusts diminished and the song of the cicadas returned. Shuo Shuo's buzzing grew louder until he plopped his tiny body onto his grandmother's lap, waking her up from her trance, nearly knocking her over.

He looked up and smirked at her. She flashed a knowing smile back. She stood up and lifted the little boy up over her shoulders, placing him on her back. Zhao ran down the street, laughing as her grandson squealed in delight. He stretched out his arms like a bird. "Fly, Grandma, fly!" the boy screamed.

And she flew.

ACKNOWLEDGMENTS

I am grateful for my friends and neighbors along Changle Lu who opened their lives to me these past six years. They granted me their trust, time, and patience, and without them, this work would not have been possible. Across the street from my home, Chen Kai shared his dreams with me over countless cups of coffee. A few blocks down, Auntie Fu and Uncle Feng had *congyoubing* and fruit from Xinjiang ready each time I arrived, and at the end of the street in their tiny flower shop, Zhao Shiling, Sun Hua, Sun Wei, Zhang Ming, and little Shuo Shuo took me in like a member of the family.

In Maggie Lane, Kang Chenggeng, Chen Zhongdao, and Xie Guozhen risked their personal safety to share their neighborhood's troubled history. I was saddened by Xie's passing just two years after her and Chen's home was taken from them.

Xi Guozhen and her son Zhu Weiqi taught me the importance of strength and perseverance in today's China, and I thank them for sharing deeply personal memories with me. I am grateful to Wei Xiezhong and Harry Wu for helping me understand day-to-day life inside China's labor camp system. And in Flushing, Wang Xuesong patiently filled in the historical gaps of his parents' letters for me while talking about his own hopes and ambitions in his adopted homeland.

Others along the street who became friends and confidantes include Zhang Naisun, Henry Shen, Tom Doctoroff, Wang Cailiang, Chu Hongsheng, Zhu Zhongling, Gong Yao, Xu Yuan, Li Zixing, Liu Xun, Qiu Huanxi, Chen Yiyi, Tu Dongxiu, and Cang Long.

I have often believed the longer I live in China the less I come to know, and I owe a debt of gratitude to the talented journalist and researcher Yifan Xie who helped me translate interviews, letters, and historical texts to accurately record the stories of those along the street. I am especially thankful for her local knowledge and for our lasting friendship.

This work began as a radio series I reported for *Marketplace*, and it wouldn't have been possible without the support of executive producer Deborah Clark, who encouraged me to report the original stories and then graciously granted me leave to write this book. Thanks also to Jon McTaggart, David Kansas, Doug Roderick, Mitzi Gramling, and the rest of the talented team at American Public Media for their support of this project. I'm indebted to foreign editor John Buckley for his sharp editorial guidance and kind supervision, as well as to John Haas, who lent his editorial talents to the stories. I am grateful to JJ Yore and George Judson for giving me one of the best jobs at *Marketplace*, and to Tina Admans for logistical support. I have also benefitted greatly from the guidance and support of my past and current colleagues at the show, and am honored to work with such a dedicated team of radio professionals. A few worthy of special note are Kai Ryssdal, Sitara Nieves, David Brancaccio, Nicole Childers, Mark Miller, Scott Tong, and Nancy Farghalli.

Throughout my career, I have been fortunate to receive guidance from veterans who have helped make me a better reporter and writer. At Columbia University's Graduate School of Journalism, Ari Goldman, Rhoda Lipton, Julie Hartenstein, and Joe Richman were excellent mentors. At Minnesota Public Radio, Katherine Smith, Euan Kerr, Gary Eichten, and Sara Meyer patiently taught me the ropes of radio journalism. At KPCC, I had the pleasure of working under the very capable Paul Glickman, Nick Roman, and Bill Davis. At KQED, Ingrid Becker, Scott Shafer, Kat Snow, Craig Miller, and Victoria Mauleon helped refine my skills, and at NPR, Alisa Barba and Kate Concannon were outstanding editors who helped provide a national platform for my work.

I am grateful to Michael Meyer, whose thoughtful reading of a draft helped me work through some early issues. Peter Hessler, another former Peace Corps colleague, was kind enough to edit an early version, too, offering helpful—and humorous—comments that helped me restructure the work. I also owe special thanks to Leslie T. Chang, whose thoughtful and thorough input improved the original book proposal, and to Alane Mason, who encouraged me to submit it to publishers. I appreciate the time of Jeffrey Wasserstrom, who helped provide valuable historical context. Thanks also to James McGregor and John Ruwitch, who reviewed the manuscript with care.

Over the years, I have benefitted from the friendship and assistance of many people whose work focuses on China, including Stan Abrams, James T. Areddy, David Barboza, Hannah Beech, Mary Bergstrom, Tania Branigan, Jonathan Browning, Mike Chinoy, Patrick Chovanec, Margaret Conley, Geoffrey Crothall, Maura Cunningham, Bill Dodson, Clayton Dube, Michael Dunne, Deborah Fallows, James Fallows, Russell Flannery, Paul French, Jeremy Friedlein, Josh Gartner, Rob Gifford, Dru Gladney, Jeremy Goldkorn, Alexandra Harney, William Hess, Duncan Hewitt, Arthur Kroeber, Kaiser Kuo, Frank Langfitt, Brook Larmer, Louisa Lim, Jen Lin-Liu, Ma Tianjie, Adam Minter, Malcolm Moore, Ching-Ching Ni, Evan Osnos, Philip Pan, Michael Pettis, Tom Phillips, David Pierson, Qiu Xiaolong, James Rice, Andy Rothman, Simon Rabinovitch, Craig Simons, Felicia Sonmez, Anne Stevenson-Yang, Kristie Lu Stout, Jason Subler, John Sudworth, Pete Sweeney, Sue Anne Tay, Alex Wang, Edward Wong, Louis Woo, Andy Xie, and Zhu Dake.

I am also grateful for the companionship of a network of friends in Shanghai and beyond: Alyshea Austern, Julian Bermudez, Kathryn Blouin, David Boggs, Steven Bourne, Brantley Turner-Bradley, Doug Bradley, Wendy Bryan, Kitty Bu, Tamy Chapman, William Chou, Elaine Chow, Sean Coady, Dan Connelly, Grace Lee Connelly, Patrick Cranley, Rob and Heidi Creighton, Fitz De Smet, Allison Despard, Arsheya Devitre, Ken and Brenda Erickson, Dan and Amy Fitzpatrick, Jerry Flanagan, Anna Gai, Jeremy and Karen Gaskill, Kevin Gibbons, Jeanne and Briand Greer, Michelle Garnaut, Mike Goettig, Adolfo Guzman Lopez, Melanie Ham, Christian and Alexandra Hansmeyer, Stephen Harder and York-Chi Harder, Steve Harris and Mercedes Valle-Harris, Julian de Hauteclocque Howe, Erich Heilemann, Rachel Ee-Heilemann, Stephen Henn, Ellen Himelfarb, Vanessa Hua, Denise Huang, John and Meg Ideker, Maile Jedlinsky, Tina Kanagaratnam, George and Heather Kaye, Melissa Lam, Julie Langfitt, Wilde Lau, Codi Lazar, John Leary, Jane Lee, Dan Levine, Dawn MacKeen, Lisa McCallum, Mary McCoy, Adam and Sara Meier, Ann Meier, Vincent Moccia, Maggie Moon, Xavier Naville, Daisy Nguyen, Richard and Karen Oothoudt, Caroline Pan, Lucia Pierce, Greg Pilarowski, Jennifer Pitman, John Rabe, David Ratner, Diana Ricciardone, Lysa Saltzman, Sarah Schafer, Clay Shirky, Alok Somani, Bill and Elena Speidel, Jason Stanard, Frank Stoltze, Christine Tan, Anh Truong, Lian Tsien, Michael Tunkey, Brett and Rebecca Wallihan, Marc and Sherine Walton, Andrew and Molly Watkins, Brian Watt, Adam Weiss, Seth Werner, Stefan and Devon Whitney,

Jennifer Wu, Ran Xu, Jiwei Ye, Almaz Zelleke, and Ami and Hayley Zweig. Special thanks to friends Richard Langone and Lei Lei Peng, whose gracious loan of a shoebox of letters led me across the world to find their owner, and to Wen Cao, who assisted in their transcription.

I am grateful to Domenica Alioto, my brilliant editor at Crown, for her patient and insightful readings of the manuscript and for helpful conversations over an *escondido* Internet connection, to Claire Potter for providing expert day-to-day assistance, and to Sarah Pekdemir and Rebecca Marsh for marketing and publicizing the book. I'm also indebted to Vanessa Mobley for taking the manuscript in and for her early guidance and support. Heartfelt thanks to Wendy Sherman, my agent, for her confidence in this project and its potential, and to Jenny Meyer for her expert handling of the foreign rights.

I am forever grateful to my wonderful mother, JoAnn, and my devoted father, Jim. They raised me to work hard, to love what I do, and to never stop exploring. These were lessons that took me far away from them for years at a time, and they've been patient, loving, and supportive through it all. I only wish my father could have lived to read these words on the page.

I am fortunate to have two brothers, Ryan Schmitz and Dan Schmitz, whom I consider my closest friends. I am grateful for their advice and companionship, and for putting up with my absence for all of these years. I look forward to the day when they, along with Denise Landeros-Schmitz, Ashley Denholtz Schmitz, and my nephews and nieces Andre, Bradley, Natalie, Scarlett, and my family live on the same continent.

I met and fell in love with Lenora Chu in graduate school in New York City. On our first date, she heard my stories about volunteering in China, and she thought I was crazy to want to return as a journalist. Little did she know that I would rope her into the deal, too. She selflessly put her career on hold, as well as a few dreams of her own, so that I could follow mine. She's my most loyal editor and partner, and she's also given me a second family: Judy and Humbert Chu, Joyce Chu Moore Kenney Moore, and Greyson and Coralai. I owe an enormous debt of gratitude to them for their generosity.

Lenora and I left Los Angeles for Shanghai with our one-year-old son, Rainer. A few years later, little Landon was born, making our family complete. I am eternally happy the four of us are on this adventure together. The love we share is the light of my life. This book is for you.

This is a work of nonfiction. I have used real names with two exceptions. The Wang family name is a pseudonym used at the son's request due to political sensitivities in the People's Republic of China. I've also used the pseudonyms "Uncle Feng" and "Auntie Fu" to protect their privacy. I've changed the street addresses of both families for the same reasons.

The majority of my research involved one-on-one interviews and personal observation. I also benefited greatly from written materials, and below I have identified the sources that were most useful to each section. Newspaper headlines from Chinese language sources have been translated into English.

Chapter 1: CK and the System

For background on the history of London plane trees in Shanghai:
"Absorbed by Time, the Phoenix Tree Is the Warmest Characteristic of Shanghai's Scenery," *Jiefang Daily*, December 6, 2013.
"A Grass-Roots Fight to Save a 'Supertree,'" *The New York Times*, June 4, 2011.
Ch. B. Maybon and Jean Fredet, *Histoire de la Concession française de Changhai*, Paris: Librairie Plon, 1929.

For background on the history of Shanghai:
Pan Ling, *In Search of Old Shanghai*, Joint Publishing (Hong Kong) Co. Ltd., 1986.
Paul French, *The Old Shanghai, A–Z*, Hong Kong University Press, 2010.
Stella Dong, *Shanghai: The Rise and Fall of a Decadent City*, New York: HarperCollins, 2000.

I am grateful to Zang Jun, Assistant to the Manager of Landscape Management, Huangpu District Landscape Bureau, for explaining the history and maintenance of Shanghai's London plane trees.

Chapter 2: Better City, Better Life

For background on etiquette campaigns both in China and the United States:

Zuo keaide Shanghai ren [How to Be a Lovely Shanghainese], The Shanghai
Commission for Cultural and Ethical Progress, 2005.

Cecil B. Hartley, *The Gentlemen's Book of Etiquette,* Boston: DeWolfe, Fiske, &
Co., 1879.

*For background on Shanghai's—and China's—increasingly influential role in the
world:*

Jeffrey Wasserstrom and Maura Cunningham, *China in the 21st Century: What
Everyone Needs to Know,* New York: Oxford University Press, 2013.

Anna Greenspan, Shanghai Future: Modernity Remade, New York: Oxford
University Press, 2014.

For background on the history of Shanghai's old neighborhoods and their destruction:

Jie Li, *Shanghai Homes: Palimpsests of Private Life,* New York: Columbia
University Press, 2015.

Qin Shao, *Shanghai Gone: Domicide and Defiance in a Chinese Megacity,* New
York: Rowman & Littlefield, 2013.

For background on the demolition of Maggie Lane:

"The Shadow of Forced Demolition Re-emerges in Maggie Lane," *Southern
Weekend,* April 1, 2011.

"New Government Policies Fail to Prevent Violent Forced Demolitions," *Legal
Daily,* April 6, 2011.

For background on both the Shanghai and the New York World's Fairs:

"Expo Offers Shanghai a Turn in the Spotlight," *The New York Times,* April 29,
2010.

Robert A. Caro, *The Power Broker,* New York: Vintage, July 12, 1975.

Chapter 3: Hot and Noisy

For background on what goes into China's GDP calculation:

"Fifth Generation Star Li Keqiang Discusses Domestic Challenges, Trade
Relations with Ambassador," WikiLeaks, March 15, 2007.

For background on China's left-behind children:

"China's 'Left-Behind Children,'" *The New York Times,* June 1, 2012.

"China Struggles with Mental Health Problems of 'Left-Behind' Children," *The
Guardian,* August 30, 2014.

"Left-Behind Children of China's Migrant Workers Bear Grown-up Burdens,"
The Wall Street Journal, January 14, 2014.

"China Raises a Generation of 'Left-Behind' Children," CNN, February 5, 2014.

For background on China's hukou system:

Kam Wing Chan, "The Chinese *Hukou* System at 50," Eurasian Geography and
Economics, Bellwether Publishing, Ltd., 2009.

"A Road Map for Reforming China's *Hukou* System," *Chinadialogue*, October 22, 2013.

"The Limitations of China's *Hukou* Reforms," *Business Spectator*, August 1, 2014.

"China '*Hukou*' System Deemed Outdated as Way of Controlling Access to Services," *The Washington Post*, August 15, 2010.

"China's *Hukou* Reform Plan Starts to Take Shape," *The Wall Street Journal*, August 4, 2014.

I am grateful to Professor Kam Wing Chan for several interviews about China's hukou system, and to Benjamin Schwall for several interviews about life in China's factory towns during the 1990s.

Chapter 4: Re-Education

For background on Jinjiang Hotel founder Dong Zhujun:
Lily Xiao Hong Lee and A. D. Stefanowska, *Biographical Dictionary of Chinese Women*, London: Routledge, July 31, 2002.

For background on Shanghai youth sent to build Xinjiang in the 1960s:
"Go to the Countryside! Go to the Remote Frontiers! Devote Your Life to Revolution—Warm Farewell to Shanghai Youth Participating in the Construction of Xinjiang," *Wenhui Daily*, June 20, 1965.

"First Batch of Shanghai Youth Embark on Trip to Xinjiang—Devoting Youth to the Construction of the Country's Remote Frontiers," *Wenhui Daily*, June 20, 1965.

"Listen to the Party and Work for Revolution in the Countryside and Remote Frontiers—Mobilizing 10,000 Youth from Shanghai to Go to the Countryside and Join the Construction of Remote Areas; Comrade Yang Xiguang on Behalf of Shanghai Municipal Government Committee Wished Youth Can Thrive in the Revolutionary Struggles," *Jiefang Daily*, May 26, 1965.

"50,000 Shanghai Youth Display Dedication to the Full Construction of Xinjiang—Two Years' Labor Cultivated Massive Pieces of Wasteland, and Resulted in the Emergence of Large Amount of 'Five-Good' Workers and Skilled Production Workers," *Jiefang Daily*, May 26, 1965.

"Four Letters Penned by Shanghai Youth from the Farms in Xinjiang," *Jiefang Daily*, May 26, 1965.

"Alongside Old Soldiers—Shanghai Youth Active in Tianshan," *Jiefang Daily*, December 7, 1963.

"Shanghai Youth's 'Flower Farm' in Xinjiang," *Jiefang Daily*, August 22, 1961.

"Passing on Advanced Technology and Advanced Thoughts—Shanghai's Skilled Textile Workers Teach Advanced Experience in Xinjiang," *Worker's Daily*, December 19, 1964.

"The Shanghai Youth I Saw in Xinjiang," *Wenhui Daily*, April 16, 1964.

"Joining the Construction of China's Remote Frontiers Is a Bright Future for Sons and Daughters—A Summary of the Speech Given by Hu Juewen at a Seminar on Shanghai's Industry and Commercial Sector's Support of Xinjiang's Construction," *Shanghai Industry and Commerce Journal*, no. 8, 1963.

"Where Lives Were Changed," *Global Times*, October 13, 2013.

Robyn Iredale, Naran Bilik, and Guo Fei (eds.), *China's Minorities on the Move: Selected Case Studies*, Armonk, New York, London: M. E. Sharpe, 2003.

"Survey of Shanghai Youths in Xinjiang," *China Daily*, November 11, 1986.

Liu Xiaomeng and Ding Yizhuang, *The History of Chinese Sent-Down Youth*, Chinese Academy of Social Sciences, 1998.

For background on religion in China, I recommend the nonfiction and journalistic work of author Ian Johnson (Wild Grass, New York: Vintage, 2005). For background on house churches and the rise of Christianity in China:

"How China Plans to Wipe Out House Churches," *Christianity Today*, February 2013.

"China's Way to Happiness," *The New York Review of Books*, February 4, 2014.

Katharina Wenzel-Teuber and David Streit, *People's Republic of China: Religions and Churches Statistical Overview 2011*, Religions and Christianity in Today's China, Vol. II, 2012.

"Global Christianity: A Report on the Size and Distribution of the World's Christian Population," Pew Research Center, December 19, 2011.

"Christians in Wenzhou Fight to Keep Church's Cross," *The New York Times*, July 7, 2014.

"China's Christians Fear New Persecution After Latest Wave of Church Demolitions," *The Guardian*, July 5, 2014.

Xi Lian, *Redeemed by Fire: The Rise of Popular Christianity in Modern China*, New Haven: Yale University Press, 2010.

For background on the Cultural Revolution, few sources compare to the depth and breadth of Roderick MacFarquhar and Michael Schoenhals's groundbreaking work Mao's Last Revolution, *from Belknap Press, Cambridge, Mass., 2008.*

Chapter 5: Box of Letters

For background on the early Mao years:

Jonathan D. Spence, *The Search for Modern China* (Third Edition), New York: W. W. Norton & Company, 2012.

John King Fairbank and Merle Goldman, *China: A New History*, Cambridge, Mass.: Belknap Press, 2006.

For background on the Anti-Rightist campaign and its impact on Shanghai:

Frederick C. Teiwes, *Politics and Purges in China: Rectification and the Decline of Party Norms*, London: Routledge, 1993.

Peter T. Y. Cheung, Jae Ho Chung, and Lin Zhimin (eds.), *Provincial Strategies of Economic Reform in Post-Mao China*, London: Routledge, 1998.

"The Issue of Taking Sides for Middle-ground Capitalist Intellectuals," *The Shanghai News Daily*, December 6, 1957.

"Anti-Rightist Movement Among Commerce and Industry Sectors Proves to Be a Sweeping Victory: Over 200 Rightists Uncovered," *The Shanghai News Daily*, December 9, 1957.

"Rightist Intellectuals from the Commerce and Industry Sectors Gradually Reveal True Colors," *The Shanghai News Daily*, December 11, 1957.

"Obliterating Great Achievements in the Construction of Socialism: Wei Zongqi Willfully Spread Rumors and Smeared Others," *The Shanghai News Daily*, December 11, 1957.

"The Grand Victory of the Anti-Rightist Struggle Among the Political Schools for Commerce and Industry," *The Shanghai News Daily*, December 12, 1957.

For background on the Great Leap Famine:

Yang Jisheng, *Tombstone: The Great Chinese Famine*, New York: Farrar, Straus, and Giroux, October 30, 2012.

Frank Dikotter, *Mao's Great Famine: The History of China's Most Devastating Catastrophe*, New York: Walker Books, September 28, 2010.

For background on life at Chinese labor camps during the Mao years:

Yang Xianhui, *Woman from Shanghai: Tales of Survival from a Chinese Labor Camp*, New York: Anchor, August 24, 2010.

Harry Wu and Carolyn Wakeman, *Bitter Winds: A Memoir of My Years in China's Gulag*, New York: John Wiley & Sons, April 3, 1995.

For background on Xi Jinping's "Chinese Dream" guiding principle:

"Chinese Dream Is Xi's Vision," *China Daily*, March 18, 2013.

Chapter 6: Auntie Fu's Get-Rich-Quick Plan

For background on Wenzhou's history of underground lending:

Hein Mallee and Frank N. Pieke, *Internal and International Migration: Chinese Perspectives*, London: Routledge, 1999.

"Shadow Banks on Trial as China's Rich Sister Faces Death," *Bloomberg*, April 11, 2012.

"Underground Lender Gets Death Sentence in China," The Associated Press, May 20, 2013.

For background on the Jade Rabbit mission:

"China Launches Lunar Probe Carrying 'Jade Rabbit' Buggy," Reuters, December 1, 2013.

Chapter 7: Bride Price

For background on typical prices for brides throughout China:

"Forget Dowries: Chinese Men Have to Pay up to $24,000 to Get a Bride," *Quartz*, June 9, 2013.

For background on Chinese president Xi Jinping, I recommend the excellent reporting of Evan Osnos, Michael Forsythe, and Chris Buckley, whose work is included below:

"Born Red," *The New Yorker*, April 6, 2015.

"Xi Jinping Millionaire Relations Reveal Fortunes of Elite," *Bloomberg*, June 29, 2012.

"Cultural Revolution Shaped Xi Jinping, from Schoolboy to Survivor," *The New York Times*, September 24, 2015.

"Portrait of Vice-President Xi Jinping," WikiLeaks, November 16, 2009.

Chapter 9: Dreams, Seized

For background on the closing ceremony of the Shanghai world's fair:
"China Holds Closing Ceremony for Shanghai Expo," Xinhua, October 31, 2010.

For background on urban land reform in China:
"Land Reform Efforts in China," *China Business Review*, October 1, 2012.
Interim Regulations of the People's Republic of China Concerning the Assignment and Transfer of the Right to the Use of the State-Owned Land in the Urban Areas, State Council of the People's Republic of China, May 19, 1990.
Property Rights Law of the People's Republic of China, National People's Congress, October 1, 2007.
"China's Next Revolution," *The Economist*, March 8, 2007.
Annual Statistical Yearbook 2004–2014, Shanghai Bureau of Statistics, 2014.

For background on Xi Jinping's "Chinese Dream" guiding principle:
"Chinese Dreams," *TheChinaStory.org*, March, 2013.

I am grateful to Chen Zhongdao for sharing dozens of police reports and court documents related to incidents at Maggie Lane from 2001 to 2013.

Chapter 10: Escape

For background on Mao's Cultural Revolution:
MacFarquhar and Schoenhals, *Mao's Last Revolution*.
Mao Tse-Tung, *Quotations from Chairman Mao Tse-Tung*, BN Publishing, 2008.

Chapter 11: *Zero* Risk

For background on China's Lost Generation:
"China's Lost Generation Coddles Its Young," *The Washington Post*, November 24, 2004.
"China's Lost Generation," *Time*, July 7, 2008.
"Chinese Police Take On 'Lost Generation' Grandparents," *The Daily Telegraph*, November 1, 2011.

For background on Liaoning Dingxu:
"157 Seniors in Ningbo Have Their Investment Dreams Smashed, Over RMB 12 Million in Pensions Poured Down the Drain," *Southeastern Business Report*, May 15, 2014.
"Illegally Absorbing Over 12 Million in Investments, Two People in Charge of Liaoning Dingxu's Ningbo Branch Sentenced," *Modern Gold Express*, May 15, 2014.
"Liaoning Publishes 9 Cases of Economic Crimes," China News Service, July 17, 2012.
"Court Verdict of Defendant Zhang Xiuying," Anyang City Beiguan District Court, August 20, 2014.
"Return on Investments in Liaoning Dingxu Never Come—Official: 'We've All Been Harmed,'"*Liaoning Evening News*, September 23, 2012.

Chapter 12: Country Wedding

For background on the water wars of Weishan Lake:
Guo Rongxing, *Understanding the Chinese Economies*, Waltham, Mass.:
    Academic Press, August 29, 2012.

Chapter 13: CK's Pilgrimage

For background on the resurgence of Buddhism in China:
China Academy of Social Sciences, *Buddhism in China*, 2010.
André Laliberté, "Buddhist Revival Under State Watch," *Journal of Current
    Chinese Affairs*, February 2011.
"30-Year Renaissance: The Revival of Buddhism in China," *Buddha Eye*, July
    2009.

*Though state statistics estimate China has had 100 million Buddhists since 1978, Liu
Zhongyuou of the Research Center for Religious Culture at East China Normal University estimated there were 300 million Buddhists in China in 2005.*

Chapter 14: Home

For background on the case of Xu Zhiyong:
"New Citizens: The Trial of Xu Zhiyong," *The Economist*, January 25, 2014.
"A Leading Chinese Human Rights Advocate Is Detained in Beijing," *The New
    York Times*, July 17, 2013.
"China Sentences Xu Zhiyong, Legal Activist, to 4 Years in Prison," *The New
    York Times*, January 26, 2014.
"The Trial of the Chinese Dream," *The New Yorker*, January 17, 2014.

Chapter 15: Chinese Dreams

For background on Gatewang:
"A Look at Some of the Rascals Involved in the Gate Concert Party," Share
    Prophets.com, April 10, 2015.
"Gatewang and Gate Ventures and Chinese Whispers," ShareProphets.com,
    April 18, 2015.